# The PERFECT SEASON

Handbook of Rational-Emotive Therapy: Volume I (with Albert Ellis)

Cognition and Emotional Disturbance

Rational-Emotive Therapy: A Skills-Based Approach (with John Boyd)

Handbook of Rational-Emotive Therapy: Volume II (with Albert Ellis)

The Rational-Emotive Therapy Companion: A Clear, Concise, and Complete Guide to Being an RET Client (with Paul Woods)

Fearless Job Hunting: Powerful Psychological Strategies for Getting the Job You Want (with Bill Knaus, Sam Klarreich, and Nancy Knaus)

The Undefeated Season: The Newspaper Story of the 1964–1965 Evansville College Purple Aces Basketball Team (with Tom Tuley)

The Couples Therapy Companion: A Cognitive Behavior Workbook

Mastering Unrelenting Drive: A Cognitive Behavior Workbook to Produce Extraordinary Performance and Results (forthcoming)

# The PERFECT SEASON

*A Memoir of the 1964–1965*
*Evansville College Purple Aces*

## Russell Grieger

AN IMPRINT OF
INDIANA UNIVERSITY PRESS
Bloomington & Indianapolis

This book is a publication of Quarry Books

an imprint of Indiana University Press
Office of Scholarly Publishing
Herman B Wells Library 350
1320 East 10th Street
Bloomington, Indiana 47405 USA

iupress.indiana.edu

Manufactured in the
United States of America

Library of Congress Cataloging-in-
Publication Data

Names: Grieger, Russell, author.
Title: The perfect season : a memoir of the
    1964-1965 Evansville College Purple Aces /
    Russell Grieger.
Description: Bloomington : Indiana
    University Press, [2016]
Identifiers: LCCN 2016018704 |
    ISBN 9780253022769 (print : alk. paper)
Subjects: LCSH: Evansville College Purple
    Aces (Basketball team)—History.
Classification: LCC GV885.43.E83 G75 2016
    | DDC 796.323/630977233—dc23 LC
    record available at https://lccn.loc
    .gov/2016018704

ISBN 978-0-253-02276-9 (pbk.)
ISBN 978-0-253-02324-7 (ebk.)

1 2 3 4 5    21 20 19 18 17 16

FOR

*My father, Russ Grieger Sr.,*
*who played catch with me by the hour,*
*rebounded for me on more occasions than I can count,*
*stood behind me through thick and thin,*
*encouraged me every step of the way,*
*cheered me through triumph and adversity,*
*and lovingly did everything any dad could do,*
*and so much more.*

If you're going to go,
go big time,
or don't go at all.

—1964–1965 Aces slogan

# CONTENTS

ACKNOWLEDGMENTS  *ix*

AUTHOR'S NOTE  *xi*

PROLOGUE  *xiii*


**PART ONE: THE ACES GET READY**

1  THE ARMORY DAYS  *3*

2  CARSON CENTER PREPARATION  *9*

3  THE IOWA HAWKEYES  *20*


**PART TWO: THE ACE GROWS UP**

4  THE BEGINNINGS  *31*

5  FROM BULLPUP TO BULLDOG  *41*

6  FLAILING AND FALLING  *53*

7  FLYING  *63*

8  ST. LOUIS BLUES  *74*

9  RETURN TO EVANSVILLE  *87*

10  A DREAM COMES TRUE—ALMOST  *96*


**PART THREE: THE ACES SUCCEED**

11  NORTHWESTERN  *121*

12  NOTRE DAME  *129*

13  A HOLIDAY FEAST  *138*

14  THE BLACK HILLS AND THE BADLANDS  *148*

15  LARRY, THEN THE HOLY GRAIL  *157*

16  FANS INTO REDSHIRTS  *165*

17    SOUTHERN ILLINOIS SURPRISE    *175*

18    DEPAUW AND MORE    *184*

19    FIVE GAMES, FIVE SNAPSHOTS    *194*

20    SOUTHERN ILLINOIS REDUX    *208*


**PART FOUR: THE ACES TRIUMPH**

21    THE NCAA REGIONAL    *219*

22    THE NCAA FINALS    *231*

# ACKNOWLEDGMENTS

As with a successful basketball team, the writing of a book requires the guidance of a great coach. My writing coach turned out to be Jay Kauffmann. I first met Jay when I attended one of his creative writing seminars. I found him to be such an outstanding teacher—intellectually astute, technically proficient, professionally inspiring—that I attended several other classes taught by him. Eventually, I prevailed upon him to edit this book. He considered every word on every page, in the process nurturing me along, encouraging me to "never settle for good enough," helping me bring out the best I had. I am happy to say that, in addition to being my writing mentor, Jay has become my friend as well.

The curse all creative writers face is a poisonous combination of ignorance and self-doubt: ignorance in that it is hard to see what is missing on the written page, the doubt that what we do see isn't good enough. I have been so fortunate to have had writing teammates who have helped me defeat these twin scourges. I will forever be grateful to Jay Varner and Sharon Harrigan, both teachers extraordinaire, who gave me the kind of information, feedback, and support I found invaluable. Then there were my fellow members of Jay Kauffmann's Baptism-by-Fire writing group—Ingrid Alewine, Jay Glick, Annabel Jordan, Sherry Hauff, Amber Marley Padilla, and Amy Wissenkerk—each of whom gave me spot-on feedback, pithy suggestions, and, most of all, generous quantities of reinforcement and humor. Thank you, one and all.

Then there was my Aces family. How does one thank someone when thanks are not enough? To Arad McCutchan, whom I owe for so much more than his talents as a basketball coach. Every day of that glorious basketball season he modeled for me what it meant to be a man—the courage to compete, the value of hard work, the virtue of perspective, the integrity of character. Assistant coach Tom O'Brien treated me and all the other guys with unflagging respect, so rare with so many coaches today, making us feel as if we were his partners as well as his players. My affection for him today is a direct result of his unflagging kindness and innate goodness back then. Dr. Paul Grabill was an unanticipated windfall. An Aces fanatic, he took me under his wing, teaching me, guiding me, and cheerleading me onto the path of psychological health and well-being. His passion for life was only matched by his inner wisdom. Each of these men, through their unique ways of being, helped mold me into the person I've become. I hope, at least in part, I have made them proud.

Boys then, men now, my Aces family included, of course, the guys with whom I shared the court that glorious season. I start with Jerry Sloan, Larry Humes, Sam Watkins, and Herb Williams, the men who filled the pages of this book, all brothers I love. But there were the rest of the Aces as well, all equally responsible for the Aces' success, each dedicated and devoted to us being the best we could be—Terry Atwater, Larry Denton, Ron Eberhard, Jim Forman, Ron Johnson, Don Jordon, Rick Kingston, Gary McClary, Earl McCurdy, John O'Neil, Jim Rubush, and Bill Simpson. Thank you, guys; thank you so very much. Go Aces!

As with every significant endeavor in my life, I have been blessed with a loving family that stood by me during the long days and late nights I wrote this book. It warmed my heart to hear my older son, Todd, say, "That's good, Dad, you put me right there on the court," or for my younger son, Gabriel, to tell me, "I've heard this my whole life, but you made it real." I love you both more than I can express. And I have been so fortunate to be on the receiving end of the love and loyalty of my wife, Patti, who not only put in countless hours typing every word of this book but also believed in me even when my confidence waned, tolerated the long hours I hunched over a writing pad, and loaned me her wisdom whenever I found myself baffled. Thank you for being my dear friend, my partner in all things big and small, and my gorgeous wife.

Most everybody thinks their mom a saint. I am no exception. Through her innate goodness of heart and her unwavering capacity for unconditional love, she laid the foundation in me to ultimately believe myself worthy of being loved and to trust in the well meaning of other people.

Finally, my dad. He devoted every day of my life, up to and through this magical 1964–1965 basketball season, to teaching, encouraging, and just loving me. I did not realize till I was well into the writing of this book the large role he played in my life that season, as a beacon, a rock, an inspiration. It is to his credit that I took his love and loyalty as a given. No man I have ever known has had the openness of heart and the unbridled affection that he had. If I can be half the father to my sons as he was to me, I will consider myself a success.

# AUTHOR'S NOTE

By my math, the 1964–1965 Evansville College Purple Aces basketball season played out fifty years ago. Fifty years, half a century. Memories fade, become fuzzy, even deceive. I would not be surprised to find that I have incorrectly recalled certain events, misremembered a conversation here and there, forgotten things that did indeed take place. I am certain, however, about the emotional truth contained in these pages.

# PROLOGUE

IT WAS FRIDAY, MARCH 13, 1964, shortly after eleven at night. It was biting and bitter outside, and 12,244 hot and steamy basketball fans had jammed into Roberts Stadium to witness the NCAA Championship game between the Evansville College Purple Aces and the University of Akron Zips. The color red dominated the eye—shirts and sweaters, slacks and skirts, sport coats and hats. It was as if a giant balloon filled with paint had exploded at midcourt, coloring everything red from the first row to the rafters.

With my game jersey soaked with sweat, I looked up from the bench at the giant black overhead scoreboard, my night's work over. It blazed time and score on each of its four massive sides, numbers that could signal either triumph or tragedy.

The clock ticked down to 1:00. Those in the stands, red-decked Aces fans, exhausted but adrenalized from almost forty minutes of racehorse action, stood and stomped and shouted: "Aces, Aces," *clap, clap . . . clap, clap, clap . . .* "Aces, Aces," *clap, clap . . . clap, clap, clap. . . .* The beat matched the pounding of my heart.

At 0:45 the Evansville College student section began to shout, "We're number one, we're number one," karate chopping their right hand to each blasted word. I glanced over my shoulder and spotted my TKE fraternity brothers, bug-eyed and red-faced, shouting at the top of their lungs. Most of the others packed in the stands joined in, and their combined chorus became so loud that the cops stationed at the intersections beyond the parking lot swore they heard each word despite the wind.

At the 0:30 mark, we Aces already removed from the action stood up, some of us bouncing on the balls of our feet, others standing and clapping, all with grins from ear to ear.

Reaching 0:10, the throng started the countdown. "Ten . . . nine . . . eight . . . seven . . . six" blasted out with the thunderous cadence of a John Philip Sousa march. "Five . . . four . . . three . . . two . . . one" came like a succession of cannon shots.

The scoreboard blinked to triple zeros. The Aces won the 1963–1964 National Championship. The stadium erupted with an explosion of noise, as crashing and enveloping as the starting lap of the Indianapolis 500. We ran to join our teammates at center court, our index fingers puncturing the sky. We danced, hugged, and high-fived, letting loose emotions long contained by our focus on the prize now ours.

It did not take long for the accolades to flow in. The Associated Press and United Press International proclaimed the Aces number one in their final rankings. Sportswriter Bill Robertson labeled us "one of the greatest teams in collegiate history." Local civic organizations honored us with luncheons and dinners, and the Evansville Chamber of Commerce sponsored a citywide "Acclaim The Aces Banquet."

But such a triumph, even one so heady and glorious, could also serve to illuminate one's secret demons and fears. For most of my twenty-two years, I'd loved nothing so much as the game of basketball. I loved the precision and poetry required to gracefully arc a basketball into the air so that it would whoosh down through the net without touching metal. I loved that it provided an outlet for my competitive instincts, the camaraderie of friends and teammates, a place to express my passion and play out the identity I had created for myself.

But that was the rub. Through those twenty-two years, I had come to define myself as a basketball player. With this self-definition came ecstasy when I shined, but also shame when I failed. Basketball held up a mirror before me, reflecting my self-worth, not only to my own gaze, but also, in my mind, for the world to peer right through my body and judge my soul.

So, here, in the closing months of my junior year, with the 1964–1965 basketball season still in front of me, I felt I had both triumphed and failed. For, while I'd played an important role in helping the Aces capture the 1964 NCAA Championship, I had not been one of the five starters. I had been one of nine, one among two platoons of four players subbed in and out around the hub of our All-American, Jerry Sloan. Bittersweet described the taste in my mouth.

It was mid-April 1964 when it happened.

I walked from my early-afternoon psychology class across campus to Carson Center, the Aces' basketball practice facility. Students strolled the walkways between the limestone buildings of Evansville College, no longer in parkas and overcoats, but sweaters and light jackets. Others, sitting in the grass or on concrete benches, lifted their faces toward the early-spring sun. The smell of wild onions pushed up amid the new grass lent a bite to the air. Flocks of birds soared from one tree to another, causing the green tips of new leaf buds to flutter.

Once inside Carson Center, I loped past the ticket window and trophy case into the locker room. The familiar odor of sweat hit my nostrils, mingled with the faint smells of rubbing liniment, foot powder, and mildew.

I took my time donning my workout gear, making sure to put my two-sided practice jersey on red-side out, the color starters wore—a statement to myself. I grabbed a basketball and dribbled it onto the court just as Coach Arad McCutchan was leaving. He wore the same midthigh shorts and gray T-shirt he had all season, only this time his shirt was stained wet under his neck and arms. Sweat dripped from his chin, pattering the floor.

"Good workout, Coach?" I asked, hoping he'd appreciate my motivation in being there.

"Sure was," he said. "What are you doing here?"

"I thought I'd shoot around a little, keep sharp."

"Good. We'll have a bull's-eye on our backs next year, you know." He rubbed sweat from his brow with his shirtsleeve.

"I know."

"Think we can repeat?" he asked, his tone friendly, but betraying a hint of something more than casual curiosity.

"I do. Sloan's back. Watkins and Humes'll be there."

Something hardened in his eyes. He looked straight at me, not pointing his finger, but I felt as if he had. "But what about you?" he asked. "You left Grieger out. Will you be there too?"

"Of course I'll be there." A knot formed in the pit of my stomach. "I wouldn't miss next season for the world."

Now he did point his finger at me, straight at my chest. "No," he said. "Will *you* be there, wearing your shirt red-side out, along with Sloan, Humes, and Watkins?"

"That's up to you, Coach." I made sure to hold his gaze, hoping he wouldn't see the fear in my eyes.

"No, it's up to you."

We both stood there a moment, neither of us speaking. "Okay, have a good workout," he said and then turned to walk away.

I sighed, dribbled the ball twice, and took a jump shot from the corner. It swished cleanly through the basket.

Coach stopped at the doorway to the locker room and shouted back at me, "Good shot. Don't forget to work on your ball handling." Then he disappeared.

I stood in the corner of the court and looked at the basketball that had settled under the basket. I walked to it, picked it up, and started dribbling left-handed, slowly, around the perimeter of the court.

At that very moment, the 1964–1965 Aces basketball season began for me.

# The PERFECT SEASON

# Part One

## The Aces Get Ready

Whenever you can or dream you can, begin it.
Boldness has genius, power, and magic in it.
Begin it now.
　　　　　　—Johann Wolfgang von Goethe

# 1

## THE ARMORY DAYS

I FELT THE TENSION THE moment I awoke. I felt it first in my chest—a dull, burning sensation that intensified with each breath, a sensation that radiated down to my stomach and then lower, all around and through my pelvis. Most painful was the sense of dread that filled my consciousness and drove my heart to beat extra hard so that I thought I could almost hear it. This fear had no focus or location; it was just a vague awareness of being in danger and under assault.

It took me but a second to connect this agony to what would take place at three o'clock that afternoon. At that hour, on this Tuesday, September 8, 1964, my Aces teammates and I would gather at the National Guard Armory to scrimmage against each other, as we would for the next five weeks until formal practices began at Carson Center. To me, these scrimmages were more than about honing my skills. My worst fear—acquired early in high school—involved failing at basketball and, as a consequence, slipping into the shameful ignominy of becoming a failure. Today the reality of my place in the team's pecking order would start to be decided—starter or sub, success or failure.

I forced myself to throw back the covers and sit up, oblivious to the sunlight from the window over my bed in my parents' house. "Day of reckoning," I muttered under my breath, rubbing my hands back over my hair and flexing my shoulders.

The tension held tight as I drove through the oppressive Ohio River heat toward Evansville College, the windows rolled down and the wind snapping my shirt. I made my way to my seventeenth-century English literature class and then to my contemporary issues seminar. I found it difficult to focus as the professors spoke. My eyes drifted to the clock over the blackboard behind their heads, then to the passing parade of students two stories below, then back to the clock.

At two thirty, I made my way to the Armory to practice shooting and dribbling before the other Aces showed up. Massive, three-storied, and red-bricked, it squatted atop a layered hill, much like an impenetrable fortress. Three tiers, some twenty-five concrete steps each, led from the street to the entrance. I knew when I walked up those steps that I'd have to sprint them—full bore, up and down, fifty to one hundred times—once Coach McCutchan took over in October. I tightened my jaw at the thought and hissed, "Shit!"

Inside there was just enough space for one full-length basketball court, surrounded by ten rows of rolled-out bleachers that could pack in 2,500 fans. The court had yellowed from the kiss of thousands of gym shoes over the decades. The dark hue from dim lights and brown walls gave the Armory the aura of a cathedral.

I paused before I stepped over the line and onto the court, feeling as if I was about to tread onto hallowed ground. This was the same court on which former Aces greats—Gus Doerner, Roscoe Bivens, and Jerry Clayton—had played. I would give anything to be thought of as their peer.

Standing there, I remembered an Aces game from the 1950s. My family and I had squeezed together hip to hip in the second row directly behind the basket. I watched Jerry Clayton's every move—the way he arched his jump shot with a flick of his wrist, how he hipped and elbowed under the basket as if every inch belonged to him, how he forced his way to the basket on the dribble. The action swirled before us when the referee whistled a foul on him. The crowd booed, and a man in front of Mom bellowed, "What's the matter, ref, you studying to be an idiot?" I doubled over with laughter, as did most everyone else around me. Clayton continued without missing a beat.

I smiled at this memory, grabbed a basketball from the ball rack, and dribbled onto the court. It gave me comfort to feel the ball's dimpled leather. I practiced my jump shot, pounding the last dribble hard to the floor, jumping into the air, and releasing the shot at the top of my leap. I had lost none of my shooting touch since last March and threaded shot after shot through the net.

At quarter to three, Jerry Sloan walked in. With his close-cropped black hair, high cheekbones, and dead-on gaze, you could easily picture him an Indian warrior, decorated in war paint, astride a horse, ready to do battle.

"Hey," I said, a grin spreading across my face. "Sure glad to see you here."

An All-American first-teamer the last two years, Jerry possessed every physical quality a basketball player could want—six feet six inches of height, spring in his legs, quickness and dexterity, speed of foot. But what I most appreciated about Jerry was his heart.

As he grabbed a basketball from the rack and dribbled toward me, I remembered the year before, the day after a Wednesday-night road game. I had walked into the Carson Center for practice to find Sloan running laps around the double courts.

"What's going on?" I asked as he sped by, lips pursed, eyes straight ahead.

Ten minutes later, dressed for practice, I walked back to the court to find Jerry still running and not stopping until Coach McCutchan whistled for practice to start. During the full-court scrimmage, Jerry dove for every loose ball, contended for every rebound, and fought through every pick. He played with even more ferocity than usual.

After practice, I sidled up next to him in the locker room and asked, "What happened?"

"I got home a little late last night," he said, slipping off his gym shoe.

"That's all?"

"Yeah."

"Aren't you tired?"

"Yeah, but we sure kicked ass today, didn't we?"

Coming back to the present, I heard Jerry say, "Whatcha gonna do, stand there all day?"

"Nah," I said and walked under the basket to rebound for him. He didn't speak as he took shot after shot, moving from one spot to the next, focusing on the basket as if nothing else existed. Only the thump of the basketball on the floor and the scratch of the ball ripping the net made a sound.

Just before three o'clock, Sam Watkins and Larry Humes walked in.

"Hey, guys," said Humes in a voice barely audible. Sam nodded hello. He grabbed two basketballs, bounced one to Larry, and turned his attention to shooting.

In came sophomore newcomers Herb Williams and Ron Johnson, along with senior Larry Denton. Soon the Armory filled with the sound of balls pounding, gym shoes squealing, and metal clanging.

At three o'clock Sloan shouted, "Let's get it going!"

Before I tossed the balls inbound to Sam Watkins to start the first play, I bounced the ball to the floor hard with both hands. "This is it," I whispered under my breath.

◆ ◆ ◆

WE SCRIMMAGED AT THE ARMORY every day for two hours. To start, we'd divide up teams by shooting free throws. The first five to make one comprised the Shirts team, the next five the Skins. Those left made up a third team that would have to sit and wait to play the Shirts–Skins winner.

Sweat drenched our bodies and bathed our faces as we thundered up and down the court like a herd of wild colts. I startled at the vehemence of everyone's effort, the ferociousness with which players battled each other, the no-holds-barred fervor with which each team played to win. I realized I didn't care. I longed to end my basketball career as a starter, to be an integral part of a legendary team. I'd do anything to make that happen.

Every ball possession took on the character of a free-for-all. I dribbled the ball up court to initiate the offense and then bounced it to Larry Humes, his back to the basket, close to the free-throw line. I knew what he would do, and he knew that I knew. I juked to my left to clear a path and ran directly at him. He stuffed the ball into my gut, quarterback style, as he pivoted out of my way allowing me to charge to the basket as hard as I could for a layup.

"Yeah!" Humes shouted, sweet music to my ears.

Hauling the ball off the backboard after an errant shot, Herb Williams fired a one-handed baseball pass to Sam Watkins that whooshed through the air like a cannonball. Sam promptly dribbled up the center of the court while I filled the right lane and Humes the left. Reaching the free-throw line, he turned his head toward me and dropped a nifty no-look bounce pass to Larry on his left for an easy layup.

"All right!" Sloan yelled from behind, giving voice to the sense of satisfaction we all felt.

On defense, I shuffled my feet as fast as I could and then stepped in front of one of my opponents as he attempted to drive past me to the basket. When he knocked me to the floor, Watkins reached down and pulled me to my feet. "Good hustle," he barked.

We kept at it every day throughout September and into October, growing stronger, more fluid, more cohesive. Sloan, Watkins, Humes, and I had been schooled in Coach McCutchan's system now for two full seasons. We not only knew his offensive and defensive strategies, we knew the nuances of each other's games like brothers who'd shared the same bedroom growing up. I could feel the bond grow between us and hoped it augured well for the future.

Yet beneath the surface my unease continued. It was mathematics. There were five starting slots, three of which were locked up by Jerry Sloan, Larry Humes, and Sam Watkins. That left two spots to be fought over by four of us—Herb Williams competed with my Bosse High teammate, Larry Denton, for the center position, while I was up against Ron Johnson for the guard spot.

Ron Johnson, a sophomore new to the varsity, stood five foot eleven and had both spring to his legs and bounce in his step. He had the moves of a natural guard, being sure with his ball handling and quick to jack up jumpers from all distances without hesitation. Despite a baby face that sported a ready smile and twinkling black eyes, he moved on the court with authority, like someone who felt he belonged there.

To me, Ron Johnson carried the patina of Aces basketball, and I could not help but look at him with the disdain of a rival. I played against him with more urgency and guarded him extra tight. I spread my legs, tilted onto the balls of my feet, and crouched lower than usual so I could shuffle with him in any direction without losing an advantage. I was determined to not only defeat him, but to break him.

But Johnson proved plucky, quick, and determined. One day, he kissed a short jumper off the backboard and into the basket over my outstretched hand. He'd held that shooter's pose an unnecessary amount of time, a grin of satisfaction on his face. The Ace in me added "Good shot" to the chorus of clapping and hooting, but the competitor in me thought, *I'll wipe that smirk off your face, you little shit.*

The constant action on the court gave me little time to think or fret, what with the ever-present need to react, almost instantaneously, to the second-by-second changing circumstances. Watkins's man might beat him on the dribble, requiring me to instantly slide over from mine to help out. Humes might unexpectedly loft one of his hook shots, and I would need to position myself to rebound. Sloan might zip a pass to me as I came off a pick, giving me but a split second to get off my jump shot.

But always lurking inside me was this demonic beast, ever alert to an unfocused moment. It was like he never slept and had no other purpose than to prey on my self-doubts and fears of failure. He lived inside my mind and took advantage of every opportunity to bedevil me with messages that would almost buckle me at the knees: "You'd better get with it or you'll lose that starting spot." "This is your last year and you're going to go out a loser." "You'll be humiliated when you have to sit there on the bench for everyone to see."

I felt beleaguered and besieged, fighting this two-front war, one on the court, the other within the confines of my own head. I desperately wanted to win both. All I knew was to soldier on.

•   •   •

FINALLY CAME OCTOBER 14, THE last day of our Armory practices. The next day, at three o'clock, my teammates and I would assemble in Carson Center around Coach McCutchan. I felt a mixture of excitement and dread.

After two hours of running up and down the Armory court, Sloan, Humes, Watkins, and I sat lathered in sweat, our legs outstretched, leaning against the wooden bleachers that had been accordioned back against the brick wall. Our muscles ached. But we were young, supple, and hopeful about the upcoming season.

"We've done good, guys," Humes said, looking around at us and nodding.

"Yeah," said Watkins.

"How far do you think we can go?" I asked.

"How about all the way," Watkins said.

"Well, it's up to us, isn't it," Sloan said, looking first at Watkins and then to Humes and me.

No one said a word.

I got up, said, "See you guys tomorrow," and walked out of the Armory. I did not look back.

# 2

## CARSON CENTER PREPARATION

I T WAS THURSDAY, OCTOBER 15, 1964, THE first day of basketball practice. It was a gorgeous autumn afternoon, the kind of day in which the deep-
blue sky seemed to reach to eternity and the patches of gold, red, and orange
made the foliage pop.

The crispness of the air bit my skin and stung my lungs as I walked to Carson
Center, the Aces' practice facility just north of campus across Walnut Street.
I saw this street as a line of demarcation that separated my two selves: on
campus, I was a college student, a fraternity brother, carefree and jaunty; at
Carson Center, I was an Evansville College Purple Ace, someone who took joy
in playing basketball but, at the same time, someone who suffered the anxiety
of possible failure and humiliation.

Unlike the Armory, with its fortress-like emanation, Carson Center looked
plain and simple, much like a manufacturing plant built more for performance
and productivity than for protection. My jaw tightened and my pulse quickened
as I approached its entrance, as if I were the subject of a Pavlovian experiment
whose autonomic nervous system was conditioned to respond to the sight of it.

Inside, I paused at the huge glass display case full of basketball trophies, plaques, and team pictures going all the way back to the 1930s. Front and center were three tall, rectangular NCAA Championship trophies, one from 1959, another from 1960, and the newest from 1964, which I'd helped put there just months before.

To the right of the trophy case ran a long hallway named the Corridor of Champions. Action photos of former Aces elected into the Athletic Hall of Fame adorned both sides of the wall. Coaches' offices and team meeting rooms nestled to the right, a basketball court to the left, behind a wall, used mostly for intramural games.

I spent most of my Carson Center time on the two side-by-side basketball courts left of the trophy case. If the Armory court nestled under a soft yellow glow, these glistened bright and white under rows of overhead florescent lights, showcasing triumph and laying bare inadequacy. In this monstrous space, the thump of basketballs, the shouts of players, and the screech of rubber on wood reverberated as if in an echo chamber.

I headed to the locker room behind the court, breathing in the familiar smell of rubbing liniment, powder, and stale sweat. Teammates sat in front of their lockers in various stages of undress, exchanging none of the banter that preceded our Armory workouts. I pulled on my white gym shorts, laced up my sneakers, slipped my practice shirt over my head, worn red-side out as an affirmation and a middle finger to my challengers.

At ten minutes to three, Coach McCutchan stepped into the gym and the air filled with a solemnity until then only implied. *Here we go*, I thought. This was for real, and I knew the stakes were high.

Arad McCutchan stood close to six foot two. Despite a receding hairline and a little softening around the middle, he kept his fifty-two-year-old body in good condition and carried himself like he could still play the game. His black horn-rimmed glasses gave him the look of a mathematics professor, which he still was, teaching one math class each quarter. He approached his players with a dispassionate, calculating eye and a mind trained to solve problems, geared to fielding a winning team.

Promptly at three o'clock, Coach blew his whistle and summoned us to center court. He cradled a basketball against his left hip and said, "Okay, boys, here's our goals for the year: one, win our holiday tournament; two, win the conference championship; three, win the national championship. Nothing more, nothing less."

He paused and leveled his gaze at us. "How about it? You in?"

I had the urge to shout "Sir, yes, sir," but thought better of it and joined the others in clapping and shouting "Yeah!" instead.

"All right. Then let's go outside. A quick lap around East Side Park and then on to the Armory," he said, meaning the dreaded Armory steps. "Go."

Coach's approach to basketball was simple—constantly put pressure on the other team, which meant run, run, and then run some more. On offense, this meant getting the ball up court lickety-split before the other team had time to set up their defense. On defense, it meant constantly hawking the other team. His strategy required that we always be in better condition than our opponents.

Off we went, with Sloan and Humes taking the lead and the rest of us bunched close behind like a pack of wolves. We ran past picnic areas with concrete barbecue grills supported by metal poles, under trees where we stimulated flocks of birds to take flight, and around strolling couples taking advantage of nature's beauty. When we made the final turn to head back toward the Armory, we skirted first the Little League and then the Pony League baseball diamonds where I'd spent many summer afternoons.

"Ain't this fun, guys?" Williams said.

"Fun, my ass," said Sloan, not looking back.

"Bitch, bitch, bitch," I said.

"I'll give you something to bitch about," Sloan said as he picked up the pace.

"See what you caused," Williams said, elbowing me.

Coach waited for us at the bottom of the Armory steps. "Good work," he said. Then, before we could catch our breath, "Let's do twenty-five." We took two or three steps at once going up, one at a time going down, angling our feet slightly to avoid landing on the edge of the step and spraining an ankle.

"Push!" McCutchan yelled.

I completed the laps and bent over, hands on my knees, gasping for air. *What is he, some kind of sadist?* I thought.

"Good hustle," he said, ambling among us. "This may hurt now, but it'll be a piece of cake by the time we start the season. Walk back to Carson Center, get some water, and stretch. Then we'll get back to work."

*If we're still alive*, I thought.

Back on the court, Coach blew his whistle and said, "Okay, three lanes, full court."

He bounced a basketball to Sloan and we broke into three lines, one line under the basket and the other two along the sidelines. Sloan passed the ball to me on the left sideline, and, with Williams on the right, the three of us started sprinting up court. I passed the ball back to Jerry, then he passed it to Herb

Williams on his right, who then passed it back to Jerry, and then again over to me. We continued this maneuver until Herb gently laid the ball into the basket. Not once did the ball touch the floor. When our group reached midcourt, Coach bounced another basketball to the next man in the middle lane for that threesome to do the same, then the next, and the next.

After maybe ten trips up and down the court, McCutchan blew his whistle and announced, "Two-man drills: Grieger and McClary, Watkins and Johnson, Eberhart and Forman, and Kingston and Rubush. You guys on this end with me, the big guys at the other end with Coach O'Brien."

Two-man drills pitted one pair against another, one twosome trying to score, the other doing what they could to prevent it. These drills tested our skills and revealed not only who was most talented but who had the stronger will.

"Grieger and McClary, you take on Watkins and Johnson first," Coach said.

I shot a glance at Johnson. I saw in his set jaw and icy stare the same resolve that I had.

Coach bounced the ball to Johnson, and I got into my defensive stance, crouching low with my knees flexed, bent forward at the waist, hands down with palms up and forward, in ready position to snatch the ball. Johnson started to dribble, scanning the court. "Pick left!" McClary yelled, and I fought over Watkins's block and kept Johnson from driving to his right to the basket.

"That's the way!" McCutchan shouted.

Johnson kept dribbling. I stayed close to him, not letting myself relax, sensing the depth of his determination. He dribbled to his left to once again try to rub me off by using Watkins as a pick. I crowded him closer and shuffled past Watkins. Johnson leaped into the air and let loose with a high-arching jumper from twenty feet, my left hand full in his face. The ball bounced off the rim and into McClary's grasp.

"Good hustle, both of you," McCutchan said.

I wiped the sweat from my forehead with my shirtsleeve and trotted to the top of the key for our turn on offense, not acknowledging Coach's praise.

McCutchan bounced the ball to me. I stood with my left foot forward, my right foot back, ready to burst one way or the other. I watched McClary come from my right to set a pick on Johnson. I faked to my left and dribbled to my right. But Johnson fought through McClary's pick, staying close. I straightened my body and slowed my dribble, causing Johnson to relax a millisecond. As he did, I lowered my head and barreled past him to lay the ball off the glass and into the basket.

McClary swatted me on the behind.

I pushed down a feeling of triumph and forced myself to concentrate on the next play.

We kept at these drills another thirty minutes. Coach watched every move and kept up his commentary: "Move your feet." "Fight over the pick." "Hustle." Finally, closing in on five o'clock, he blew his whistle and said, "Okay, boys, enough for today. Good work. See you tomorrow."

I stood near center court, bent over at the waist. Sweat dripped from my eyebrows and chin as I breathed deep to fill my lungs. I glanced over at Watkins, who held a similar pose. We both rolled our eyes as if to say, "We gotta do this again tomorrow?"

Wrecked from putting my all into every play, I slouched into the dressing room. I felt encouraged from this first day's effort, but I knew that perilous and treacherous days lay ahead, and all I could do was take them one at a time.

* * *

COACH McCUTCHAN HOSTED A PICNIC in his backyard on the last Sunday of October. I brought along my girlfriend, Joyce, in part as a distraction from having to engage in basketball talk.

I'd met Joyce at a Tau Kappa Epsilon rush mixer the fall before. She was blond and fair and quietly sexy. We'd danced to the rock-and-roll of The Four Most, drank beer from red plastic cups, and had been a couple ever since. After too many complicated and drama-filled relationships, I found her laid-back ways and undemanding nature refreshing.

We both arrived at the picnic in jeans and sweatshirts. I took Joyce's hand and led her behind Coach's house, where I found Coach and various other Aces with their girlfriends, all gathered around a cooler full of soft drinks and a long table with a white tablecloth. On the table were pretzels and chips, cookies, and hot dogs, burgers, and buns. A grill stood to the side, smoldering white-hot charcoal. A badminton net occupied the center of the yard.

In jest, I challenged Coach to a game. To my surprise, he accepted. Despite our age difference, Coach sprinted to a quick 8–3 lead. He hit passing bullets into corners and drove me to the back of the court with high-arching volleys, only to drop a floater just over the net that I couldn't reach. When he drew me to the net, he'd then lob the birdie over my head, which fell harmlessly at the back of the court. I felt like I was up against Rocket Rod Laver.

My teammates gathered around the court and began to cheer for McCutchan, while I took on the role of stooge.

"Great shot, Coach!" bellowed Herb Williams as Coach blazed another passing shot.

"A little more hustle, Russ," teased Larry Humes as I failed another attempt to catch up to a lob that barely cleared the net.

"Go, Coach! You're the man!" Johnson shouted.

I stole a glance at Joyce, who grimaced and turned her palms up as if to say, "I don't know what to tell you."

*Damn,* I thought. *I'd better hit the accelerator before this gets uglier.*

And it did. The cheering section began in unison to announce the score after each point. "Eleven to five." "Fifteen to eight." "Nineteen to ten." And mercifully, "Twenty-one to fourteen."

As the cheering died, Coach walked under the net and draped his arm around my shoulders. "Thanks for the game, Russ," he said. Then, to the crowd, he added, "I'm just grateful that Grieger is better at basketball than badminton."

I smiled, pretending it was no big deal, but I felt embarrassed.

Later that afternoon I drove Joyce home. She sat close to me, anticipating, I figured, that I needed some extra support to buck up my nicked dignity.

"That was a nightmare," I said.

"Why?" she asked. "They're your friends and could care less about badminton."

We rode in silence a few minutes, dusk settling around us.

"Well," I said, "I'd better do better on the court tomorrow than I did in that damn backyard."

◆ ◆ ◆

ON MONDAY OF THE THIRD week, Coach McCutchan gathered us at center court and announced, "Today we put it together—five on five." Then, looking around and pointing a finger at each of us in turn, he called out, "Sloan . . . Humes . . . Watkins . . . Grieger . . . Williams, you run first team. Let's get it going, half-court offense first."

I stifled what I really felt, but inside I screamed, *Yes!* I looked down, happy to see I was wearing my practice jersey red-side out.

The yellow-shirted second-teamers took their defensive positions. Coach admonished them to make us work and then shouted, "Let's go!" My heart quickened a beat or two.

Sam Watkins and I started the offense at half-court, with Humes down low on the right side of the free-throw lane and Sloan and Williams stacked across from him on the left. Watkins bounced the ball to Humes just right of the free-throw lane and cut past him hard to the basket. The yellow shirts knew the offense as well as we did and cut off all the lanes. This forced Humes to pass the ball to me at the top of the key. I immediately rifled the ball to an open Sloan on the left, whose defender had been blocked away by Williams. He swished the ball through the basket as if that's where it wanted to go.

"Again," Coach commanded.

This time I initiated the offense by flipping a pass over my defender's shoulder to Sloan on the left, close to the free-throw lane. I feinted toward the middle to open up a path down the line and then barreled straight ahead. He pivoted out of my way as I shot past him and in the process picked off my man behind him with his hip. This left Sloan's man to guard one of the two of us. He chose Sloan, and Jerry left-handed a push pass to me near the baseline. I jumped, shot, and watched the net dance.

"All rights" rebounded off the walls of the gym. *Two for two,* I thought, stoked that I'd had a hand in both of these plays.

We repeated our offense over and over, pushing hard against our teammates, who played as if their lives were at stake. Coach McCutchan paced the sidelines and provided a steady flow of instruction: "Cut hard." "Hit it." "Hustle." At the end of each play, he grunted, "Again."

After a full thirty minutes of this, he blew his whistle and said, "Okay, boys, take five for water, then let's go defense to offense."

With sweat dripping from my chin to the floor, I loitered with the guys in front of the water fountain, waiting for my turn to get a drink. On my left, Humes said to Sloan and me, "We work good together."

"Yeah," agreed Sloan.

I drank some water, picked up a basketball, and dribbled to center court, feeling encouraged. The "we" in Humes's simple sentence included me. But I knew better than to relax. This was only the beginning. *Bear down,* I told myself.

Defense to offense was an excellent practice method since it simulated game conditions. It started with the first team playing defense against the second team. If the second team scored, we'd have to play defense again. If we stopped them, we'd either race down court on a fast break or slow the ball down to run our offense. Once the play ended, we'd return to defense.

I took my defensive stance against Ron Johnson. The strongest part of his game was his shooting. I knew he could wear out the net, and I didn't want to give him the chance. I admired his quick first step, the spring in his legs, his feathery shooting touch. I knew him to be a real threat to my starting position and the one to delegate me to being a benchwarmer.

When Johnson started the offense by dribbling the ball across midcourt, I crowded him tight. I forced him to pass the ball to Gary McClary, then dropped back to protect the middle from an inlet pass. Seeing this, McClary hustled the ball back to an open Johnson, who let fly a twenty-footer that rattled through the rim.

"Good shot," said McCutchan.

"Shit," I hissed under my breath, recognizing that my boneheaded decision had left Johnson open.

Johnson started the next yellow-shirt offense by again passing the ball to McClary. This time I stayed tight to Johnson, denying him the ball. Moments later, McClary clanged a long shot off the side of the rim that I corralled between the free-throw line and the sideline. I slung the ball two-handed to Watkins at center court, who immediately led a fast break with Sloan filling the left lane and me the right. Watkins dribbled to the free-throw line, turned his head toward Sloan, and bounced the ball to me on his right. I took the ball on the run and laid it in the basket without breaking stride.

"That's the way to do it!" boomed McCutchan. Then, "Again."

Practice took on a familiar pattern over the next few weeks. After warm-ups, we rehearsed our offense, then ran defense to offense, and followed that with a full-court scrimmage. We ended practice working on our out-of-bounds plays and free throws. With each passing day, I developed a growing appreciation for my running mates, for both their personalities and how they played their games.

Jerry Sloan went to battle every second he spent on the court. A two-time All-American, he knew he was good, the best in every game he played. Raw-boned and wiry at six feet six inches tall, he fought for every rebound, dove for every loose ball, and got in the face of any man he guarded. Best of all, Jerry didn't care who starred or scored, so long as each of us put out the same 100 percent effort he did on the court.

If Sloan was a warrior, Larry Humes was a ballet dancer. Slender and loose-limbed at six foot four, Larry ran the court effortlessly, consuming yards of hardwood with each fluid stride. Though soft-spoken and understated, he liked nothing better than to gather the ball under the basket, contort his body this way and that, shucking off opponents, and loft a soft, sylph-like shot that always seemed to find its way into the basket. What pleased me most was to watch Larry make one of those beauties and then glide down the court with eyes glazed, as if he inhabited a place of ecstasy no one else could access.

Off the court, Sam Watkins had a smile that could warm any room and a chuckle that could lighten any mood. But, on the court, he acted like a cold-blooded assassin. He said little, maintained a poker face, and stared with piercing, black eyes. Sam always challenged the man he defended, stood ready to pull the trigger of his jump shot, and forced his way to the basket through the smallest openings. The only words he used on the court were "Let's pick it up," "Let's finish them off," or "Let's get with it."

Herb Williams had the bounce of a kangaroo in his legs. At six foot three, he could stand flat-footed under the basket and leap up to slam the ball through the basket two-handed. He bounded up and down the court as if he had coiled springs in each ankle. He leaped up so high that one would swear he stood six foot eight. He came to practice every day with a wide smile, a warm greeting, and tons of enthusiasm. It was hard not to be affected by his cheerfulness.

The more we played together, the more familiar I became with my teammates' games. With familiarity came predictability, then efficiency, and finally trust. I could actually feel the connection between us grow.

Coach McCutchan must have felt it as well. When asked in mid-November how this team compared with last year's championship team, he said: "I won't say this is a better team. But they seem to be a little further along in their development than the team was at this time a year ago. They seem to work well together."

The Friday before Thanksgiving was the kind of winter day you dreaded if you lived in Indiana. Branches extended stark and naked toward thick gray clouds. A biting wind gusted at will and spit occasional icy splatters. Though the temperature hung in the low thirties, it felt colder than that.

Despite the weather, I felt good. I had just left The Indian, the fast food restaurant in the basement of the student union building where my fraternity brothers and I had made plans to meet at our favorite bar later that night after we'd dropped off our dates. I felt confident about life and myself as I dressed for practice. But I wasn't prepared for what was about to come. On the court, Coach McCutchan announced, "Johnson, you run with the first team today in place of Grieger."

The air turned suffocating. Time froze and sound evaporated. I felt a burning sensation fill my chest, as if someone had poured molten lead down my throat. It seemed like every one of my teammates stared at me. I didn't know what to do except just stand there. If I could have become invisible, I would have.

I did my best to hide my shock. I took off my practice shirt and inverted it to the yellow side, the side of the second team. I felt ashamed, embarrassed, humiliated, having no choice but to soldier on.

McCutchan devoted most of that day's practice to a full-court scrimmage. I know not how, but I posted a good practice, hitting several jump shots from the perimeter, tipping in a missed shot with my left hand, and setting up the yellow team's offense with the right passes.

At a break in the action, I sat on the floor under the basket, legs outstretched, leaning back against the wall. Larry Humes plopped down to my left, our shirts soaked with sweat. He slapped my leg and said, "I think we're much better with you than without you."

"Thanks," I mumbled.

I drove home after practice, picked at my supper, and retreated into my bedroom. I laid on my bed, my forearm draped over my eyes, my mood dark and confused. I begin to think that what drove Coach McCutchan to demote me was the same thing that had caused my failed high school romance and that had prevented me from breaking free from the platoon system the season before: There was something deeply wrong with me, something missing and inadequate, some secret defect in my broken self that McCutchan had perceived.

My frustration and anger came out of nowhere. I bolted up, swiped my books off my desk, and shouted, "Goddamn it!" Then I kicked them across the room.

A moment later, Dad stuck his head in my room and asked, "What's going on?"

"Nothing," I said, more stridently than necessary.

"Want to talk?"

"No!"

Late that night, after my parents had gone to sleep, I tried to get a grip. I felt devastated. It wasn't enough to do my best, to contribute, to be a part of the team. I had to succeed, which meant being on the starting team. To fall short of this made me a failure.

I leaned back and sighed, looked around, and replaced my books on my desk. I flipped the pages of my three-ring binder and came to the notes that I had taken in Dr. Paul Grabill's contemporary issues class. Under what I had titled, "The Wit and Wisdom of William Shakespeare," I found: "It is not in the stars to hold our destiny, but in ourselves."

That quote caught my attention. I remembered the discussion Dr. Grabill had led just that week about the differences between taking a victim stance in life and taking charge of one's own future. I rolled these thoughts over in my mind, knew that this very moment represented such a choice, and wondered if I had the strength and courage to take charge. More out of bravado than conviction, I told myself: *You're not going to roll over and play dead. Go claim what's yours tomorrow.*

At the next Monday's practice, Coach put me back on the starting team. I never discovered his motivation for my demotion, but this episode taught me never to be cocky or complacent. Maybe that was Coach's message the whole time. I'll never know.

• • •

I SAT IN MY BEDROOM THE night before our opening game against Iowa and fiddled with a business-sized card that displayed a photo of myself in purple ink, my name printed below it, and, underneath that, "6'2" Guard." The other side listed the Aces' twenty-four-game schedule. These cards, with my picture and those of my teammates on them, could be found all over Evansville and beyond, in banks, bars, and businesses.

It struck me that some sadist must have front-loaded our schedule with games against the toughest teams. Whenever I bragged about that season, I rarely mentioned the small schools we'd played, like Ball State, Kentucky Wesleyan, or Valparaiso. I only mentioned the behemoths—Iowa, Northwestern, Notre Dame, George Washington, Louisiana State University, Massachusetts, and Butler.

I looked out my bedroom window at the concrete expanse between my house and the backyard that had served as my private basketball court since childhood. I pictured myself wearing blue jeans and a sweatshirt, throwing up jump shots and fighting for rebounds against my neighborhood playmates. I saw how intensely I played, contesting every shot, fighting for every possession, attempting to score every time I got my hands on the ball. Whenever I played on that court, sometimes unconsciously, sometimes with full awareness, I fantasized about playing big-time basketball.

I moved to my bed, slipped under the covers, and thought, *Tomorrow night I'll be a starter for the Evansville College Purple Aces.* I closed my eyes and heard the steady thump, thump, thump of the basketball bouncing off concrete until I drifted off.

# 3

## THE IOWA HAWKEYES

I SAT IN MY LIVING room on the morning of Saturday, November 5, 1964, and slowly read the *Evansville Courier*, even the obituaries. Then I tossed the paper aside with a flick of my wrist and shot a glance at the big gold clock shaped like an exploding star that hung on the wall over the TV. It read ten o'clock, a full ten hours before tip-off. The second hand ticked in slow motion, seeming to take its time as it moved from one digit to the next.

"Hurry up, dammit," I spat out.

What I went through that morning was in no way unusual. It had happened the morning of every game I'd played since grade school. I awoke with a knot in my stomach the size of a cantaloupe, feelings so electric and untamed that the hair on my head could have stood straight up like a Saturday-morning cartoon cat with its tail stuck in an electric socket. Back then it could have been Holy Rosary Elementary School or Central High School, but today it was the Iowa Hawkeyes.

The University of Iowa belonged to the Big Ten, one of the most high-profile and feared conferences in the country. It shared headlines with such powerhouse programs as Michigan, Ohio State, and Indiana. During the week, whenever someone said, "Good luck against Iowa," the dread in my gut reminded me of what was at stake—a test of whether or not I was good enough.

At eleven thirty, my best buddy and TKE fraternity brother, Gene Hahn, knocked on the front door and walked in without waiting. "I knew you'd be uptight," he said in his soft voice that bordered on a mumble. "Come on, let's get out of here."

Gene and I drove to the Coral Drive-In, the high school hangout I'd cruised hundreds of times as a teenager. We found a parking space beside a squawk box but then walked inside to sit at a booth near the back where we wouldn't be disturbed. I glanced out the window and spotted a huge water tower that sat high over the landscape. I noted peace signs, obscene phrases, and hearts with lovers' names painted in them. I remembered scaling its metal ladder, painting my own words, and peeing off the side.

I smiled at the memory, feeling my tension evaporate some.

"What's so funny?" Gene asked.

"See that tower over there?" I pointed out the window, then shared my memory.

"What a dumbass!" he said, grinning.

"You think?"

We sat for a minute, studying the menu. I hadn't eaten yet, and I suddenly felt hungry. Our waitress took our order of burgers and fries.

"How about after the game?" Gene asked. "Want me to come by the locker room and then head to Art and Helen's? The guys will be there."

"Yeah, sure. How about bringing Joyce along?"

The waitress brought our food. Gene held his burger in his left hand and slid French fries into his mouth with his right, first dipping each into a glob of ketchup. Between bites, he said, "I took Kathy out last night."

"Yeah, where'd you go?" I asked, but with little interest.

"We went to the Rocca Bar for pizza and beer before heading to the parking lot behind the frat house. Didn't get home till after midnight."

"All right!" I said, giving him a thumbs-up, the kind of response I thought he wanted.

We shot the breeze for another hour or so as if we had nothing better to do. There was an unspoken understanding that talk of the game was off-limits. As we walked to the cash register to settle our bill, I felt a hand on my shoulder, turned, and saw a man with a small boy. The boy was maybe twelve and was wearing jeans, a gray Evansville College sweatshirt, and a New York Yankees baseball cap.

The man held up a menu. "Will you sign this for my son?"

"Sure," I said, jolted back to the reality of game day.

I signed it, took the boy's hat, and put it on my head. "Can I keep this?" I asked, quickly adding "Just kidding" when I saw him dart a fretful glance at his dad. I tussled his hair and replaced the cap where it belonged.

"Thanks, and good luck tonight," the dad said, and then he and his son walked away.

"Aren't you hot shit," Gene said.

We paid our bill, got into the car, and eased out of the parking lot into traffic to head back to my house. I flipped on the radio to hear the broadcaster say, "Don't forget the game at the stadium tonight at eight o'clock, the Aces opening game against the big, bad Iowa Hawkeyes."

"Like I could forget." I turned off the radio with a flick of my wrist.

"Ready for tonight?" Gene asked.

"Yeah, I guess."

"Who're you guarding?"

"Only their star, Jimmy Rodgers," I said, throwing a glance at Gene.

"You can take him."

I kept my doubts to myself but was grateful for the words of encouragement.

The closer we got to my home, the tenser I felt. When we pulled up to the curb, Gene jabbed my bicep and said, "Be cock tonight."

"I will," I said, more assuredly than I felt. I got out of the car and slammed the door behind me.

I went inside the house and straight to my bedroom without speaking to anyone. Fear filled my stomach as it had before Gene rescued me. Reason told me that this was just a game, not, say, the war in Vietnam. If only I could have listened to reason. All I knew to do was to accept my suffering as the price I had to pay to play the sport.

◆ ◆ ◆

THE SUN HAD FINALLY SET WHEN I slid into my parents' blue 1962 Ford Fairlane and, with the radio turned to the Aces' pregame broadcast on WGBF, drove to Roberts Stadium. Temperatures hung in the low thirties. Blustering winds rattled tree branches and swirled leaves. A full moon almost made headlights unnecessary.

Leaving the safety of my parents' home was frightening. I motored to the stadium with the sense of dread astronaut Alan Shepard must have felt the hour before blasting off into outer space. I took a deep breath when I came upon Roberts Stadium across Division Street—red-bricked, one-storied, rectangular, like a giant warehouse. Row upon row of parked cars already surrounded it, a full hour before tip-off. Fans jammed ten deep in huge semicircles around the stadium's entrances, pressing toward the turnstiles. I thought of them more as wild beasts ready to devour me than rabid Aces fans.

Sitting there, taking it all in, I heard Marv Bates, the WGBF play-by-play announcer, remark, "Ladies and gentlemen, these Aces games have become more than just about basketball."

*No kidding,* I thought.

"In fact," he went on, "they have become an event around which family and friends gather—at the stadium, at neighborhood bars, around their radios at home—to solidify their connection with each other through the Aces experience. More than that, they have become an opportunity for the residents of the entire Evansville area to collectively affirm their community pride."

There is no way I could have put those thoughts into words, but I knew them to be true and felt the weight of them on my shoulders.

I crossed Division Street, drove through the parking lot, and eased downhill to the players' entrance at court level, three stories below ground. There I walked through the same metal door as had all prior Aces, as well as Elvis Presley and Frank Sinatra, Minnesota Fats, John Kennedy, and Richard Nixon. Stadium employees and security guards greeted me with slaps on the back and well wishes as I passed.

"Go get 'em, big guy!"

"Good luck tonight!"

"Get it done, fella!"

Being there in the reality of the stadium quieted my nerves; I didn't know why and didn't care. I reached the court and looked out over the brightly lit space. Thousands of fans had already taken their seats. Others walked around the space between the bench seats and the bleachers high above the court, while still others descended the aisles to find their seats. It reminded me of the ant colony that had sat on a table in my Bosse High School biology class years before.

The mood in the locker room was tense. Sloan sat shoeless, staring at the floor. He looked up and nodded at me when I entered. Humes, already outfitted for the game, said "Hey" in a soft voice. Watkins walked past me on the way to the bathroom without saying a word. Williams stood in the middle of the room, bobbing up and down on his toes and checking his image in the full-length mirror in the adjacent shower room.

I put on my home whites, watched as the trainer taped my ankles, and settled between Sloan and Humes. The arena hummed like a jet airplane waiting to thrust down the runway for takeoff. Just as I was about to ask "Where the hell is Mac?" Coach walked into the dressing room. He wore a natty outfit—black slacks, black-checkered sport coat, and red socks. *Dressed for battle*, I thought.

"Everybody ready?" he asked, not expecting an answer. He glanced around the room. "Okay, get on out there and get loose."

We ran onto the court and into a blast of noise that would've singed our eyebrows had it been heat. We formed into two lines for layups. After ten minutes we broke into pairs to practice our shooting, one of us rebounding for the other, then reversing our roles. Mostly to settle myself, but also to relax my teammates, I kept up a steady stream of encouragement.

"Looking good, Larry."

"Nice shot, Sam."

"You're the man, Jerry."

"The Kangaroo Kid, Herbie."

At the end of our warm-ups, we performed an old Aces ritual that I had watched way back in high school. The first Ace dribbled straight to the basket, followed single file by the rest. Instead of laying the ball into the basket, he leaped up and bounced the ball softly off the backboard and trotted off court toward the dressing room. A second and third Ace then followed suit by leaping and rebounding the ball against the glass without letting it touch the floor. They too trotted to the dressing room without looking back. The other Aces waited their turn with Herb Williams taking up the rear.

Some of the fans noticed this, stood, and cheered. This caught the attention of others, and the shouts of excitement grew in number and decibel until they reached a deafening roar as each succeeding Ace took his turn.

Finally came Herb. Instead of repeating what the others had done, he leaped high, grabbed the ball with both hands, and slammed it full force down through the basket. The exploding roar reverberated throughout the stadium as he too disappeared from sight. Once in the dressing room, he let out a loud whoop and said, "Ain't I something?"

I looked at Sloan and said, "Unbelievable."

Ten minutes later I sat on the bench alongside my teammates, my heart in my throat. After the announcer had introduced the Hawkeye starters, 12,500 red-clad Aces fans stood and cheered in anticipation of our turn.

"And now, for the Aces, starting at guard, Russ Grieger," he bellowed. With what I hoped was a modicum of panache, I loped onto the court for my brief moment of singular glory, soon joined by Larry Humes, Sam Watkins, Herb Williams, and Jerry Sloan. The clamor that greeted me grew until I could hardly hear Sloan's name when he was introduced. I felt on fire, couldn't wait for the game to begin.

Moments later, Herb Williams toed up against Iowa's six-foot-eight center, George Peebles, at center court. The referee tossed the ball up, and Williams leaped high to tip the ball to Jerry Sloan. He grabbed it and dribbled over the centerline. We passed the ball around the perimeter until Watkins tossed the ball to Larry Humes in the pivot. With his back to the basket, Larry faked to his right, dribbled to his left, and lofted a soft hook shot over his defender's outstretched hand and into the basket.

*Yes!* I thought, clenching my right fist.

Coach McCutchan preached up-tempo basketball, and nothing delighted him more than a well-executed fast break. Williams grabbed a rebound, and I heard Coach yell, "Outlet!" Herb complied by firing the ball to Sloan at center court with Watkins and me filling the outside lanes. He pounded the ball on the dribble to the free-throw line, glanced left and then right. Without picking up his dribble, he barreled past his Iowa defender to lay the ball in himself.

When Iowa made a basket, the Ace closest to the ball quickly inbounded it to move it up the court as fast as possible. This often prevented Iowa from setting up their full-court press. When they did, we fired the ball past their first wave of defenders to Sloan, Humes, or Williams at midcourt to create what amounted to a three-on-two fast break.

Both teams ran at every opportunity, and the lead changed hands several times. Sweat drenched our jerseys. Five minutes into the game, I knew something was wrong. I gasped for breath so deeply and desperately I wondered if I was having a heart attack. At breaks in the action, I bent over with my hands on my knees and struggled for air. No one else on the court looked to be laboring like I was. I didn't realize it yet, but I was playing tense and hadn't relaxed into the rhythm of the game. I had made each offensive cut, each defensive maneuver, and each attempt for a rebound as if I was running a hundred-yard dash.

"Keep pushing!" Coach yelled as I ran past the bench.

"Yeah, right," I mumbled, stifling the urge to throw a hostile look at him.

Right then, a minor miracle took place. It turned out that the stadium custodian had attached brand-new nets to the rims that afternoon. The one at Iowa's end of the court had yet to stretch out, so the ball periodically got stuck rather than dropping freely to the floor after a basket.

When it happened for the third time, the referee blew his whistle and said to me, "Hey, Number Twenty-four, how about jumping up and stretching out the net?"

*Are you nuts?* I thought, too oxygen deprived to catch my breath.

I turned my back on him and meandered down the court with my hands on my hips till I could breathe normally. Then I walked under the basket, jumped up, and, hanging from the net with both hands, jerked it from side to side. That move stimulated my biggest applause of the evening.

When I dropped down, the referee bounded the ball to me. I banked the ball into the basket a couple of times. Each time the ball dropped cleanly through the net.

The crowd roared. I relaxed. The running commenced.

Two minutes later, Sam Watkins picked up his third foul and slouched to the bench. Three minutes after that, Jerry Sloan also committed his third foul and joined Sam courtside. A murmur filled the stadium as if the entire crowd had just witnessed a car crash.

I looked up at the scoreboard, noted our slim 21–20 lead, and uttered the first word that came to my mind: "Shit!"

But I had yet to fully appreciate the talents of Larry Humes. With Ron Johnson and Larry Denton filling in for Sloan and Watkins, we continued to feed the ball to Humes so he could work his magic from under the basket. His play could only be described as otherworldly. He made every shot in the playbook—long and short jumpers that floated through the net like feathers, hook shots with both his right and left hand that softly kissed the glass and dropped into the basket, rabbit-quick twisting and turning drives that left his defenders a half step behind. I noticed the satisfied, ethereal expression on his face after each move and remembered the days when I'd dominated games as he did. I felt a visceral connection with him as I watched.

Fortified by Larry's nineteen first-half points, we took a 40–38 lead into the dressing room at halftime. Glancing around at the crowd as I walked off the court, I thought the fans must share my exhaustion. They had jumped up and sat down so many times, shouting and pleading and exhorting, they looked as if they had run up and down the court with us for the last twenty minutes.

While we guzzled water and Coca-Cola, Coach applauded our effort and instructed us to box out better, cut down on errors, and avoid unnecessary fouls. Then, with a slight smile, he said, "If we keep running, boys, this game will be ours. Let's go out there and bring it home."

The second half unfolded just as intensely as the first. Iowa must have realized they couldn't keep up the pace because they tried to slow down the game. But, schooled as we were to run, run, run, we charged down the court at every chance, often sending three attackers down the floor against two defenders.

We led 53–49 midway through the second half when we made our move, a sensational two-minute flurry that left Iowa reeling. Humes hit a short jumper, Watkins drilled a twenty-footer, and Humes banked in another ten-footer to give us daylight. The crowd sensed the kill, rose to their feet, and roared. Before they had a chance to settle back into their seats, Williams intercepted an Iowa cross-court pass, dribbled uncontested the length of the court, and slammed the ball down through the basket. The roar increased to a deafening level. Another basket by Sloan and one more by Humes put us ahead by ten. The noise became so loud I couldn't hear the referee's whistle signaling Iowa's desperate time-out.

We assembled around Coach McCutchan. "Isn't this fun, boys?" he said.

The scoreboard displayed the final verdict: Aces 90, Iowa 83. But the score didn't communicate our second-half dominance. We ran them into the ground. Some of our passes were beyond belief, and, for the game, we hit thirty-three of our sixty-two shots for a remarkable 52 percent shooting average.

The locker room resembled Times Square on New Year's Eve just before the ball drops. I had to slither between people to get to the shower, a towel cinched around my waist.

I stood in the shower beside Herb Williams and let the hot water relax my muscles and settle the adrenaline still coursing through my body. Peeking out at the mayhem, Herb darted a glance at me and said, "If you can't find a towel, grab a fan to dry off."

Coach McCutchan held court before a group of reporters just outside the dressing room. He noted that Humes had hit sixteen of his twenty-one shots and seven of nine from the free-throw line. "He has the moves to get open if they play him one on one. In fact, he'll have a big night on anyone who tries to play him one on one."

One of the reporters asked, "Were you worried about the outcome of the game at halftime since both Sloan and Watkins had three fouls?"

"Actually, no," Coach replied. "I felt confident then. I was convinced if we could stay that close with Sloan and Watkins resting, I was pretty sure we could handle them later on."

After showering, I squeezed through the pack of visitors, again with a towel around my waist, and sat next to Jerry to dress. A ten-year-old kid wearing a yellow sweatshirt stepped on Jerry's bare foot. "Careful, son, those are my toes you're smashing," said Jerry.

I looked at Jerry and we both laughed.

"One down," I said.

"Yeah, only twenty-three more to go," he answered.

◆ ◆ ◆

GENE FOUND ME WITHIN THE mayhem and, together, we collected Joyce and walked out the stadium door. Joyce settled into my car, and we followed Gene to Art and Helen's, the neighborhood bar adopted by my fraternity brothers as our favorite watering hole. We walked through the smoke and honky-tonk music to a corner table where three of my fraternity brothers sat—Klee Wilson, Terry Cyson, and Eddie Paxton—along with Eddie's girlfriend, Suzanne.

I sat with my back to the room and took a long swig of beer. Leaning back, I felt a hand on my shoulder. I turned and saw a man wearing tan khaki pants and a red sweatshirt. "Hey, man, great game. Can I buy you a beer?"

"No, thanks," I said. "I'm in training." This was received with guffaws from the guys at the table.

This brief encounter drew my mind back to the stadium. I saw images of red-shirted fans standing and clapping, heard the ceaseless roar rising and falling. I remembered hands touching me on my back and shoulders, somewhere between a pat and a strike, as I left the court.

Klee Wilson interrupted my reverie. "Hey, frater, no kidding, you played a good game," he said.

"Yeah," said Eddie. "You made us proud, buddy."

"Thanks, guys," I said.

I appreciated these words of support from my brothers. I knew I'd done okay. I'd played every one of the game's forty minutes, maneuvering through Iowa's pressing defense with dexterity, doling out assists, and playing solid defense. Yet I'd connected on only two of my nine field-goal attempts, scored only six points, and made my presence felt only marginally. I was happy to be a starter, but I wanted so much more. I wanted to be valuable, indispensable. I wanted the team to be incomplete without my presence. I wanted the full respect of my teammates. I knew I'd have to do better.

"Hey, Russ," shouted Terry, bringing me back to the table once again. "You know you're our hero, don't you, you sweet thing?"

We all laughed, me the loudest. I put my arm around Joyce and gave her a hug. Then I took off my Aces uniform and became a fraternity brother for the rest of the night.

# Part Two

## The Ace Grows Up

In the arena of human life
the honors and rewards fall to those
who show their good qualities in action.
                                        —Aristotle

# Part Two

## The Ace Grows Up

# 4

## THE BEGINNINGS

I MUST HAVE BEEN FIVE or six the first time I picked up a basketball. I lived on Covert Avenue, directly across the street from a coal yard where trains stopped to refuel. The trains provided an endless source of fascination, but I was banned from visiting them because of the dangers posed by the elephantine boxcars that thunderclapped as they stopped.

That left the humdrum backyards as my playground. One fall day I roamed these unkempt yards, past soiled concrete stoops, clotheslines that drooped empty between rusted poles, and weather-beaten doghouses. Down the block, I came upon a dilapidated wooden backboard and hoop topping a pole stuck into a barren patch of ground. God only knows how many previously played basketball games made the earth beneath it smooth and indented.

As if to beckon me further, an old rubber basketball, worn slick and shiny through many seasons of use, lay lifeless on the ground. I picked it up and tried every possible way I could to launch it up and into the basket—underhanded from between my legs; backward, two-handed, over my head; one-handed from alongside my right ear; two-handed from my chest; a sideways sling vaguely resembling a hook shot. No luck. *This is stupid*, I thought and meandered back home to my toys.

The arc of my life changed forever the spring of my eighth year when my family moved from the concrete of Covert Avenue to the grasslands of Evansville's east side. At about four thirty one day, Dad retrieved my brother, Gary, and me from the St. Benedict convent where the nuns babysat us after school. He drove us east on Lincoln Avenue through what seemed like a hundred stoplights. The further we drove, the bigger the houses grew and the more manicured the lawns became. He finally slowed and turned down a narrow street completely shaded by large trees. After a few blocks, he turned again and stopped in the middle of the road.

"This is our street, Chandler Avenue."

I inched forward to the edge of my seat, my hands on the dashboard and my forehead close to the windshield. There were no sidewalks. The lawns fronting the houses extended all the way to the street, some mowed, others neglected and wild.

"Where's our house?" I asked.

"There," Dad said, pointing at the next-to-last house on the block and then pulling into the driveway.

I bounded out of the car, ran into the front yard, and looked at my new house. It stood single story, flush to the ground, and was painted white with a dark-gray-shingled roof and a redbrick chimney. Another house sat just across the driveway to the right, but there was no house in the empty lot to the left, only a field of knee-high weeds.

Mom opened the front door and stepped out onto the tiny front porch, only a step above the grass. Wearing a blue dress belted at the waist, she extended her arms wide open, smiled, and said, "Welcome home, dearies."

Gary and I ran through each of the rooms as if on an Easter egg hunt, pausing only a second or two before scooting on to another. We laid claim to our bedrooms and bolted out the back door. There we found a covered porch that extended to a single-car garage. Looking right, I saw a concrete expanse the width of the house connecting the driveway to the garage. Behind all this was a luscious green backyard that looked as big to me as a football field.

"Wow!" I sprinted around the garage, threw myself onto the ground, and rolled over and over in the grass.

Dad stood on the concrete and smiled. He said, "Come on, let's get Mom and explore the neighborhood."

Out the front door and across the street sprawled Dexter Grade School's huge playground, large enough to accommodate two baseball diamonds. Behind them spread a full-length, concrete basketball court, nestled close to the school itself. Cattycorner from Dexter, left of our house and across the street, sat Christ the King Parochial School. It too occupied a whole city block and sported its own ball field.

"Think you kids'll have enough room to play?" Dad asked.

The neighborhood was loaded with kids about my age, all eager to play sports. On weekends and every day during summer vacation, I woke early, ate a quick breakfast, and went hunting for my friends to play ball—baseball in the spring and summer, football in the fall, and basketball year around. We went at it all day, stopping only for a quick lunch, supper, or when it was too dark to continue playing.

When I was ten, I came home from school to find that my dad had erected a backboard and hoop in the driveway behind the house. Spotting me through the window, he came outside wearing a big grin and carrying a new leather basketball.

"Let's play some ball," he said.

Dad threw a two-handed chest pass and invited me to pass the ball back to him by trotting toward the basket with arms extended. Pushing fifty with graying hair, he was still loose limbed and fluid as he must have been as a youthful basketball player himself. I felt the texture of the basketball in my hands and led him a step or two with a bounce pass. He took it in stride and laid the ball off the board and into the basket.

"Your old man still has a few moves, doesn't he?" he said.

He retrieved the ball, passed it back to me, and said, "Now, you shoot."

I peppered away at the basket from every angle. Dad worked me by throwing the ball to my left and to my right, as if I were being set up for a shot in a game.

Ten minutes in, I had yet to make a basket. Frustration kicked in, and I must have made a scornful face. Dad caught the ball off the backboard and walked out to me in front of the basket.

"Let me show you," he said, facing the basket. "Don't push the ball—flick it with your wrist. The flick produces backspin and gives softness to the shot. Look, like this."

Dad took two dribbles, lifted off the ground, and lofted the ball toward the basket, exaggerating what he'd just told me.

"That's how it's done," he said. There was a smile of self-satisfaction on his face when the ball dropped into the basket.

I kept at it, constantly trying to loft the ball with my wrist rather than my forearm. I clunked a few more before I swished first one, then another, and then another.

"Good shooting, son. You're getting the hang of it. Now, arch it more. You want the ball to fall down through the basket like it was dropped from heaven."

I loved the feel of the ball's leather in my hand, the thump it made bouncing on the concrete, the sandpapery sound of it scratching through the net. I loved the feeling of mastery every time I propelled the ball through that metal cylinder high above me.

Starting the next day, and most days over the next few years, I practiced shooting by the hour—right- and left-handed hooks, twisting layups from every angle to the basket, and jump shots from all distances. My routine never varied. I dribbled once or twice, stopped on a dime, jumped, and shot. If I missed, I hustled to the ball, shot again from that spot, and kept it up until I made the basket. Once I hit the shot, I dribbled back to the perimeter to start the process over at a new location. To the chagrin of our neighbors, Dad installed a spotlight on our roof that flooded the court so I could practice in the dark.

I also invented games to challenge myself. I had to make five shots in a row before I could shoot from a new location. I had to hit shots consecutively from each of seven spots around the perimeter before I could stop for the day. I had to make ten driving hook shots in a row, alternating right-handed and left-handed ones, before taking a different kind of shot. Eventually I convinced Dad to purchase a reducer rim that fit inside the real one and required more precision for the ball to fall through the net.

It wasn't long before the bounce, bounce, bounce of the basketball served as a tom-tom to summon my playmates for a game. Soon we figured out who stood where in the pecking order, and we divided into teams that made the games as competitive as possible. The first team to score twenty-one won.

Our personalities dictated how we played. Larry Collins, two grades ahead of me, wore jeans pegged at his ankles, a T-shirt with sleeves rolled up at his biceps, and a peroxided tuft of yellow-white hair combed to a point halfway down the middle of his forehead. He liked to dribble the ball behind his back, toss up twisting over-the-shoulder layups, and make no-look bounce passes.

Harold Altmansburger, nicknamed "Rug" because of his thick head of nappy hair, played the game precisely and conservatively, much like he did his homework and lawn mowing. Coordinated but not athletically gifted, Rug had an annoying habit of reacting a split second slower than expected. Once, with the ball in both my hands, I faked to my left, expecting him to shift to his right so I could drive to the basket unmolested. But he just stood there, his feet not shifting, as if glued to the concrete. I barreled straight into him, knocking him down, and sprawled forward over the top of him.

Jim Dougherty cared about music more than basketball, having recently moved from Memphis to Evansville. He joined me on the court more to socialize than to compete. His "you alls" mixed with our own "yous guys," and he sounded funny when he said things like "You all sure take your basketball serious around here."

I played to win each possession. I stood at the top of the key, holding the ball low and to my right with both hands. I bent forward at the waist, hunched my shoulders forward, and swayed my upper body back and forth, assessing what to do. Larry played a few feet off me, so I elevated without dribbling, as high as I could, and released the ball at the top of my jump with a feathery flick of my wrist. I knew the moment I let the ball fly that it would fall through the basket. The climactic meeting of leather on twine confirmed my anticipation.

"Good shot," he said.

I said nothing but drank in the pleasure of the moment.

Rug bounced the ball to Larry to start the next play. Larry immediately dribbled to his right toward the basket. He leaped off his left foot for a driving layup, and I leaped with him to try to block his shot. I deflected the ball into the backyard and bumped his body so hard we both flew airborne.

"My foul," I said and then retrieved the basketball.

The score stood 20–18, in our favor, and I desperately wanted to get to 21 first. Dougherty bounced the ball to me on the right wing. Collins defended me close so as to stop me from scoring the winning basket. I dribbled once to my left, crossed the ball over to my right, and drove hard along the baseline, marked by the edge of the concrete and the beginning of the backyard. I elevated full speed off the ground while slightly behind the backboard, dipsy-doodled my arms back and forth in midair while holding the basketball in both hands. I spun the ball with my left hand up and behind me off the backboard with just the right amount of English to slide it into the basket: 21–18.

I slapped Larry on the behind and said, "Good game."

"Yeah, you too," he said. "Ready to go again?"

Over time, I realized I could outplay kids my own age and more than hold my own against the older boys. The more I practiced, the better I got; the better I got, the more competent I felt. After a while, the act of playing basketball became an expression of this sense of mastery. Then, gradually, imperceptibly, the playing and the pleasure merged and gave a coherent definition to my emerging sense of self. At some unremembered moment on the court behind my parents' house, I became, to me, a basketball player.

After my friends scattered to their houses for supper, I walked through the back door and into the kitchen. There stood Mom, a full-length apron cinched around her neck and waist.

"Have fun, dearie?" she asked.

"I did," I said, and meant it. I was hungry for supper but hungrier for the next day on the court.

• • •

IT WAS LATE OCTOBER, COOL and crisp and dark outside. I was eleven years old. The four of us—Mom, Dad, Gary, and myself—sat at the dining-room table, finishing our burgers sided by Mom's homemade coleslaw and German potato salad. I ate fast, my head down, concentrating on cleaning my plate, eager to get out back to shoot baskets before the evening frost set it. If there was conversation, I didn't hear it.

"All done," I said. "Can I be excused?"

"Hold on a minute," Dad said. "I have a surprise."

He reached into his shirt pocket, pulled out four small booklets, and held them up, splayed out like a winning poker hand.

"Season tickets to Central High's home games," he said, a look of triumph on his face.

Gary and I looked at each other, not comprehending the significance of this announcement. Mom held her hand to her mouth, her eyes big and wide. "You didn't!" she said.

"I did," Dad said. "Central is ranked third in the state in preseason polls, boys, and their star, Jerry Clayton, is an All-Stater in the making." Both these facts were lost on me, but not on Mom and Dad.

A few weeks later, with our collars turned up, scarves cinched around our necks, and gloves on, we made our way into Central Gym, the epicenter of Evansville high school basketball. The aroma of fresh popcorn followed us up the concrete staircase to the second tier. We found our seats behind the bleachers, two-thirds of the way between the court and the rafters. The noise and energy generated by choreographed cheering and rhythmic foot stomping from the students in the bleachers vibrated the entire building. I felt my heart pound like it had never done before. I knew in that instant that I wanted this for myself, to do what I did behind my house in this gym, to experience this excitement with the possibility of glory right there on that yellowed court.

"There's Jerry Clayton," Dad said, pointing in the general direction of the white-shirted team, with the same reverence in his voice that he might have reserved for Roy Rogers. Twelve players warmed up, some shooting, others gathering rebounds.

"Which one?" I asked.

"There," he said. "Number three."

I zeroed in on number three and studied him. He stood six foot seven and had strong legs, but he moved smoothly and fluidly, almost gliding as if on ice. He never smiled or said a word. He focused on each shot, oblivious of everyone and everything except the basket. Sometimes he dribbled once or twice before launching his shot; other times he took the pass from his rebounder, faked, and shot without dribbling. He worked his way around the perimeter, taking three shots at each spot before he traded places with his partner and became the rebounder.

Once the game began, the Central guards took pains to get the ball to Clayton at every opportunity. He looked to shoot first and pass second. He rained high-arching jumpers that left his fingertips and touched nothing but net. He banked shots that glided softly off the glass and into the basket. He made floating hooks on the run across the front of the basket that always found their mark. He roared like a tornado, leaving devastation behind him through the full thirty-two minutes of the game.

Dad sat to my right and Gary to my left. As the game wore on, Dad leaned toward us and kept up a steady stream of instructional comments. "Watch how Clayton holds his defender on his hip to get positions for the inlet pass." "Look how soft his shot is." "Did you see that cross-over dribble that got him open for the shot?" I wondered if he'd keep up the same patter with Mom if Gary and I weren't there.

I watched Clayton's every move, oblivious of the long-skirted, bobby-socked cheerleaders dancing on the sidelines and the bleachers filled with cheering students. I saw him hold his right hand up, signaling he wanted the ball. I took note of how he bumped his opponents under the basket as if to say "I own this space." I sensed his confidence, a deep belief that he commanded the court. As the game wore on, I tried to absorb Jerry Clayton into myself, tried to will what he possessed into my being. I wanted to rush home that very night and replicate what he was doing before my eyes. I saw him as what I aspired to be.

My family and I attended every Central home game that year and, game by game, my admiration for Jerry Clayton grew. Somewhere near the end of the season, a week or so before the beginning of the state tournament, Mom announced that she had contacted Mr. and Mrs. Clayton and expected them for dinner the next night.

Stunned, I asked, "Jerry's parents? Will Jerry be here too?"

"Uh-huh," said Mom, nodding her head. "Pretty special, huh?"

Special didn't capture it. "Think he'll shoot baskets with me?"

"Slow down, fella," Dad said, coming into the room. "Jerry'll be here after his practice, and he'll be pretty tired. We don't want to wear him out, now do we?" He looked at Mom and gave her a wink.

The next night, Mr. and Mrs. Clayton showed up all alone without Jerry. My heart sank. Moments later, Jerry walked in, ducking a little to not bump his head on the door. As I stood on equal footing with him for the first time, he looked like a giant, as if he didn't quite fit into our living room. I looked at him and took in his penny loafers and white socks, khaki pants pegged at the ankle, and a long-sleeved, checkered shirt open at the neck.

We sat for dinner with me at one end of the table and Jerry Clayton at the other. Mom, Dad, and Gary sat on my left and Mr. and Mrs. Clayton on my right. I stared at Jerry throughout dinner as he and the adults made small talk. I wished they'd shut up so I could take him out back and play ball.

Finally, after what seemed like an eternity, dinner ended and Dad said, "Jerry, I know you've got to get home and get some rest, but how about taking young Russ out back and shoot a few hoops with him?"

I darted a look at Jerry, hoping he'd say yes, holding my breath.

When he said "Why not?" I practically ran to get my basketball, turned on the spotlight, and hustled to the court.

Once outside, he said, "Okay, let's see what you got."

It was nippy outside, but I didn't care. I clunked my first shot. He hauled it effortlessly off the rim and bounced it back to me without saying a word. I swished the next one and banked in the one after that. He took that shot out of the net, dribbled as far away from the basket as he could, and then took the jump shot that I'd seen him take a thousand times on the court. The net scorched as the ball went through without touching the rim.

"All right," he said. "I gotta go." Just before walking into the house through the back door, he turned and added, "Wish you were older so you could play on my team at Central." With that, he winked and disappeared.

It would be no exaggeration to say that, at that moment, my feelings for Jerry Clayton turned into full-bloom hero worship. I looked upon him as if he were a god, and I fantasized that, if I could be like him, I too could be like a god.

What I failed to realize at eleven years old was that, by elevating Jerry to hero status, I was doing myself a disservice. For, if I couldn't live up to the godlike standouts like Jerry Clayton, I would see myself as a failure.

◆  ◆  ◆

IN THE EIGHTH GRADE, I played organized basketball for the Christ the King Monarchs. They belonged to the Diocese of Evansville's Parochial League and competed against other Catholic schools such as Sacred Heart, Holy Rosary, and St. Teresa. I thought it funny to picture cheerleaders waving pom-poms and shouting, "Beat St. Teresa," or better yet, "Beat St. Teresa's ass."

We played our games in a compact downtown gymnasium called the Agoga Tabernacle. Brick walls bordered three sides of its shiny hardwood floor. Thick cushions hung from the wall behind the baskets to absorb a player's impact when flying out of bounds. Bleachers rose all the way to the ceiling on the fourth side, each seat polka-dotted gray and white from missing paint chips. Behind the bleachers were two locker rooms, both with concrete floors, splintered benches, and the smell of sweat, rubbing liniment, and foot powder.

But I could have cared less about the ambience. We wore honest-to-goodness basketball uniforms—shiny gold shorts and tank tops, "Christ the King" scripted in black lettering across the front. We had an actual coach who drew up real plays and gave impassioned pep talks. We submitted to the rulings of referees who wore black-and-white-striped shirts and ran the court blasting their whistles. We performed in front of actual fans who yelled and clapped just like those in Central High.

On the court, the Christ the King Monarchs played their hearts out, modeling themselves after the Central Bears in every way possible. We ran and cut and set picks as we had seen our elders do at Central Gym. We raised our hands to the sky in guilty confession when the referee called a foul on us. We popped each other on the fanny after a well-executed play. We felt like basketball players.

Bigger and more skilled than the other players, I dominated the games. Something happened to me on this Agoga Tabernacle court one Wednesday evening that had never occurred to me before. I lost all sense of myself within the confines of the rectangular black lines. It was like my mind left my body. I parried and attacked on pure, unconscious instinct. I took jump shots from the wing, stormed to the basket for layups, and fought the boards with the feeling of total mastery and control. I felt exhilarated and powerful.

These feelings stayed with me long after the final horn sounded. I replayed the game over and over in my mind, falling asleep well after midnight. The next day at school, I sat at my desk as Sister Carmelita paced up and down the aisles, carrying her yardstick. I found it difficult to focus on my studies. I had experienced something momentous the evening before, and the universe felt somehow different. Yet my classmates just sat there as if nothing had happened, seeming to be thoroughly oblivious to what I had experienced. I had no idea what it was and wondered if I was crazy.

I glanced at the round, white-faced clock that hung on the wall behind the sister's desk a hundred times that morning. Its big hand clicked ever so slowly, taking its sweet time. All I could think about was bounding out of that building, running across the street to my house. Forget the grilled cheese sandwich and tomato soup my mother would have prepared for me. Outside, behind the house, the basketball court called me.

•  •  •

IT HAPPENED ON SATURDAY, JANUARY 28, 1956. That afternoon, Jim Dougherty and I were shooting baskets behind my house when he said, "Ever hear of Elvis Presley?"

"Who?" I asked, launching another jumper.

"He's a singer. I saw him at a state fair in Memphis. He's on TV tonight. He's wild."

That night my family and I watched the Tommy Dorsey show on our seventeen-inch black-and-white Philco. Elvis stormed the stage. Wearing a black shirt, a white tie, and a sparkling black jacket, he grabbed the mike, tilted it back to his mouth, and let loose with Big Joe Turner's "Shake, Rattle, and Roll," then quickly segued into "Flip, Flop, and Fly." When he came to the instrumental breaks, he rose on the balls of his feet, spread his legs wide, strummed his guitar as hard as he could, and pulsated every muscle of his body. At the end of the song, he backed away from the microphone, bowed, flopping his hair over his forehead in the process, and hustled off the stage.

We sat without a word. I didn't realize that I had moved to the edge of my chair.

Mom finally broke the silence. "Oh, my."

My brother laughed.

Dad asked, "What's his name, pretzel something?"

I had no appreciation of the musical or social significance of what I had just seen. I knew, though, that I had just watched someone who expressed a passion that originated from somewhere deep within himself, for the sheer joy of just doing it. *Like me,* I thought, sensing a visceral connection to this dark, menacing figure, no longer feeling so weird.

# 5

## FROM BULLPUP TO BULLDOG

IT WAS A LATE APRIL evening in 1956 when I sat at my bedroom desk, leaning back in my chair and jiggling a pencil between my fingers. A small record player behind me dropped a forty-five onto the turntable, making a soft clicking sound. The Platters' "My Prayer" gave way to Elvis Presley's "Heartbreak Hotel." I looked down at my eighth-grade geography book, then up to the window over my desk where I could see the backboard behind the house. It stood tall and at attention, as if waiting for me.

Just as I stood to open the window to check the temperature, Dad stuck his head into the room and said, "Come on out. Your mom and I want to talk to you."

*Now what have I done?* I thought. Finding Mom sitting at the dining-room table with a smile on her face gave me relief.

"Son," Dad said, "you've got quite a basketball career ahead of you."

I took a deep breath, relieved that this wouldn't be one of those come-to-Jesus lectures or the birds-and-bees talk other neighborhood kids had to endure.

"We're thinking," he said, "that, with your basketball ability, you need the best coaching possible."

"Yeah?" I said, waiting for the punch line.

Dad glanced at Mom.

"We've been thinking . . . You might be better off at Bosse rather than Memorial High. They have a coach who's won two state championships."

The room went silent. I neither felt the chair beneath me nor smelled Mom's meatloaf cooking. I only saw Dad's eyes on me.

"But I don't know anybody at Bosse," I said, fighting to keep from raising my voice.

"Sure you do, honey," Mom said. "You know Larry Collins and Jim Doughtery. They're already there. And your cousin Nancy will be a freshman along with you next year."

"I guess."

"Well, let's not get too far ahead of ourselves," Dad said. "Here's the deal. We need to get permission from the bishop anyway, and that'll take a while. Let's all think about it and then talk. Okay?"

I didn't say anything, sensing that my life would take this new direction whether I liked it or not.

When I walked back to my bedroom, everything looked the same: the geography book still open, the backboard illuminated by the moon, Elvis warbling "Heartbreak Hotel." But none of it mattered. I flopped back on my bed, laid my arm across my forehead, and stared at the ceiling till tears blurred my vision.

◆   ◆   ◆

SOME FOUR MONTHS LATER, THE Tuesday after Labor Day, Dad pulled up to the curb in front of Bosse High School for the first day of school. I had passed by Bosse hundreds of times but had never appreciated how big it was. I had to turn my head to take in the expanse of the two-story building. Two huge entranceways divided the building into thirds, with each doorway recessed under a white sandstone archway. Above, brick turrets rose like lookouts for foreign invaders.

I must have sighed because Dad put his hand on my leg and gave a squeeze. "You'll do just fine."

"I don't know," I said.

"Sure you will. You'll see."

I got out of the car, took a deep breath, and walked inside Bosse High School. Dozens of students darted left and right. I heard high-pitched laughter from a group of girls clutching books tight to their chests. A boy wearing a short-sleeved blue shirt cinched tight at his biceps sidled behind another boy, pinched his butt, and scurried ahead. Some students stood close to the wall, freshmen, I guessed, with their heads hunched forward, looking at the same hall map I carried.

The hallway extended some twenty yards to my right and at least forty to my left. Its size overwhelmed me. As if drawn by a magnet, I found myself standing in front of a huge trophy case built into the wall across the hall. It contained trophies, pictures, and memorabilia of past Bosse team triumphs. I spotted pictures of the 1953 Bosse basketball team, the team I'd watched play against the Central Bears. Wearing scarlet uniforms, they stared straight at the camera, unsmiling. I touched my finger to the glass in front of the one Bosse player I recognized, Bunky Holt, as if he would somehow infuse me with his spirit and confidence.

I checked my map, walked down the hall to my right, and took a left at the end of the hall. The scuffle of hundreds of feet, the din of constant chatter, and the bang of gray metal locker doors reminded me of Central Gym. I looked to see if I could spot Larry Collins or Jim Dougherty among the students hustling the opposite way. No luck.

The map proved reliable, and I soon found my homeroom on the second floor. In the doorway stood a man I judged to be in his early thirties. He had a crew cut and wore a bowtie clipped at the collar of his white oxford. He had the chest and shoulders of a former football player. He paused for a minute as he looked me over. Then he introduced himself as Don Williams, put a check next to my name on a list attached to his plastic clipboard, and directed me to my desk on the far side of the room. Much later, I learned he'd recognized me from his side job refereeing parochial league basketball games. After homeroom, he hustled to tell the head basketball coach, Herman Keller, that I had enrolled at Bosse.

Later that morning I hit the jackpot. I walked into my third-period algebra class and there sat Jeanne in the front row. She wore a dark-green dress cinched at the waist. Her brown hair curled over her forehead and hung in back almost to her shoulders. Lipstick and eye shadow gave her a hint of maturity and intrigue. An involuntary smile came to my face, and I felt my mood brighten.

I'd first met Jeanne the summer before eighth grade. She'd stood straddling her bicycle, chatting with two girlfriends as I'd cruised toward them on my red Schwinn. As I approached our eyes locked, and then she quickly dropped hers to the ground. In the next instant, she looked up, as if she had made a conscious decision to do so. Something in my chest gripped.

"Hey," she'd said as I braked next to her.

The four of us had talked for the better part of an hour. But, like a rubber band pulled taut, my eyes had kept snapping back to her. She'd looked so pretty in her white shorts and blue sleeveless blouse. She had a throaty laugh that came without hesitation. At times her eyes darted, betraying, I sensed, a hint of self-doubt. I'd felt a visceral attraction I'd never experienced before and couldn't have described in words. I had the feeling that if she asked, I'd ride off with her anywhere.

Dusk came and Jeanne said she had to go home. She'd smiled, turned her bicycle around, and pedaled away. After ten yards or so, she'd turned in her seat, looked at me, and waved. I'd had the urge to call out "Wait!" but didn't.

I couldn't believe my luck in seeing her now on this first day of school. I hesitated a moment and then walked up to her. "Jeanne?"

She looked up, and her eyes crinkled into a smile.

"Remember me?"

"Of course," she said. "What are you doing here?"

Before I could answer, the teacher walked into the classroom carrying his algebra book. I said, "Wait for me after class" and held her eye till she said, "Okay." I nodded, took a seat near the back of the room, and flipped open my textbook. No matter how hard I tried, I could not keep my eyes on the teacher as he chalked numbers on both sides of equal signs on the blackboard. Instead, I studied the texture of Jeanne's hair, the gentle slope of her shoulders, the smoothness of her skin.

I hustled to the hallway as soon as class ended to find her waiting for me, not realizing I had already fallen in love for the first time in my life. She said, "I gotta find my next class, but here," and handed me a folded piece of paper. I watched her walk away until she turned the corner, then opened the note. Above her phone number, it read, "Better call me tonight."

I did. This phone call led to many more conversations, before and after class, and finally to dates. Sometimes we were chauffeured by my dad, and sometimes we double-dated with Larry Collins, my neighborhood pal, who drove us in his first four-door Ford.

On a Saturday night late in October, my parents dropped Jeanne and me off at a hayride outside Evansville. It started just before dusk and was to conclude midevening around a huge bonfire. The glaze of gray clouds, the smell of fresh-cut hay, and the crispness of the air stimulated in me such a sense of affection and sensuality that I felt my head would burst.

Jeanne and I snuggled in the back left corner of the wagon under a soft blanket we tucked tightly around our shoulders. The driver flapped the reins and made clicking sounds out of the corner of his mouth. The horses pulled the wagon at a slow, steady pace over a gravely path that made a steady crunching sound under the wheels. Night fell and we passed under branches that looked like long, skinny arms. From somewhere deep in the woods, we occasionally heard a dog bark and an owl hoot. We jostled against each other when the wheels passed over potholes and bumps. We could hear the voices of other couples chatting, but we burrowed into ourselves.

Darkness descended, as did the temperature. Jeanne scooted her hip tighter against mine, angled her upper body toward me, and nuzzled her face into my neck. "Brr, it's cold," she whispered.

I said nothing, but I put my arm around her to pull her tight against me. I moved my hand to grasp her shoulder, but what I felt was soft. Without intending to, I had cupped her breast.

Jeanne did not move, except to press her face more firmly into my neck. Realizing what I'd done, but ignorant of what to do next, I moved my hand away and hugged her. I was thrilled that she'd accepted my unintended act of intimacy without protest.

After the hayride, we sat on a log close to the bonfire.

"Let me fix you a plate," she said.

I watched her as she walked to the picnic table, skewered two hotdogs onto a stick, and, kneeling, held them over the fire. She glanced sideways at me and smiled, a look that went straight to my heart and filled me with feelings of protectiveness and possession.

I was devastated when, three weeks later, out of the blue, she broke up with me for a senior fullback on the football team. It came during the last of our nightly phone conversations. The hesitancy in her voice turned to sobbing as she told me. When she hung up, the click of the phone sounded like the crack of a rifle shot.

I lay on my bed, stunned, feeling like an anvil had fallen onto my chest. I had never felt so lonely and lost. All I knew was that I had given myself totally to her, and that wasn't enough. I felt that I had somehow failed, not been good enough. I wanted to lock my bedroom door and stay there forever, knowing I deserved to think of myself as a failure.

◆ ◆ ◆

MY DAD AND I DROVE toward Bosse High the night of the freshman basketball tryouts. We settled behind a string of cars inching toward an open metal door where young hopefuls entered, one by one, into a dim yellow light. I wondered if this was what it looked like when you died and went to heaven.

Halfway to the door, I asked Dad, "Think I'll make the team?"

"Are you kidding?"

"You really think so?"

"Let me put it this way. If you don't make the team, I'll sit through church on Sunday wearing nothing but my jockey shorts."

I walked into the building and followed other freshmen up the staircase to Bosse's second-floor basketball court. A glass backboard jutted out from the wall on each end of the court, leaving just enough space for a player driving for a layup to put on the brakes before colliding into brick. Benches lined the wall on one side of the court where coaches and players sat during games. Those riding the bench had to keep their feet tucked under them lest they trip the players on the court. Only about three feet separated the inbounds line from the wall on the other side of the court, and this served as the only pathway for students to walk between classes. Every yell made a gargantuan sound as it echoed within the walls.

At exactly six thirty, freshman basketball coach Al Buck blasted his whistle. He stood at center court, cradling a basketball against his hip and looking as commanding and powerful as a drill sergeant. Thirtysomething, he wore his black hair close cropped and had eyes that flashed with competitiveness and authority. Under a red T-shirt with *Bosse* on the front, he wore gray sweatpants so snug he would later be nicknamed "Buns" Buck.

To this point, basketball for me had been self-directed, limited to freewheeling in the privacy of the court behind my house. The only judgment that mattered was my own. My only yardstick was making more baskets than the other guy, getting to twenty-one before the other team. As I trotted to the circle of thirty or so boys forming around Coach Buck, I realized that my neighborhood standards no longer counted. Now only his judgment mattered. He had the power to make or break me.

One at a time, Coach Buck had us dribble from center court to the baseline with one hand and then back to midcourt with the other. After that, he had us dribble to the basket, lay the ball in, and then run to a particular spot on the court and shoot a jumper. Finally, he had us jump as high as we could to rebound a ball one of the student assistants careened off the backboard and put it back into the basket. Between turns we mostly stood around and waited while the coach jotted notes down on his silver clipboard. I too watched my classmates, anxious to see if I measured up.

After about an hour and a half, Coach called us together at midcourt. "Okay," he said, "that's it. I'll post the names of those who make the team on my office door first thing in the morning. Good luck."

*That's it?* I thought, wondering how he could rely on such scant information to make his decision.

I skipped breakfast and pestered Dad to drive me to school early the next morning. I hopped out of the car, trotted up the same stairs as the night before, and hustled down the hall to the basketball office. There on Coach Buck's office door hung the list. I ran my fingers down the typed names and found mine nestled alphabetically between Chuck Garner and Don Katterhenry.

"Yessss!" I hissed and pumped my fist for emphasis.

Practice began that afternoon at three thirty, the freshmen at one end of the court, the junior varsity at the other. Guards Chuck Garner and John O'Connor could be relied on to bring the ball up court, initiate the offense, and score. Mike Dale made up in scrappiness what he lacked in finesse. Dick McCool's chunky body betrayed his smoothness and grace. Standing at only five foot ten, he was a born shooter and dropped fifteen-foot bombs through the basket like clockwork.

My team lost two of its first three games, but we then found our rhythm and ran off eleven straight victories to lead the race for the city championship. I took up where I'd left off at Christ the King, scoring in double digits in all but one game and scoring twenty-five points against the best freshman team in southern Indiana, New Albany.

After freshman practice one afternoon in early December, varsity coach Herman Keller summoned me, along with sophomores Jim Newcomb, Paul Utley, Dave Crosley, and Ron Volkman from the junior varsity team, to scrimmage against the varsity after our practices ended. I felt heroic going up against the older boys who drove cars, boasted of sexual exploits, and strode the hallways cocksure and commanding. Though they played the game a notch faster, and were more physical than my freshman teammates, I found I could run the court as their peer.

That night at supper, I told Mom and Dad about the scrimmage. "How'd it go?" Dad asked, darting a quick glance toward Mom, who responded with a slight smile.

"Good."

"Well, great. We're proud of you, son. Keep working hard."

These scrimmages continued through December and January until the afternoon of Tuesday, January 29, 1957, when my freshman team captured the Evansville City Championship by beating Central High at Central Gym. The game held special meaning for me because, for the first time, I ran the same floor as my hero, Jerry Clayton. I now felt my turn had come.

That night we ran into the dressing room after the game, our scarlet jerseys wet and clinging. We traded congratulations and whooped and hollered.

Into this celebration strode varsity coach Herman Keller, my father trailing a few steps behind. The room went quiet.

"Boys," he said, "take a seat."

He paused as we settled onto the wooden benches lining the periphery of the room. "Great job. You're city champs, and we're proud of you."

Looking around, he asked, "Russ, where are you?"

"Over here," I said, raising my hand. He looked at me and nodded.

"Boys, I want you to be the first to know. As of today, I'm promoting Russ to the varsity. He'll play with us Thursday night against Mater Dei."

He again paused, as if not knowing what else to say. "Okay then, congratulations again on a great season." He then left the locker room as abruptly as he'd entered.

I sat slumped on the bench, my hands dangling between my legs, a glazed look on my face. I felt stunned, as if I had been hit flush on the chin by heavyweight champ Floyd Patterson. An image of myself out there on the Central Gym court, under bright lights, in front of thousands of people, formed in my mind, causing my mood to teeter between exhilaration and fear.

The dressing room slowly returned to life. Mike Dale tousled my hair. Dick McCool said, "Way to go, buddy." Other teammates shook my hand, punched my arm, or gave me a "Congratulations." Waiting his turn, Dad patted my shoulder and just nodded, tears in his eyes.

Two nights later, I found myself on this same Central Gym court, now surrounded by bleachers that hugged the court and filled with students crowded hip to hip, all standing and chanting in unison. Bosse cheerleaders danced in front of a mass of scarlet on one side of the court while the Mater Dei cheerleaders danced in front of a mass of gold on the other. The noise and motion and color both thrilled and overwhelmed me, and my stomach fluttered with nerves.

I dared not turn my attention from the warm-ups for fear of seizing up. Despite my resolve, I searched for my family in the bench seats above the bleachers and found them at midcourt where we used to sit to watch the Central Bears. Mom gave a little wave and a smile. I locked eyes with Dad. He gave me an abrupt nod, as if to say, "You can do it." My brother, Gary, sat next to him, scanning the crowd, oblivious to the turmoil inside me.

The horn at the scorer's table blared. I trotted to the bench, relieved that the moment had finally arrived. I stripped off my warm-ups and joined my teammates around Coach Keller. Immediately, the announcer introduced the players—sophomores Newcomb, Utley, and Crosley, and senior Danner. While waiting my turn, Coach Buck jerked me close to him. "You belong here," he said and shoved me onto the court as I heard my name called.

Bill Danner controlled the opening tip. I ran up and down the court as the two teams strove to exert their will upon the other. After two or three minutes, I settled into the rhythm of the game. Just outside my focus, I could hear the eruption of cheers after each basket, and I felt elated when one of my passes, rebounds, or defensive moves ignited a visceral response. That night, for the first time, I felt the symbiotic bond between myself and those in the stands. My playing stimulated their response, and their response reinforced my playing.

I hadn't scored a point in either quarter of the first half, and we trailed 28–24 when Bill Danner toed the centerline to start the second half. I felt it important that I show what I could do. The referee tossed the ball up, and Danner tipped it forward to me. I grabbed it in both hands, pivoted, and saw that only one Mater Dei player stood between me and the basket. I dribbled straight toward him. When I reached the top of the key, I paused in my dribble and straightened my body, trying to trick him into relaxing for a moment. It worked. I flew forward, closing in on the basket. Even with my opponent, I suddenly stopped, gathered myself, and faked forward with my upper body. The Mater Dei guard leaped up and past me, helpless, as I gently laid the ball off the glass and into the basket. I had scored my first two varsity points, and they pulled us to within two points of the lead only moments into the third quarter.

Bosse and Mater Dei traded baskets throughout the third quarter. In the closing seconds, I swiped the ball away from my Mater Dei opponent as he crossed midcourt, sending it rolling free near the centerline. I dove and collared the ball. Sitting up, I faked to my left and bounced the ball to teammate Paul Utley on my right. Utley dribbled toward our basket and tossed a perfect pass to the streaking Bill Danner, who laid the ball into the hoop as the buzzer sounded. This move brought the Bosse crowd to its feet. It brought my teammates on the bench to their feet. It brought my mother and father to their feet. Bosse led 36–34 at the end of the third quarter.

The five of us ran back to the huddle. Larry Collins swatted me on the butt and said, "Great play." I took this to be my official anointment into the Bulldog family. The rest of the juniors and seniors crowded around as Coach Keller gave us instructions for the fourth quarter.

I made three of Bosse's fourth-quarter baskets as we pulled away for a 55–45 win. I finished with eight points, well below my freshman standard, but points

I had made when they counted. The baskets seemed to count more for me than my freshman team baskets and gave me a special pleasure.

I found it difficult to sleep that night, unable to shut off the adrenaline and excitement from the game. Tired, but still hyped up, I walked to the breakfast table the next morning. Dad sat reading the paper while Mom puttered in the kitchen, making eggs and bacon.

Peeling off the sports section from the rest of the paper, Dad handed it to me and said, "Here, read this." Under a big, bold headline, "YOUNG BOSSE TEAM SCORES 55–45 WIN OVER MATER DEI," sportswriter Larry Saunders wrote:

> The three sophomores—Jim Newcomb, Dave Crosley, and Paul Utley—and the freshman—Russ Grieger—were all outstanding. Along with their own sterling contributions, they kept Danner well supplied with sharp passes under the basket to make most of the scoring easy for the night.

I felt thrilled and elevated as I rolled the words "outstanding" and "sterling" around in my head. I looked at Dad and grinned as wide as a circus clown. Little did I know then that this game had caused a seismic shift in me. Basketball would no longer be a private experience; I could no longer play solely for enjoyment. From now on, my playing would be something shared with hundreds and thousands of strangers, something that could give pleasure or pain to others, something that carried others' desires and expectations along with and intertwined with my own. The pleasures and joys I experienced through basketball would intermingle with the rewards and punishments of judgment, both theirs and my own.

• • •

FIVE NIGHTS LATER, THE BULLDOGS again took the Central Gym to play Memorial, the school I had been slated to attend before the decision for me to enroll at Bosse. Warming up, I spotted three burly Memorial students standing shoulder to shoulder in the bleachers, each wearing a dark-blue sweater with a white "M" stitched on their chest. They held up their right hands with their middle fingers pointed to the sky and thrust their arms in my direction.

I felt calm and fluid and in control during the game. The action seemed to slow down compared to the Mater Dei game. Paul Utley and I led the way as Bosse opened up a 13–11 lead by the end of the first quarter and extended it to 29–21 at the half. I hit jumpers off the pick and drove to the basket when I found an opening. Our big men held their own on the boards. We defeated Memorial 65–47. I played the whole game and scored fourteen points.

Sportswriter Jack Schneider headlined his *Evansville Courier* column the next morning: "BOSSE'S KIDS LEAD ALL THE WAY IN BEATING MEMORIAL, 65–47." In the *Evansville Press* that evening, Bill Robertson wrote:

> Danner, a fixture from the start of the campaign, led the Bulldogs last night with his tireless rebounding and his 14 points. But he got some noble assistance from all sides, notably young Russ Grieger, a gifted freshman forward who rolled in five of his ten shots from the field plus two free throws, broke up Memorial advances half a dozen times and looked almost as if he had been playing all season.

A week later, the highflying Madison Cubs came to town. They were state ranked and featured all-state senior guard candidate Bobby Orill. Oddsmakers declared them a nine-point favorite and gave us little chance of victory.

Both teams started with a hot hand. The game felt easy and simple to me. I slid off pick after pick, took passes around the perimeter, and either turned without dribbling to swish a fifteen-foot jumper or slashed to the basket for a driving layup. The first half turned into a shooting match between Bobby Orill and myself. Wiry and fearless, he shot with artistry and daring and blistered the defenseless net with fourteen first-half points. I did my best to match him, hitting six of my eight shots and scoring twelve points myself.

In the second half, Madison coach Bud Ritter put Bobby Orill on me. He bird-dogged me all over the court. He got in my face when I held the ball. He grabbed my shorts when I tried to run. He bumped me with his hip and jabbed me with his elbow. I couldn't get rid of him and, after a while, I became less aggressive, no longer cutting hard to get the ball, no longer fighting to get open for my shot. I let my grit dissolve and my fight evaporate. For the first time ever, I felt myself listless on the basketball court. I became invisible and irrelevant. Bobby Orill broke my will and limited me to two points in the second half. Madison pulled away and won.

In bed that night, unable to sleep, I dwelled on my second-half letdown. I knew I had been bested, the first time ever in my basketball life. I took no comfort from the fact that Bobby Orill was three years older and had up to one hundred varsity games under his belt. Worse, I knew that I had backed down from a challenge. I felt ashamed and humiliated that I had done so in front of thousands of people.

I laid there for the longest time, brooding, wallowing in self-loathing. Finally I swore, with all my might, to be the kind of bold, take-no-crap ballplayer a Bobby Orill would never intimidate again.

The remaining four games of the season ended with a whimper. I came down with the flu for the Bulldogs' final regular-season game against Bloomington and played only sparingly against Mater Dei in the first game of the Evansville sectional tourney. The next afternoon, the Bulldogs lost to the Lincoln Lions, who went on to win the championship. My first varsity season ended as suddenly as it had begun.

I sat in the living room on Saturday night a week later as Mom busied herself in the kitchen preparing supper. Dad reclined in his La-Z-Boy, reading the *Evansville Press*, a beer on the table to his right. I sat on the love seat to his left and watched the sports news on television.

Leaning sideways toward me, he held the paper out and said, "Here, read this." Sportswriter Bill Robertson had written in his column, "The Firing Line":

The basketball season is over but actually there is no end to this immediate irresistible Hoosier force and already the blueprints are being drawn and the strategy planned for another season six months away.

While most of the bright stars will be graduated and new ones may not be immediately forthcoming, the long summer weeks ahead will be filled with promise for several coaches because southern Indiana had an unusual number of outstanding players this season.

One of them is Bosse's Russ Grieger, a talented forward who came up in midseason to win a starting post on the rebuilt Bosse team that turned out to be better than it was in its original state.

Already this 6'0", 150-pound yearling is being marked for future stardom and one of the good reasons why Bosse basketball prospects now are the best since Broc Jerrell, Bud Ritter, Norman McCool, Norris Caudell, and Jack Mathews were sophomores.

I looked at my dad.

"Now, don't let this go to your head."

"I won't."

We sat there for a minute, neither of us speaking. I felt thrilled by what Bill Robertson had written, but I also remembered my act of cowardice against Madison a few weeks before. I sensed the road ahead would be treacherous, but I knew I had no choice but to walk it. I played basketball. I was a basketball player. What else could I do?

I leaned forward and said to Dad, "Okay, here I go." I walked to my bedroom, put on my gym shoes, and grabbed the basketball from the floor of my closet. I flipped the switch just inside the back door to illuminate the court behind my house. I went outside and took my first jumper of the evening.

# 6

## FLAILING AND FALLING

I CLIMBED THE CIRCULAR METAL staircase that led from Bosse's first floor dressing room to its second-floor gymnasium. Steep and rusted, it wobbled with each step. I trailed behind Paul Utley, with Larry Collins following just below.

"Don't anybody cut the cheese," Collins said.

It was October 15, 1957, the first day of basketball practice. I stepped into the gym and crossed paths with my former freshman teammates who had just finished their junior varsity practice and waited to descend. I got a "Hey" from Mike Dale, an "All yours" from Dick McCool, and a nod from Chuck Garner.

Their tepid greetings reminded me of the canyon that had developed between my classmates and me since my promotion to the varsity the year before, a void not filled as yet by any of my upperclassman teammates. Sadness shot through me, and I remembered a Saturday afternoon last December. Chuck Garner's parents had dropped us off at Reitz Bowl on Evansville's west side to watch the Refrigerator Bowl, a second-rate college football game between Sam Houston State Teachers College and Middle Tennessee State.

The football field sat below ground level. Though shielded from the wind, the cold and gloom of that December day settled around us as we sat in our concrete seats at the thirty-yard line. Despite three layers of clothing, we found it impossible to keep the frigid air from penetrating our bones.

By the end of the first quarter, discomfort overwhelmed us. When the public address announcer bellowed, "Sweeney enters the game for Middle Tennessee State," Chuck and I looked at each other and shouted at the same time, "Sweeney!"

A few plays later we heard: "Pass caught by Sweeney. First and ten for the Blue Raiders on the 40 yard line." That did it. We burst out laughing and we Sweeneyed each other the rest of that day and for weeks to come.

"Let's get some hot chocolate, Sweeney," I said.

"Okay, Sweeney," he replied.

At the concession counter, I said, "After you, Sweeney."

Chuck responded, "No, I insist, you first, Sweeney."

We carried this back to Bosse High. Spotting Chuck in the hallway between classes, I saluted him with, "Hey, Sweeney."

"What's up, McSween," he replied.

Coach Herman Keller interrupted my brooding with a sharp blast of the whistle. He wore black polyester sweatpants that made a whooshing sound when he walked and a long-sleeve yellow jersey that he never tucked in. Tall and lanky, he had the look of Abraham Lincoln before the presidency wore him down—an elongated, slightly craggy face, hair short on the sides but fuller on top, and black horn-rimmed glasses that often slid to the front of his nose. He moved fluidly, but his gestures were awkward, and he spoke with a twang in his voice that betrayed his Indiana background. Though he tried at times to act gruff and demanding, he could never quite overcome his innate sweetness.

All thirteen of us Bosse Bulldogs—four seniors, eight juniors, and me, the lone sophomore—trotted over to join him at the center of the gym. He got right to the point. "I expect a lot out of you boys this year, so let's get right down to work."

We did. We battled hard in practice, knowing that how we performed in October would determine our status later on. By early November, Coach Keller settled on the starting lineup—senior Bill Danner at center, senior Larry Collins and junior Paul Utley at guard, and junior Dave Crosley and myself at forward. It became clear that I would be expected to play a pivotal role. In his *Evansville Courier* column, reporter Jack Schneider wrote before our first game:

Grieger, 6'1", has almost limitless potential with only inexperience likely to keep him from complete stardom this season. He has a splendid shooting touch and the actions of a true thoroughbred.

Coach Keller wasted no time calling me into his office that day. "I know that there's a lot of pressure building on you, what with what those darned sports-writers put in their newspapers," he said.

"Some, I guess."

"Well, I don't want you to pay any attention to that nonsense. You just go play your game, you hear?"

"Okay, Coach," I said, feeling appreciative, but having no clue how not to feel the pressure.

"All right, then," he said, standing up. "Go get dressed and I'll see you in a few minutes."

We started the season fast, winning eight of our first ten games. I soared in these games, stroking in jumpers at a steady pace and gunning in fourteen against both our first two opponents, Huntingburg and Tell City, thirteen against both Memorial and New Albany, fifteen against Jasper, and seventeen against Reitz.

I remember only fleeting impressions of these games, a blur of running and positioning, shooting and rebounding. One sequence of plays, however, stands out, because it came at a decisive moment during the championship game of the Evansville Holiday Tournament in the newly built Roberts Stadium. Trailing the Reitz Panthers 56–52 midway through the fourth quarter, I connected on two free throws to bring Bosse to within two points at 56–54, then hit a jumper from downtown to tie the score at 56. With 2:39 left, I found myself with the ball at the top of the key, facing the basket. I dribbled once to my right, saw my defender lean in that direction, switched the ball to my left hand, and bar-reled full bore past the Panther guarding me straight toward the basket. When another Reitz defender stepped out to block my path, I veered slightly to my left, averted his leaping attempt to block my shot, and, in full stride, arched a soft left-handed running hook off the backboard and into the basket. We led 58–56. I then added two more free throws before Bill Danner and Larry Collins contributed field goals to clinch our 64-58 victory.

I hit my peak against Boonville. Covering this game, *Evansville Courier* sportswriter Jack Schneider headlined, "GRIEGER PACES BOSSE'S 79–37 VIC-TORY OVER BOONEVILLE," then wrote,

> With brilliant sophomore forward Russ Grieger spearheading the charge, Bosse romped past Boonville, 79–37, last night at Central Gym.
>
> Grieger, displaying the kind of finesse and shooting accuracy that belies his tender age and lack of experience, scored 23 points, including nine field goals in 14 shots.

Young Russ connected on his first three field goal attempts, helping Bosse spurt to a 13–2 lead after four minutes and a 23–3 advantage at the end of the opening period.

And after the Bulldogs bogged down a bit in the second quarter when the Pioneers played them on even terms, Grieger got them back on the right track again in his 14 shots.

Following the intermission, the 6'1" youngster scored 10 points and hit four of his five shots before leaving the game with two and one half minutes left in the third frame. He sat out the rest of the game.

I hardly had time to digest these remarks when the same Jack Schneider laid it on even thicker the morning of our January 17, 1958 home game against the Daviess County Panthers, the team ranked number one in the state of Kentucky. I sat at the dining room table, my Cheerios turning the milk in the bowl from white to tan, and read:

> It would be foolhardy to underestimate the potential of this Bosse team. The Bulldogs have size, speed, and scoring ability. They are rapidly accumulating the only ingredient they weren't well stocked with when the season began—experience. They have a tremendous rebounder, plus a steady scorer, in 6'4" Bill Danner. They have added rebounding prowess in 6'5" Dave Crosley. And they have one of the greatest young prospects in the city's hardwood history in 6'1" sophomore Russ Grieger who already may be the very finest among the present crop of Evansville prep cagers. Grieger displays the kind of finesse and shooting accuracy that belies his tender age and lack of experience. He is averaging almost 14 points per game and is the leading scorer on the team. But more indicative of his effectiveness has been his brilliant shooting. In the ten games played, young Russ scored 52 field goals for a blazing .509 percent.

I slumped back in my chair while Mom puttered in the kitchen, clanging silverware into the utensil drawer and clinking plates, saucers, and cups into the cabinets. Rain spattered against the window and thunder rumbled from far away, somewhere behind Dexter School. From the bathroom, I heard Dad hack phlegm from his throat and flush the toilet.

Right then, the thought flashed through my mind, like an electrical shock that propelled itself from the top of my head to my loafered feet, that maybe, just maybe, I wasn't up to all this. I sat frozen in my chair, feeling as scared as I ever had in my whole life. *One of the greatest young prospects in the city's hardwood history, the very finest among present crop of Evansville prep cagers.* "Oh, God," I said out loud.

Mom must have noticed something odd about me, maybe the blood draining from my face, my long deep sigh, the "Oh, God" under my breath. "Something wrong, dearie?" She asked.

At school that day, students and faculty went out of their way to offer encouragement. Teachers in two of my classes wished me luck in front of my classmates. After lunch, two thousand Bosse students and teachers packed the school's auditorium for a pep rally. From the wings, I watched the cheerleaders twirl their scarlet skirts almost waist-high and kick their bobby-socked shoes high into the air. I felt the floor shudder from the clapping and stomping and heard two thousand students yell at the top of their lungs, "Bulldogs, Bulldogs, Bulldogs."

I walked single-file onto the stage with my teammates and took a seat in a row of folding metal chairs. Every single person stood and cheered. I looked around the vastness of the room, the lower level bigger than any movie theater in Evansville, with not an empty seat. A balcony hung from the back of the room halfway to the stage, also packed. I spotted Don Williams and my homeroom in the middle of the main floor. Next to them sat diminutive Miss Poohl, my prim, elderly Latin teacher, along with her homeroom, cheering along with everybody else. I had to yell into the ear of the teammate next to me to be heard.

I sat in my metal chair and did my best to look cool and collected, wearing my favorite pair of pegged jeans, a long-sleeved white shirt turned twice above my wrists, and a gray button-up sweater-vest that hung open and loose below my waist. I fidgeted with my Vicks inhaler, which I had taught myself to unscrew, unsheathe, bring to each nostril, resheathe, and rescrew all in one continuous motion, all done as part of a quick-draw contest Larry Collins and I had invented. I couldn't relax.

David Dudley, Bosse's white-haired, bespectacled principal, walked to the podium and quieted the crowd by raising his hands above his head Richard Nixon style. He introduced Coach Keller by saying, "Here's the man who tonight will lead our Bulldogs to their greatest victory ever, Herman Keller."

Coach Keller strode to the podium to a standing ovation. He took a small piece of paper from his shirt pocket, cleared his throat, and said, "We'll do our part tonight. Will you do yours?" The crowd roared. "If you do, I promise all of you that we'll make every one of you proud."

*Oh shit!* I thought, and wanted to shout, "No, don't say that!

That night my right arm felt like it was weighted down with ball bearings. Jump shots I normally would have dropped hit metal and bounced away. Driving layups I usually slid off the glass and into the basket circled the rim and spun off. I found the basket growing smaller and smaller as the game progressed. With each missed shot, my spirits sagged lower.

We lost 52–49. I left the stadium dazed, bedeviled by a labyrinth of black thoughts and gloomy emotions. I drove toward home, down familiar streets that now looked alien and menacing. I paid no attention to the beams of moonlight that sneaked through breaking clouds and naked tree branches to slither in front of my path.

When I pulled the car into the garage, I walked to the basketball court where I had always felt so powerful and invincible. The moon now illuminated it so brightly I could have shot baskets had I the heart to do so. Instead, I sat down and leaned back against the metal pole that supported the backboard. The cold concrete bit the back of my legs, but I didn't care, what with the whirlpool of self-disgust churning in my chest.

Just then, the backdoor rattled and opened. With her hair wrapped loosely in a hair net, Mom stuck her head out of the door. "Russ, is that you?"

"Yeah," I said.

"What are you doing out there? Come on in here out of the cold. You'll catch your death."

I slid through the back door, slunk into my bedroom, and flopped down on my bed. I didn't bother to turn on the light or take off my coat or shoes. I laid my arm across my forehead and stared at the ceiling, wanting more than anything to be left alone.

No such luck. I heard steps coming through the kitchen toward my bedroom. Before I could shout, "Go away," Dad prattled his fingers on the door, stuck his head in, and sat down at my desk. "Pretty rough shooting night, huh?" he said. "Don't worry, it happens to everybody."

"Yeah," I said, not taking my arm off my eyes, "but I'm not everybody."

"Well, you'd be the first ballplayer to never have an off night."

With that, I bolted to a sitting position, leaned forward, and practically shouted, "Two for fourteen! Are you kidding me? I was pitiful!" What I didn't say was: *I'm supposed to be the best ever, that's what they say. But I'm not. I'm a loser.*

Dad stood there, saying nothing. Maybe he didn't know what to say. Maybe he realized that anything he might say would be futile. He walked to me, put his hand on my shoulder, and said, "You'll see, everything will look better in the morning."

"Yeah, right!" I said.

• • •

WHEN YOU'RE BROKEN, YOU RUN. But you don't always run away. Sometimes you slow down, scale back, try to become invisible. That's what I did.

Although I didn't comprehend it at the time, in some dark place deep in my brain I reasoned that, if I didn't put out to the best of my ability, then I hadn't really failed. If I hadn't really failed, then I was spared the shame of being a failure.

Four nights after the Daviess County game, I crept along, three-quarter speed, against the North High Huskies. I didn't defend my man on the balls of my feet, claw for rebounds, or thrust to get open for my shot. Once again I made only two baskets and watched as inferior players drove the action. I continued this lethargic play a week later against Memorial. The two baskets I hit near the end of the game, the second a jumper from behind the free-throw arc with just ten seconds on the clock for the victory, did not hide the fact that I coasted throughout the game.

The next Tuesday night, we defeated the Reitz Panthers 61–52. I was not a factor, taking only five shots the whole game and scoring a paltry two points. Midway through the third quarter, Bill Danner grabbed a defensive rebound and fired an outlet pass to me on the right sideline near midcourt. When I turned with the intent of streaking toward the basket, I accidentally dribbled the ball off the side of my right foot. Disgusted, I watched it roll out of bounds, not even trying to retrieve it. Coach Keller pulled me from the game a minute later, where I sat on the bench the rest the night.

I slunk down the side of the hallway close to the lockers between classes the next day, hoping not to be noticed. Midway through my third period biology class, Coach stuck his head into the room and asked the teacher if he could borrow me for a few minutes.

I walked alongside him down the empty hallway, up the stairs, and into his office, more a cubbyhole than a working space. On one side of his desk was a file cabinet, on the other, a movie projector. On top of his desk I spotted several film canisters, his whistle, and a clipboard holding diagrams of plays.

Coach Keller settled into his wooden swivel chair, which squeaked when he turned to me. "Things pretty rough for you, aren't they?" he said, as he motioned to me to take a seat.

"Yeah, I guess so," I said, not knowing what to do with my hands.

"Lookit, Russ, you haven't been yourself for a few weeks now. I can see it. You've been going through the motions. I'm worried about you. Is something bothering you? Problems at home maybe? Or, God forbid, girl problems?"

I sat silent for a few seconds, my head bent forward, my eyes tracing the lines between the floorboards in front of me. "No, nothing," I said.

He paused and sat with his hands clasped in front of him on his desk, seeming to study me. I wanted to bolt.

"Listen, Russ, you're an outstanding basketball player and you will leave this school one of the best ever to wear a Bosse uniform. But you're only a sophomore. Don't expect so much of yourself. You can't always be on your game. Lighten up on yourself."

Tears filled my eyes and I had to work hard to keep from crying. I couldn't say whether they came from shame or relief.

Keller looked at me. With a soft voice, he said, "Listen, more than a basketball player, you're one of the finest young men I've ever coached. I don't care whether or not you score another point the rest of the season. Rebound, get the ball to the open man, play defense. Just forget what those guys write. Just play ball. Okay?"

"Okay, Coach," I said, taking in and releasing a deep breath while wiping my eyes with my sleeve.

"Okay, then," he said. He walked out from behind his desk, put his arm around my shoulder, then tousled my hair. "Get yourself back to class, and I'll see you this afternoon at practice."

I got up and turned to walk out. "Hey," he said from behind me, "don't forget to bring your smile with you."

Three nights later we traveled to Vincennes to play the Alices. Their strange nickname did not do justice to their 14–2 record and their ranking as the third best team in Southern Indiana. They designed their defense to keep me on the perimeter without the ball and held me scoreless the first half. But I took Coach Keller's words with me onto the court, reminding myself, "Work hard, just do what you can to help the team." I kept my head in the game and collected seven rebounds and played solid defense through the first two quarters.

We left the court at halftime tied 24–24. The ten-minute break provided little time except for encouragement. I peppered Larry Collins, Bill Danner, and the others with "Good going." Coach Buck walked past me and said, "Good hustle." On my way out the door to the court, Coach Keller grabbed my arm and said, "Atta boy."

Relaxed and energized, in the third quarter I ran the court with nine other Indiana boys in the racehorse style of basketball that gave substance to the term Hoosier Hysteria. In the first minute of action, I came off a screen and lofted a twenty-footer that knocked the bottom out of the net, then on the next possession another twenty-footer from the other side of the court. A minute later I drilled one from the right corner and, shortly after that, banked one in off the dribble from right of the free-throw lane. I felt liberated and played fearless, lost in the flow of the game.

After a nip-and-tuck third quarter, I tied the game 37–37 at the beginning of the fourth with another fifteen-foot jumper from the baseline. Then Collins,

Danner, and a flurry of others, me included, scored for the Bulldogs to run away with a 55–46 victory.

Sportswriter Jim Frazier opined two days later: "Sophomore Russ Grieger takes pride in his marksmanship and doesn't understand that sometimes he must miss." The next day, under the headline, "Grieger Emerges From His Slump," Jack Schneider wrote in his weekly column,

> Bosse's success against Vincennes clearly was a "team" victory but the thing that most impressed me was the way Russ Grieger reasserted himself. After a fine start, young Russ fell into a bit of a mid-season slump, no doubt due to his inexperience. But he snapped out of it brilliantly with his 6-for-10 shooting performance in the second half against the Alices. When at the top of their game, the Bulldogs have many attributes that lead to success. But to my thinking, the lad who could elevate this Bosse team to true greatness is Grieger. He doesn't yet have the polish and aggressiveness that only experience can provide, but he possesses the latent explosiveness in his gifted shooting touch that can pull a team out of nearly any kind of hole.

I didn't need to read these words to feel like my old self. I played the next three games with the same abandon I did on the concrete driveway behind my house, the Bulldogs winning all three to complete the regular season with fifteen wins against only three losses.

Then, suddenly, it ended. In our opening game of the Evansville Sectional, the first leg of the Indiana basketball tournament, we lost to the Lincoln Lions. My 1957–1958 basketball season was over.

I shuffled out of the gym into the cold February night, my coat collar turned up and my hands dug deep into my pants pockets. A gust of wind slapped me in the face, causing me to blink. I spied Dad leaning against our car, his coat collar also turned up, holding a cigarette between his fingers.

"You okay?" he asked as I walked toward him.

"I guess so."

"Well, what a year you've had," he said, flipping his cigarette away as miniature embers trailed behind and disappeared.

"Yeah, sure," I said.

"No, I'm serious. You had a lot of pressure on you all year. You did just fine."

I dropped my head and walked to the passenger side of the car. Just before sliding in, Dad looked at me over the car's top and said, "I can't wait till next season."

"Not me," I said. "How about if I let it rest for a while? I need a vacation from basketball."

"Sure, son," he said, "give it a rest. You've earned it."

Dad drove toward home, not hurrying. I leaned my forehead against the cool window and looked at the houses that passed by, recessed behind tan yards and green shrubs, warmed by the muted lights from windows, all oblivious to the drama of my life.

As we cruised, my mind wandered over the season. I knew I had ridden a roller coaster, reaching thrilling heights and dropping to disheartening lows, all connected, I saw clearly, to my performance on the basketball court. Out of blindness, though, I had little understanding of the driving force behind both my exhilaration and my despair, both of which had to do with my sense of self as much or more so than with my basketball performance.

Dad turned left into our driveway, crawled past the basketball goal behind the house, and inched into the garage. "Be it ever so humble," he said and opened his door to go inside. I sat there, staring ahead, not moving.

"Are you coming in?" he asked.

"You know what," I said, "I think I'll turn on the spotlight and shoot a few before going to bed."

"Okay," he said. "Give me a few minutes and I'll come back out and rebound for you."

# 7

## FLYING

EARLY SEPTEMBER 1959. TEMPERATURES HOVERED in the high eighties. Twenty of us gathered on the quarter-mile track surrounding Bosse's football field. A high brick wall hugged its perimeter, blocking any possibility of breeze, funneling the sun directly on top of us.

I stood with three of my senior basketball teammates: Lewis Browning, Chuck Garner, and Allen McCutchan. We wore white gym shorts, scarlet tank tops, and high-top Keds, all except McCutchan, the city mile champion, who wore spiked track shoes. Our shirts clung wet to our chests before we ran our first step.

"Is this nuts or what?" Garner said.

"Yeah, nuts." Browning rolled his eyes.

I looked down and pawed at the black cinders with my gym shoe. To me this was serious business. What I had accomplished before—the wins, the points, the newspaper clippings—was not enough. This was my senior year, the culmination of all I had started three years before as a freshman. I wanted to accomplish something I could carry with me into the future, glory and stardom for sure, but also the self-validation I craved and vindication for my lost junior season.

Just the year before, a junior, I had grown to six foot two and added ten pounds to my frame, weight that gave me more upper-body strength and spring in my legs. More importantly, I had made a commitment to myself: I would banish my fear of failure. I was determined to be the best basketball player I could be, one who played with joy and abandon.

As a visual aid, I'd chosen an image of myself as a locomotive barreling down two tracks, each track necessary for the train not to derail. On one, I was to simply play basketball, full out, oblivious to the time, the place, the competition, exercising all my physicality and passion without contemplation or judgment. On the other, I would fill myself with empowering thoughts meant to buck up my confidence.

In preseason practice, I honed my mantras as fervently as I did my moves. I sounded like one of those old men who sat on Evansville's downtown streets, mumbling incoherent sentences only they could understand. I dribbled slowly up the court and told myself, "Nobody can stop me." Playing defense, I whispered, "You're mine." If I missed a shot, if my opponent scored a basket, or if I made an error, I grunted, "Forget it. Next time."

We played Huntingburg at Central Gym to open my junior season. Getting dressed for the game, I absorbed the smell of the laundry detergent that saturated my game uniform, the thunder of stomping feet muffled by distance and brick, the butterflies colliding in my stomach. When we ran onto the court, the students exploded into yelling and dancing. I could feel the spring in my legs as I ran the layup line and the softness of my touch when I practiced my shooting.

My preseason work paid off. I felt relaxed and for three quarters roamed the court as if I owned it. I battled the boards against the Hunters' frontline: three boys—one six feet and six-and-a-half inches, another six foot six, and a third six foot three—all with thick legs and broad shoulders. I streaked down the court, dribbling left- and right-handed, between and around my black-clad opponents, pushing the fast break. I rained long jumpers from the outside and shorter ones from close in that often required midair adjustments. I played with the daring of a warrior and the lightness of the innocent. By the end of the third quarter, I had tallied fifteen points, snared twenty-one rebounds, and limited their high scorer to a mere four points.

We gathered around Coach Keller at the break, holding a slim lead. The Bosse student body made so much noise I had difficulty hearing his instructions.

When I turned to walk back onto the court, he grabbed my arm and shouted into my ear, "Win it for us."

Then, less than a minute into the fourth quarter, it happened. Leaping as high as I could for a rebound, I came down on the outside of someone's gym shoe, rolled my weight onto the outside of my left ankle, and fell to the floor still holding on to the ball. A teammate pulled me to my feet, and I limped to the bench, expecting to walk off the injury as I had dozens of times before.

A minute later, Coach Keller looked down the bench and yelled at me, "You okay?"

I nodded.

"Get back in there," he said.

When I threw off my warm-up jacket and stood up to report to the scorer's table, I practically fell to the floor.

"Shit," I said.

An x-ray the next morning confirmed the worst: a torn ligament in my left ankle. By noon I wore a cast that started inches below my knee and extended to just above my toes. I had to walk with crutches for six weeks. For the first time in my life, it dawned on me that my life could be derailed through circumstances beyond my control. The universe seemed vast and I a mere speck.

I attended every Bosse practice and sat at the end of the bench each game, watching my teammates run the court, unrestrained and colt-like. Though I charted statistics, handed out towels, and rooted with all my might, I felt as useless as a spectator.

The cast finally came off, and I began rehab. I felt a bit wobbly at first but gained strength and stability with each workout. I scored eight points my first game back, then eleven, sixteen, fourteen, and again sixteen as we closed out the regular season.

By this time, I had worked myself back into playing shape. I could run the court for a whole game without being winded. The bounce in my step, the spring in my legs, and the feathery touch of my shot returned. We defeated the Central Bears in the first game of the Evansville Sectional on Wednesday night, with me contributing fifteen points. Then we destroyed the North High Huskies on Friday night, 73–50. I hit nine of my twelve field-goal attempts and tallied a game high twenty-two points.

The next afternoon we took on the Lincoln Lions in the semifinals. I felt the same sense of unrestrained freedom I had three months earlier against Huntingburg. I played relaxed and ran wherever I wanted on the court. I scored only one basket in the first quarter but made five free throws, having been fouled repeatedly en route to the basket. The game felt like playground basketball, and I eagerly wanted more.

At the beginning of the second quarter, I intercepted a pass at midcourt, right in front of our bench, and dribbled straight toward the Lincoln basket. I heard Coach Keller yell, "Go!" I saw an opening, barreled toward the basket, and leaped to lay the ball off the glass. While in midair, one of the Lincoln defenders had slipped underneath me and lifted up as I hurdled over him. As he rose, he propelled me beyond the edge of the court, headfirst onto the surrounding concrete.

The Bosse students under the basket stood, pointed, and yelled obscenities at the player who did this. I got up, prepared to shoot my free throws. But when I tried to flex the fingers of my left hand, I couldn't.

Coach Keller called time-out and our team physician, Doc Wilhelmus, hustled over to me. He took my left hand in his and examined each finger one at a time.

"I think this bone's broken," he said, holding the index finger of my hand.

"Tape it up," I replied.

"Can't do that. What we're going to do is get you to the hospital for an x-ray."

Someone had rumpled my hair, someone else had squeezed my shoulder, yet another patted my bottom as I followed Doc Wilhelmus off the court. He draped a terry-cloth Bosse robe over my shoulders and led me through the driving rain to an Evansville police car. With sirens blaring and wipers thumping, the policeman hustled me to the emergency room. I listened to the play-by-play of the game while waiting for the results. When the doctor came out and reported, "You have a broken metacarpal on the index finger of your left hand and three severely strained joints on your right," I slumped my shoulders and gave him an "are you shitting me" look.

That ended my junior season. Now, in my senior year, I was determined to get into the best shape of my life. Track coach Max Smith walked from the shade of the redbrick grandstand to the track. He was decked out in gray sweatpants and T-shirt. His close-cropped hair and rimless glasses gave him a nerdy look that detracted from the loose-limbed, athletic way he carried himself.

Standing with a clipboard pressed against his hip, he said, "Boys, we're going to begin winning the conference championship today. Allen, you lead. Three-quarter-mile intervals at a seventy-second pace. Then we'll do three miles. On the count of three: one, two, three, go!"

McCutchan led us out on the first lap, all twenty of us packed tight, two and three abreast. No one said a word. The only sound was the crunching of cinders underfoot and a chorus of quick, sharp breaths. Once around the track, we jogged a slow lap, then repeated this process two more times.

My legs felt like rubber. I walked with McCutchan to the end of the straight-away, breathing hard and trying to stay limber. "Can we go home now?" I said.

Allen grinned. "Yeah, after three more miles."

We ran the three miles, twelve laps around the cinder track. Lewis Brown-ing struggled alongside me. Between quick gasps, he said, "Did you know . . . Jeanne's . . . back at Bosse?"

"She is?"

"Yeah. Becky told me . . . to let it slip . . . that . . . she'd like . . . you to call . . . so . . . I let it slip."

"Hey, thanks," I said, doing my best to sound casual. I had tried to forget about Jeanne since my freshman year but hadn't fully succeeded.

That night after supper, too keyed up to do my homework, I called her. Ner-vousness quickly changed to longing when I heard her voice, husky and halt-ing. "I'm glad you called," she said. I kept the conversation short, not wanting to spoil anything before it got started, and arranged a date for Saturday night.

That Saturday, when I pulled into the circular driveway in front of her house, I noticed that it looked the same as it had three years before—three steps lead-ing up to a concrete porch, a waist-high redbrick wall surrounding it, and a two-person swing hanging from the ceiling. I felt the same butterflies I did before tip-offs. She opened the door as I was about to knock. She wore her thick auburn hair down to her shoulders, a soft curl swept over one eyebrow. Her eyes sparkled when she smiled. Her voluptuous figure, in a red plaid skirt and soft gray sweater, took my breath away. She took my arm as we walked to my car.

After we sat through a movie, we drove to the Coral Drive-In. She sat close to me and we ordered burgers and fries from the squawk box next to the car. I sat behind the wheel, she angled toward me, and we poured out our hopes and dreams as if we both hungered to make up for three whole years of silence.

"We better go," I said, noticing the clock inching toward midnight.

I walked her to the front door and we embraced. I wanted to hold on to her and not let go. When she raised her face to mine, I gave her a kiss. Looking into my eyes, she said, "You better call me tomorrow."

"I will," I said.

September snuck into October. Our first date led to many others. We met before school and at lunch. After school, I ran the cinder track, gradually building up to ten successive intervals and long-distance runs of six miles. Then, at night, after homework, Jeanne and I would talk for hours on the phone.

By the first day of basketball practice on October 15, I was in the best shape of my life. Jeanne wore my class ring on a gold chain around her neck. I felt full of confidence, powerful and eager. Everything necessary for success seemed to be in its proper place. Eager for the season, I thought, *Bring it on!*

◆　◆　◆

IF EXPECTATIONS RENTED A ROOM in a boarding house, those for the 1959–1960 Bosse Bulldogs would have lived in the basement. We lost nine players to graduation, me being the only varsity returnee. As Coach Herman Keller put it, "We're an unknown quantity."

To the surprise of Bosse students and teachers, the Bulldogs started the season by running off four straight victories. I scored a workmanlike sixteen, fourteen, eighteen, and twenty points in these games, all the while garnering such newspaper accolades as "Russ Grieger's brilliant all-around play led the Bulldogs" and "Russ Grieger has been sparkling as a scorer, playmaker, rebounder, and defensive man." I relished every word, yet I knew deep down I could do better. I had yet to unleash the creativity and dominance for which I longed.

Then magic happened.

In the fifth game of the season, we played the Central Bears at Roberts Stadium. I started fast, hitting all seven of my first-quarter field-goal attempts and scoring sixteen points. By halftime, I had tallied twenty-four points, one more than the entire Central team. At the end of three quarters, leading 62–35, I had amassed twenty-nine points. Coach Keller pulled me from the game only moments into the fourth quarter. I knew I could have obliterated Bosse's single-game scoring record of thirty-three had I played to the end.

But those were just the facts.

While gliding over the court, feeling in total control, my reality altered. The fans receded to a faraway place and seemed to shrink to gnome size. The rich colors and the bright lights in the stadium took on a sepia hue. The screech of gym shoes, the blast of whistles, the shouts of players all seemed muted, as if from miles away. The attacks and parries of each team slowed. I felt alone, but not in a bad way. Every second belonged to me. Nothing else mattered but what I was doing. I felt I could do anything I wanted. I felt capable of floating above, around, and even through the other players if I wanted to.

I showered and dressed after the game, tired but fully alive. I felt as if I were built out of pure energy, electricity on bone. Jeanne waited for me outside the locker room. She looked prettier than usual, in a skirt, wearing her loafers and bobby socks, my class ring hanging in the V of her sweater.

"Hey," she said, flashing a smile.

I helped her on with her coat, took her arm, and walked her to my car. Nestling close to me, she asked, "Well, how did it feel?"

"How did what feel?" I asked, deadpan, knowing full well what she meant.

"Oh, you know," she said and elbowed me in the ribs. "Being the big star tonight?"

I paused, searching for the right words. I realized something strange had happened to me that night. It seemed too crazy to tell anyone. Finally, I said, "It felt like I could fly."

One week after the Central game, a capacity crowd of four thousand packed New Albany's Death Valley Gym to witness a battle between two undefeated teams. People pressed in on the court from all sides. The lights shone down dimly, as if the school had exhausted its budget. The heat felt oppressive, and a faint smell of perspiration permeated the gym.

The crowd greeted the Bulldogs with jeers the second we trotted onto the court. Lewis Browning shouted in my ear, "Think we'll get out of here alive?"

I relished the mayhem, feeling alive and carefree. I had been thinking about my mysterious experience against Central throughout the week. It made my life of schooldays and sodas seem trivial and irrelevant.

I challenged New Albany much like I had the guys from my neighborhood. I took long shots from the wings and running jumpers off the drive, the ball swishing through the net with the sound of paper tearing. I posted twenty points by halftime and thirty-one before game's end. Though New Albany gradually pulled away and won, I knew I had ruled the gymnasium and grudgingly won the respect of the crowd.

We won four of our next six games. I scored nineteen in a loss to Jasper, sixteen and twenty-five in wins over Columbus and Daviess County, twenty-eight in a loss to North, and then twenty-five and twenty in wins over Lincoln and Memorial.

Next up, Springs Valley, the night of January 29, 1960. Journalist Jack Schneider wrote in anticipation of that game:

Aside from the game itself will be the attraction of the Bulldogs' Russ Grieger apparently getting even better as the season progresses.

I took charge from the opening tip. I scored seventeen points by halftime and thirty at the three-quarters mark. After I tied the Bosse record of thirty-three a minute and a half into the fourth quarter, I took a pass on the right wing, dribbled left-handed as fast as I could to the top of the key, jumped, and shot from twenty-five feet while being bumped hard by my defender. The roar of the crowd as I lay flat on my back told me I had broken the record. My free throw gave me thirty-six. Then, with 5:15 left in the game, I took a pass above the paint, faked to my left, and barreled to the basket for a layup to jack my total to thirty-eight. I could have scored even more had Coach Keller not emptied the Bosse bench after I scored the last two points.

In the locker room, I sat in front of my street clothes hanging from a hook on the wall. I leaned back, spent but satisfied. Teammates and coaches gave their congratulations and pats on my shoulders and knees. Dad walked in, shook hands with Coach Keller, and squeezed my head inside the crook of his arm. I flashed on the day four years before when he'd dropped me off for my first day at Bosse. I remembered wandering to the trophy case and fantasizing that one day my picture would hold a place of honor there.

We won three of our next four games before traveling to Madison to play the Cubs in our final regular-season game. They ranked number two in the state. Their star, Buster Briley, averaged thirty points a game to my twenty-four. He and I had played against each other in our first two high school years, but not the year before when I was hurt.

Accompanied by our cheerleaders, we rode our Greyhound bus along Indiana Route 66. I sat by myself, looking out the window, but paying little attention to the low-hanging gray clouds, the dormant cornfields, the darkened farmhouses. I didn't notice that Coach Al Buck had slipped into the seat next to me and startled when he said, "Some people say Buster Briley is a better basketball player than you."

I glanced at Buck and said nothing.

"They say you're not in his league."

"Well, we'll see, won't we?" I said, more with annoyance toward him than venom toward Briley.

"Well, okay then," he said. He patted me on my leg and went back to his seat. I figured he meant to motivate me, but I resented that he thought this was necessary.

Madison coach Bud Ritter walked over to me before the game while I stood in the layup line. He grabbed my arm and said, "I wanted to say hello from one

Bulldog to another." Tall and elegantly dressed, he had starred on Bosse's 1944 and 1945 state champion teams.

Coach Ritter put sentimentality aside once the game began. He harried me from start to finish with two pint-sized ball hawks. In tandem, they crowded me everywhere. But I was not to be denied. In front of Al Buck, Bud Ritter, and Buster Briley, I made plays on both ends of the court, one after another, as if timed by a metronome. I felt the court to be my own fiefdom.

I surged around my defender along the right baseline and, when under the basket, leaped and spun the ball left-handed and backward off the backboard and into the basket. I intercepted a pass, dribbled the length of the court in front of the Madison student section, and, sliding between two defenders, floated a running hook shot into the basket with my right hand. I arched feathery jump shots over outstretched hands, ones that fell through the basket as if from outer space. I finessed four-, six-, and eight-foot jumpers off the glass, often surrounded by two and three white shirts. Before game's end, I had hit fourteen field goals and three free throws for a robust thirty-one points, handed out six assists, and collected five rebounds.

Somewhere amid all this action, I was once again transported to a different reality. No one existed in this world but me. All the shadowy figures on and off the court existed for my purposes. The court, the basket, the basketball—all were an extension of me. Joy filled me, and I would have happily played this game for eternity.

I sat slumped on the dressing-room bench after the game, my jersey soaked, sweat running down my face. Teammates and coaches walked by congratulating me and giving their condolences for our narrow defeat. Buster Briley, who'd also worked his own magic that night, bounded into the locker room and grabbed my hand. "Best I've seen all year."

"You too," I said.

I appreciated the accolades but found it distracting. I wanted to stay in the afterglow of my special reality as long as I could. I stood, peeled off my uniform, and slowly walked to the shower, a towel wrapped around my waist. After I dressed and settled into the bus for the ride back to Evansville, I spoke to no one.

As soon as I got home, well after midnight, I tiptoed into my bedroom and called Jeanne. She answered on the first ring and said in a half-whisper, "Hey, big guy."

"Did you listen to the game?"

"Yes. I wish I had been there."

"Yeah, me too."

We talked for the better part of an hour, our voices hushed so as not to awaken our parents. I never mentioned my out-of-body experience. It was all mine, and I didn't want it to be trivialized or diluted by words.

. . .

CLOSE TO SEVEN THOUSAND FANS POURED into Roberts Stadium for our first-round state tournament game against the Central Bears. I ran onto the court to find fans divided into four colors—red for Bosse and gold for Central, purple for Lincoln and blue for Memorial, the teams to play the game that followed ours. There was a sense of mortality to this game for me. If we lost, my high school career would end. Yet I also felt a peculiar sense of immortality, as if the pure playing of the game had come to matter to me as much as the winning.

The Bears must have harbored bad memories of the twenty-nine-point savagery I had unleashed against them only five games into the season. They double- and triple-teamed me every time I touched the ball and taunted me throughout the game. They took charge from the opening bell. They ran to an 18–13 first-quarter lead, kept ahead 32–28 at the half, and took a 52–46 advantage into the fourth quarter.

With 4:06 remaining, and Central leading 56–48, I gathered my teammates around me at midcourt and said, "We're not going to lose this game, dammit. We're going to shut them down, and we're going to score every time we get the ball."

An icy calm came over me, everything inside me perfectly in sync with winning. I made ten of Bosse's next twelve points to tie the game at 60–60—three jumpers from long range that I knew to be true the moment they left my hand; a runner off the dribble from the left side that slammed off the backboard and through the rim; and then a short jump shot from the right baseline that snapped up the net. After a basket put the Bears back ahead, I hit my twelfth basket of the night to tie the game at 62–62. The clock read 1:20.

Everyone in red and gold stood and cheered. Cheerleaders jumped and twirled. Noise filled the stadium.

Central decided to hold the ball for one final shot. With eleven seconds left on the clock, they took their chance and missed. One of the Bulldogs ran down the rebound in the right corner. I ran toward the referee to call a time-out to set up a winning play. As I closed in on him, I saw that the teammate who had snared the rebound was about to commit one of basketball's cardinal sins. Before I could shout "No!" he whipped the ball along the baseline under Central's basket toward another of our players. Like a pickpocket, one of the Bears darted in, intercepted the ball, and laid it into the basket for an abrupt, merciless end to the game, our season, and my high school career. I stood under the basket, looked to the rafters, and walked off the court.

The dressing room could not have been more quiet. The teammate who had made the pass walked over and said, "I'm sorry."

I showered, dressed, and called Jeanne from a payphone. She was home with the flu.

"Hi," she said in a raspy voice.

"We lost."

"I know. I listened to the game on the radio. You should've heard what they said about you."

"Yeah?"

"Yeah. You're my hero."

I walked from the phone to the stands and sat with my Bosse classmates. I looked around the stadium. Its vastness struck me. Then I looked out on the court, at the Lincoln and Memorial teams now playing. It looked familiar but surreal, like finding someone else living in my house.

Sitting in the stadium, with my legs outstretched and my arms hanging over my chair back, a peace settled over me. Basketball had been so many things for me. On one level, it was just a sport. On another, it was a passion. And, finally, it had come to define me as a person. I inhabited this identity so fully that at times this senior year I'd played in what seemed like an alternate reality.

I took a deep breath, exhaled, and nodded to no one in particular. I knew I had the happiness trifecta firmly in my hands. I had fulfilled the promise I'd first shown behind my house on Chandler Avenue. I had a girlfriend who loved me. My sense of self felt solid and steady. *It's all good*, I thought as I got up to go home.

Little did I know that, by year's end, all of this would disappear.

# 8

## ST. LOUIS BLUES

I SAT IN MY LIVING ROOM a few minutes before noon, my hair slicked back and dressed in my Bosse letter sweater, tan slacks, and penny loafers. I tapped my foot on the carpet and sat up to see out the front-room window. Mom, wearing her powder-blue skirt and jacket, placed bowls of peanuts and pretzels on the coffee table. Dad put the finishing touches on his tie in front of the bathroom mirror. We were all waiting for St. Louis University's freshman basketball coach, Fred Kovar.

Many colleges had expressed interest in me throughout my senior basketball season—Vanderbilt, The Citadel, Louisville, Indiana, and Evansville College. I felt attracted to Evansville College, but St. Louis, as in the St. Louis Cardinals and the St. Louis Hawks, gave off an aura of the big time, the higher rolling, the powerful and glamorous.

At exactly twelve noon, Fred Kovar approached our glass storm door, and I sprang up to greet him. He stood about my height, with an angular body and a slight paunch. He wore his light-brown hair short. His small, black eyes gleamed when he smiled, but they could, I thought, become beady and penetrating when angry. He might have been handsome, in that homey Midwestern way, except that, below his eyes, his nose and mouth angled noticeably to the right.

He raised his hand to greet me through the glass. When I opened the door, he grasped my hand in both of his. With a wide grin, he said, "You must be Russ. So glad to meet you."

We settled in the living room. Mom served drinks. After what seemed like endless small talk, Kovar looked first at Dad and then at Mom, sitting together on the love seat. In solemn tones, he said, "Mr. and Mrs. Grieger, I think you know why I'm here. We want Russ to play basketball for the St. Louis University Billikens."

He then scooted to the edge of his chair and leaned forward. He painted St. Louis University in glowing terms, emphasizing his points by grabbing one after another of his fingers. He listed the names of the teams I would play against if I became a Billiken, including Ohio State and Iowa from the Big Ten; Kentucky, Louisville, and Notre Dame from close to home; Stanford and California from the West Coast; St. John from the Northeast; and other big-league basketball schools, Marquette, Cincinnati, Bradley, and Kansas. He said that SLU housed a premier psychology department, so that a degree from that program would launch me into a career that would make the world take note. He told Mom that head coach John Benington, nicknamed "Old Dad," was soft-spoken in the Gary Cooper mold and took his players under his wing like family. Coach Benington, he vowed, would guide me into becoming a great basketball player and a great person. Fred Kovar reminded my parents that the Jesuits, "the Cadillac of priests," guided St. Louis University so that no student could help but be molded into a person of the highest character. For his grand finale, he reminded us that Benington was good friends with the St. Louis Hawks' coach, "Easy" Ed McCauley, a direct pipeline to the NBA for deserving Billikens.

I absorbed every word. Then he spoke directly to me. He referenced stats from my senior season. He passed on a "hi" from Buster Briley, whom he had met the day before in Madison and whom he quoted as saying I was the best he had played against that year. He told me I was one of the purest shooters to grace the hardwood. He detailed the ways I would fit into a Billiken uniform. He practically dangled stardom in front of me.

He took a deep breath and said, "Russ, I think you'd look great in a St. Louis uniform." Then, turning to Mom and Dad, he said, "How about we schedule a weekend, see the campus, meet Coach Benington, maybe take in a game?"

"Absolutely," I said before Dad could respond.

Two weekends later, my parents and I drove out of Indiana and through the rolling farm fields and small hamlets of Illinois. When we crossed the Mississippi and rolled onto the concrete streets of St. Louis, I felt awestruck. When I stepped out of the car at our hotel, I had to crane my neck to see the top.

The next afternoon, Coach Kovar gave us the grand tour of St. Louis.

He took us to Busch Stadium, the home of the St. Louis Cardinals. He drove us out of the downtown area to the Anheuser-Busch Brewery, where I watched Budweiser beer being made and petted the Clydesdale horses. He chauffeured us through Forest Park, a giant expanse in the middle of the city that housed both a zoo and an eighteen-hole golf course. We finally went to the St. Louis University campus, which sat in the middle of several major thoroughfares.

"What do you think about St. Louis?" Kovar asked.

"It's big," I said. "A guy could get lost."

That evening we drove to Kiel Auditorium in downtown St. Louis to watch the Billikens play. Huge, limestone, and fronted by a row of white columns that rose two stories high, it occupied, along with the St. Louis Opera House, a whole city block.

Kiel's interior was mammoth, not so much for its seating capacity but for the height and grandeur of its domed ceiling. A giant scoreboard extended halfway from the dome's apex above midcourt, and brightly lit panels directly over the court illuminated the floor below, leaving the rest of the auditorium in relative darkness. I took a deep breath as we walked to our seats, feeling the kind of reverence I experienced in church.

We sat in the first row behind the Billiken bench, so close I could hear Coach Benington when he shouted instructions. He was tall and gangly, almost gaunt, with a receding hairline, a long, narrow face, and dark bags under his eyes. With every Billikens error, he sunk his face into his hands. Occasionally a smile lit up his face, but rarely.

Near halftime, one of the student managers squatted down in front of me and said, "Harry Caray wants to interview you at halftime."

"What?" I said. Harry Caray announced St. Louis Cardinal baseball games on the radio, and his voice provided the backdrop to almost every one of my summer evenings.

"Yeah, over there," he said, pointing to a man sitting across the court in front of a microphone. He looked nothing like what I expected, given his rich, sonorous radio voice. He was short and squat, with large jowls beneath his chin, and wore glasses with thick black rims that gave him an owlish look. "I'll take you to him once the half ends."

Harry Caray motioned me to sit next to him and handed me a pair of earphones to put on while he finished reading a commercial. When done, he welcomed me and then, to my surprise, reviewed the highlights of my senior season from a typed piece of paper. Without missing a beat, he turned to me and said, "So, what's your impression of St. Louie U basketball?"

I got through the interview, dazed and sputtering, just trying not to sound stupid. I felt awed to be talking on the radio with this famous man and marveled that people in Evansville might be listening.

After the game, Coach Benington escorted me and my family to a postgame dinner at Stan Musial and Biggie's Steak House, co-owned by Cardinal great Stan "The Man" Musial. The dining room was huge and semirustic with thick wooden beams, paneling, and tartan-patterned wallpaper. A giant chandelier hung over the middle of the room along with faux-candle sconces along each wall.

We sat at a corner table covered with a white tablecloth. I remember a trapezoid lamp, a salt-and-pepper set, and a scarlet ashtray. We ordered steak, baked potato, and salad. Coach Benington asked how I'd liked the game and told me that St. Louis's two starting guards would be graduated by the time I became eligible as a sophomore. Then he asked me if I thought I could handle the full-court pressure the opposing guards had applied that night.

"I think so," I said, meaning it. The confidence with which I gave my answer was absolute, with the memory of my on-court prowess still fresh from the season. I could visualize myself freewheeling on the Kiel Auditorium basketball court.

Halfway through dinner, Benington glanced over my shoulder and waved someone over to the table. I looked behind me to see Stan Musial approaching. He had a deep tan, and the corners of his eyes crinkled from squinting into the sun. He looked the same as he did on the baseball cards I had collected in grade school, except that he wore a powder-blue sport coat and a pink dress shirt instead of Cardinal whites.

*Oh, my God!* I thought. My breath caught in my chest.

Benington made introductions all around. The Man stood by my side and rested his hand on my shoulder. When he took his leave, he said to me, "Hope to see you in St. Louis come September. Maybe you can even take in a World Series game if we make it."

"Thanks, Mr. Musial," I said.

I hardly had time for my adrenaline to settle when Coach Benington again waved someone over to us. This time it was Bob Pettit, the six-foot-nine star forward of the St. Louis Hawks, one of my basketball idols. Lean and sharp-featured, he had a movie-star face with close-cropped dark hair, the same penetrating gaze he wore on the court, and a perpetual five o'clock shadow. When I saw him playing on TV, I admired the way he came hard off picks to bury his jumpers, drove determined to the basket for left- and right-handed layups, and fought the boards for second and third shots. He made it clear he owned the court.

I stood up to shake his hand and felt dwarfed by his height. Holding my hand in his, he said, "You won't find a better coach than this man right here," nodding at Benington. "I hope you join me in St. Louis next year."

I returned to the hotel wired. Totally seduced, my mind labored to put the events of the day into perspective. *Harry Caray! Stan Musial! Bob Pettit!* I wouldn't have been surprised if Marilyn Monroe knocked on my door.

The next day, Coach Kovar drove us to the West Pine Gym on the St. Louis University campus, where Benington had his office. The Billiken practice court occupied the middle of the building. A brick wall surrounded the court, with large windows, waist to head high, where coaches could watch the practices. High above, around the perimeter, was a deck where spectators could stand and watch the action.

Coach Benington waited for us in his large corner office. Team pictures covered the wall behind his desk. A basketball signed by President Dwight Eisenhower sat mounted on a small table in the corner. Various trophies and signed photos of sports luminaries shared the bookcase with sports books across from his desk. He invited us to sit.

Benington got down to business. "Russ, Florence, we want your son to play basketball for St. Louis University. I'm offering him a full four-year scholarship. We think he belongs here with us. What do you think?"

Dad glanced at Mom and said, "It's up to Russ." They both looked at me, as did Coaches Benington and Kovar.

I didn't hesitate. "I'd love to come here, Coach," I said. I had to restrain myself from leaping up and shouting "Yeah!"

I lounged in the backseat on the ride home to Evansville that afternoon. The Illinois towns and farmhouses looked so much smaller driving east to Evansville after being among the bustle and towering buildings of St. Louis. My mind wandered over the last two days. I envisioned myself romping on the hardwood of Kiel Auditorium while Harry Caray described my prowess to a rapt radio audience spread over several states. I rolled the words *College Basketball Player* over and over in my mind, savoring them like that last mouthful of butter pecan ice cream. In the quiet of the backseat, the only sound the humming of the tires, the reality that I would once again be a freshman, needing to prove myself all over again, did not cross my mind. Nor did the fact that Jeanne would not be there with me.

• • •

THERE ARE TIMES IN LIFE when you are confident that things will unfold just as you imagined. And then there are times when that's not the case. Life denies, disappoints. And you become confused, lost, not knowing whether to surrender or continue to fight.

Early Sunday morning, September 4, 1960, Dad backed out of our garage, over the concrete basketball court behind my house, and onto Chandler Avenue. He looked at Mom and then said to me and my brother, Gary, in the backseat, "Well, here we go."

The sky was gray and the air prematurely cold. The night before, I had said a long, plaintive goodbye to my high school sweetheart. For the last twelve months, Jeanne had been my daily companion, my emotional support. I had no idea how I would be without her.

Three hours later I stepped out of the car in front of Clemens Hall on the St. Louis University campus. I took a deep breath and slowly let it out. Rectangular, four-storied, and red-bricked, it looked like an army barracks. It gave off none of the warmth and security of my family house, which, up until now, was all I had known.

It took Dad, Gary, and me three trips to carry my belongings up the three flights of stairs to room 322. Mom busied herself hanging up shirts and pants in the closet and putting socks and underwear in drawers. Double sets of beds, chests of drawers, and desks made it clear I would have a roommate. The white plaster walls were bare. I could hear the slap of our shoes on the tile floor, and our voices reverberated just short of an echo.

I expected my family to spend the evening with me before going home. When Dad said, "Well, we better get going," I practically yelled, "You're going?"

I walked them to the car. Dad reassured me that I was about to begin the best years of my life. Mom told me to call any time, day or night. "See ya," Gary said. When they drove out of sight, I walked up to my room and sat on my bed. For the first time in my life, I felt the full weight of loneliness.

I knew I had to get out of that room. I wandered the urban streets surrounding the St. Louis University campus, knowing nothing else to do. I saw no front lawns, no families barbequing hamburgers, no playgrounds. I passed dry cleaners, clothing stores, specialty shops, liquor stores, and assorted other businesses, all dark and locked up. Few people walked the streets, and the only sound I heard were car engines.

I walked for hours, wanting to wear myself out so I could sleep. Time crept, darkness descended. I felt such aloneness I wondered if I would disappear if nobody noticed me.

Head down and my hands stuffed into my pants pockets, I heard impassioned shouting coming from an open doorway. I stuck my head in and locked eyes briefly with the man who had shouted. He wore a black suit, a thin black tie, and a white shirt that glared in contrast with the rest of his garb. His pockmarked face, slicked-back hair, and blazing eyes gave him the look of a maniac as he thrashed the Bible up and down like a tomahawk, all the while ranting. A smattering of people sat before him in rows of folding metal chairs, some dressed casually but neatly, others shabbily and wrinkled in stained pants and shirts.

With a nod, he directed me to sit. Half intimidated and half grateful, I slid onto an empty chair in the last row near the door. The room smelled of sweat and alcohol. He held my gaze, and, with the look of a prophet who had just witnessed the apocalypse, spat out, "You are doomed if you don't repent."

He paused, inhaled, raised his Bible toward the heavens, lowered his chin to his chest, and, with closed eyes, said, "Let's pray." I used that opportunity to make my escape. Back on the street, I feared that all my old anchors and strategies would no longer be of use to me.

I woke early the next morning and walked to the dining facility at the far end of the block. A foul odor made me pull the neck of my shirt over my nose. Later I learned that the smell came from a meatpacking plant just north of campus.

After breakfast, I hiked the half-block back toward Clemens Hall to the West Pine Gym, temporarily converted from the Billiken practice facility into a space to register for fall classes. I then found my way to the SLU bookstore, bought my books, and lugged them up the three flights of stairs of Clemens Hall. Just as I slipped my key into the lock, the door burst open and there stood a gangly boy about my age, a good head taller than me. He wore khaki pants, a buttoned-down shirt, and black horn-rimmed glasses. He smiled and said, "Hi, I'm Gil Beckemeier, your roomie and teammate. Here, let me help you with your books."

Gil took me some four blocks off campus to a neighborhood pub called Garavelli's. Dark and narrow, with a rectangular bar down the middle, it smelled of bratwurst and beer. College kids sat at tables along the walls on either side of the bar. All had bottles of beer and bowls of pretzels in front of them. Gil and I found a table and ordered sandwiches.

We made small talk. Gil told me he had played basketball at Roosevelt High in St. Louis, where he lettered three years and earned all-city honors his senior year. He wanted to be a lawyer. He had a girlfriend, Sue, whom he professed to love, adding, "I can't wait to see her this weekend."

I told Gil about Jeanne, how empty I felt without her, how much I wanted to see her. I told him about my family, my ambitions to be a psychologist, and my basketball history. Then, I said, grinning, "More than anything, I miss my mother."

Gil put his hand on my forearm. "Don't worry, roomie. I'll share my mom with you."

I smiled and felt my first sense of comfort since my parents had left the afternoon before. I knew I had made my first friend outside the state of Indiana.

When we returned from Garavelli's, we found a note from Coach Kovar slipped under our door. It was typed on stationery that read "Billiken Basketball" and instructed us to come by the West Pine Gym that afternoon at three o'clock to be assigned a locker, fitted for game uniforms, and introduced to the training-room personnel. He reminded us that, although formal practices didn't begin until October 15, great things were expected of us, and we were to work out every afternoon on our own until then.

"Guess it gets serious now," Gil said.

I showed up with Gil at three o'clock that day, and we met our other freshman scholarship teammates. There was six-foot-ten Gary Garrison, also from St. Louis, a blond burr-headed behemoth with broad shoulders and a goofy smile that made him instantly likable. Illinois farm boy Stan Leuchtefeld and movie-star-handsome John Cunneen from Kansas City—both six foot six, both built thick and strong like fireplugs—looked like they relished the battle under the boards. Jerry Strange, a high school teammate of Gary Garrison's, stood eye to eye with me and had the raw-boned look of a street fighter. We all gave awkward hellos and sized each other up as bulls might when competing for the only heifer in the corral.

Each day thereafter I worked out at three o'clock with the other Billikens. I played half-court, two-on-two and three-on-three, sometimes with my freshman teammates, often with varsity players, perhaps out of habit from high school. In these freewheeling games without structure or coaches, basketball came easy, as I made jump shots, hauled down rebounds, and executed crisp, precise passes. I more than held my own and felt confident and powerful. From time to time I noticed Fred Kovar and John Benington watching through the portals and imagined them wowed by my prowess.

On October 15, I stepped onto the West Pine court and right into the harsh realities of St. Louis University basketball. In the first week of formal practice, I pushed the ball up court on a two-on-two fast break and let fly a fifteen-foot jump shot that sandpapered the nets. Coach Kovar blew his whistle to stop play. "We don't want that here," he said. "That's playground basketball. You didn't have the numbers. Slow it down and set up the offense for the high-percentage shot."

I wanted to say, "Hey, I made the basket," but I just nodded and trotted back to play defense.

Another time, I brought the ball up court to start the offense. I scooped a one-handed pass off the dribble to Stan Leuchtefeld and cleared out to my left. Again he blasted his whistle. "One more pass like that and I'll send your ass right back to Evansville," he shouted.

I struggled through the preseason, never able to get into a comfortable groove. I lost the sense of mastery I had gained at Bosse. My frustration mounted. SLU basketball felt wrong, like a too-tight shirt worn inside out, too uncomfortable to wear as is, too awkward to pull off and turn right-side out. I had doubts about the St. Louis system, but I also doubted myself, and my self-doubts started gaining more and more of a foothold.

I hit bottom the night of the annual varsity-freshman scrimmage. It took place in the West Pine Gym with a few hundred onlookers standing on the overhead running deck that surrounded the court. We wore our blue Billiken travel uniforms. Real referees, decked out in black pants and black-and-white-striped shirts, officiated the game. John Benington, though coaching the varsity, settled back to watch our performance with the cold-blooded gaze of a hanging judge.

The tip went up and the senior guards smothered me. I had a difficult time advancing the ball over the centerline and found it almost impossible to get off a shot. I made only one basket, an awkward layup I should never have taken and was lucky to make. For the first time in my life, I felt overwhelmed on a basketball court. My sense of inadequacy and incompetence knew no bounds. I carried the full weight of shame on my shoulders, worse than any time in high school.

Later, in the dormitory, after most of the residents of the third floor had settled into their rooms, I slipped to the hallway payphone and called my parents.

"How'd it go tonight?" Dad asked.

"Not good," I said. "I was awful."

"Well, it's your first game. It'll come. You'll see."

"No, it won't," I blurted. "I don't think I'm good enough to play here."

"Nonsense. It'll work out. I know it. Just keep doing your best."

As my self-esteem tumbled, I came to rely more and more on the multipage letters from Jeanne to bolster my spirits. Without realizing it, I crossed the line from thinking I loved her to believing I needed her. She became for me the sole source of my self-worth.

Two weeks before Thanksgiving, I hustled to my dorm before practice to find a letter from Jeanne in my mailbox. I raced up the three flights of stairs to my room, threw off my coat, and ripped the pages from the envelope. Inside I found my worst nightmare. She wrote that she needed to break off our relationship, citing pressures from her parents and her studies, none of which made sense to me.

My mind went numb and my body went slack. My chest felt empty, as if life had been sucked from me. A future without meaning instantaneously took over my mood. Without realizing it, I was in shock.

I read the letter again, and then again, hoping to find some word or nuance that could offer a glimmer of hope. Out of desperation, I grabbed the change I always kept in my desk for the payphone. I paced while I waited for her to come to the line, taking deep breaths to keep my emotions under control. When she answered, her voice sounded distant and guarded, carrying a wariness I had never before heard. She gave no explanation of what had changed. When I asked her how I had failed her, she broke into sobs that made further conversation impossible.

I hung up the phone and, without going back to my room, walked down the staircase and out the door to go to practice. Heading in, Gil stopped me and said, "Where you going?"

"To practice," I said without looking at him or stopping.

"Hey, wait a minute, roomie, it's freezing out here. You forgot your coat. Are you okay?"

"Jeanne just dumped me," I said, almost whimpering.

"No!" He put his arm around my shoulders. "Come on upstairs. Let's get your coat, and we'll walk to practice together and talk about it."

I stumbled through practice, my body present but not my mind, as if I were disassociated from my surroundings. After practice, I skipped dinner and called my parents the moment I got back to the dorm. When I heard my mother's voice, I began to cry, as quietly as I could so as not to embarrass myself in front of my dormmates.

"What is it, dearie?" Mom asked. She told Dad to pick up the extension in my bedroom.

"It's Jeanne, Mom," I said between stifled sobs. "She broke up with me."

"What?"

"This'll straighten out, son," Dad said. "If not, there are a million fish in the sea."

"Not like her, Dad," I said.

"Sure there are," he said. "Everything will be okay. You'll see."

That night, I couldn't sleep. Jeanne's awkward and anguished voice echoed in my mind. I'd given her everything I had to offer, and that still wasn't enough. *There must be something terribly wrong with me*, I thought.

•   •   •

I SPENT CHRISTMAS IN EVANSVILLE and returned to St. Louis the first day of the New Year an emotional mess. Clemens Hall felt like a ghost town—dark, empty, and eerily quiet. The rest of the students wouldn't return for another ten days. Freezing rain alternated with blowing snow. The weather outside felt as oppressive as the emptiness I carried within. Desperate for relief from the pain, I wondered what I was doing there. Maybe I had made the biggest mistake of my life. I longed to feel detached, invulnerable, but had no idea how.

That Friday, Jerry Strange gathered the six of us together after practice in the locker room. "Hey, guys," he said, "how about we go howling tonight?"

The six of us had slowly bonded into the best of friends. We had become so close we called ourselves The Guys. That night, we roamed farther and farther away from campus, into squalid neighborhoods where winos loitered in alleyways, trash bags piled on the sidewalks, and iron bars protected store windows. Down the block, we spotted a neon sign above a doorway. It blinked on and off: *The Tic Toc Friday Night Club*. Strange and I stopped walking and raised our eyebrows at each other.

Gil looked at us and said, "Tell me you're not thinking what I think you are."

"We sure are," Garrison said, and we all walked into dim lights and loud music from a band on the stage across the room. When our eyes adjusted, we saw that we were the only white people there. Dark-skinned ladies in tight skirts and low-cut blouses sat at tables, some with men, others not. *Oh, shit*, I thought.

Before we could turn to leave, the bandleader pointed at us and drawled into the microphone, "Ladies and gents, let's welcome the St. Louis Hawks. These guys must be the Hawks, they're so big."

Laughter broke out and we settled at a table next to the bandstand. After we ordered Budweisers, Cunneen said, "Hey, let's get dancing." And we did.

I held tight to ladies who smoked cigarettes and drank cocktails and who, I fancied, had done the kinds of things of which I only dreamed. No one refused my overtures, and some even pressed full-body close to me as we slow danced. At some point, as I surveyed the women in the room, a startling thought hit me: *She has nothing that these women don't have.* I meant Jeanne. I felt lighthearted and powerful for the first time in months.

The basketball season continued, and I worked hard. I concentrated on shuffling my feet on defense so as not to let my opponent get an angle to the basket. I accepted that it was my role to start an offense geared to get the ball low to the big men, not scorch the net with high-arching jumpers. I worked to improve my ball handling. I got better, though not to the breakthrough level I craved. I longed to run the court as a free spirit, not a piston in a car engine.

On a mid-February afternoon, the freshman team took the court at the Robertson Memorial Field House in Peoria, Illinois, to play the Bradley University frosh. From the outside, the field house looked like a giant airplane hangar, with a roof that curved from ground level on one side to ground level on the other. Inside, the playing floor stretched from one end of the curve to the other, with bleachers slanted gradually upward from courtside to the ceiling, giving the fans the look of a wheat field swaying in the breeze. The smell of popcorn hung in the air, and an organist cranked out carnival tunes when there was no activity on the court.

Maybe it was because this was the last game of the season. Maybe it had to do with the relaxed atmosphere in the gymnasium. I didn't know and didn't care. All I knew was that, as soon as I ran onto the court, I felt loose, at home, relaxed. Early in the game, I fought under the basket for a rebound, crowded on all sides by bodies in white uniforms. Scrambling for the ball, I thrust my arms out to create space and felt my left elbow smash first against soft tissue and then bone. It felt good. I failed to snare the rebound, but I did grab hold of something I had not held on to for ever so long: the sweet feel of basketball power.

That afternoon, Jerry Strange and I worked the backcourt as if we were twin brothers, taking care of each other whenever the other one got in trouble. Stan Leuchtefeld and John Cunneen crashed the boards as if they were charging the beaches of Normandy. Gil Beckemeier and Gary Garrison floated hooks from both sides of the baskets. I popped seven jumpers from around the perimeter that made the net dance. My fifteen points were not show stopping, but they gave me a hint that maybe, just maybe, I could still find magic in this game.

•  •  •

FRIDAY, MAY 12, THREE O'CLOCK. Gil and I sat slumped, bleary-eyed and hangdog at a table near the back corner of Garavelli's. The light from the front window barely reached us, making it hard to see the faces of the men who sat at the bar, only their dusty jeans, sweat-stained shirts, and work boots. Before us sat a pitcher of Busch Bavarian beer and a basket of onion rings drenched in ketchup. We had just finished our final exams and were too tired to celebrate but too wired to go back to our dorm room.

Gil grabbed an onion ring and said, "Well, roomie, we survived our freshman year."

"We sure did," I said, then I added, "barely." I held my glass up as a salute and drained my beer.

"What are you doing this summer?" he asked.

"Nothing special. Work for the Rec Department with little kids, work on my game."

The waitress came from around the bar toward us. She wore a tight-fitting white blouse that hugged the well-rounded contour of her body. She had auburn hair pinned into a bun and friendly brown eyes. I wished she'd take off her apron and sit next to me. "Another pitcher?" she asked.

"Yeah, why not," I said.

We both watched her walk away. Then Gil said, "Well, we got a whole three months of fun and sun coming up. We sure deserve some good times, after what we've been through."

"We sure do," I replied. "But, I gotta tell you: September feels so close."

"I know," he said, taking a deep breath.

What I didn't say but thought was, *Making it on the varsity feels so far away.*

# 9

## RETURN TO EVANSVILLE

SOMETIMES YOU KNOW THAT THINGS won't work out. You can feel it, sense it, but still you don't quite comprehend it. That's where my head was when I returned to St. Louis for my sophomore year. At exactly three o'clock on October 15, we Billikens—seventeen of us in all—gathered around Coach John Benington at center court of the West Pine Gym. He wore shiny white sweatpants with a thin black stripe down the side of each leg, a white V-neck with SLU embossed in blue on the left breast, and a whistle dangling around his neck. Even at this first practice, he had bluish-black bags under his eyes and deep lines at their corners.

I slid the bottom of my shoe back and forth against the hardwood, trying to ignore the tension in my gut. "Gentlemen," he said, "today we start becoming a lean, mean marauding machine."

I liked the sound of that. The word "marauding" brought to mind daring, audacity, and the specter of surprise attacks and midnight raids. I glanced around at the other six guards, all of whom had been groomed to play the SLU system. They could protect the basketball like armed sentries and had the mentality of true playmakers. With my strength being my feathery shooting touch, I figured that my only chance was if we played a wide-open game. With his words, I allowed myself to feel hope.

By the end of the second week, I realized that Benington's operative word was "machine," not "marauding." We repeated half-court moves over and over—two-on-two pick and rolls, inlet passes to the big men, defensive foot shuffling—but rarely fast breaks or scrimmages, nothing creative. I fell into the middle of the pack of guards and alternated between berating myself and damning John Benington.

The Billikens won their first two games and then lost in succession to Kansas State, Kentucky, Ohio State, Louisville, Stanford, and California. I mostly sat on the bench, wearing my warm-ups and rarely seeing any action. I watched the SLU cheerleaders. They leaped, swirled their pom-poms, and danced Rockette style in their white sweaters, dark-blue skirts, and bobby socks. None of it was for me. I spotted Harry Caray sitting across the court, at the press table, before a microphone. I realized he would never mention my name on the air. It seemed that the bright overhead lights shined down directly on top of me, spotlighting my irrelevance. I felt a strange mixture of resignation, shame, and bitterness, a brew of emotions I could not have sorted out had I tried.

On the bench, Jerry Strange and I worked to keep our spirits up. "Hey," he said, "we've got the best seats in the house."

"Yeah," I said. "Being humiliated sitting here is better than being humiliated out there."

I still showed the proper support for my teammates. After delivering one of my obligatory cheers, I said, "We're lucky. We don't have to shower after the game. We haven't worked up a sweat."

"You know what," Jerry said, "I don't even know what the hell I'm doing here."

"Neither do I."

Weeks passed. Our record stood at eleven wins and twelve losses when we traveled to Drake University in Des Moines, Iowa, to play our third-to-last game of the season. I sat on the bench and watched our guards repeatedly pass up open shots, laboring to get the ball to one of the big men under the basket. I'd made thousands of those shots behind my house, at Central Gym, at Roberts Stadium. I wanted to yell, "Shoot the ball." When they did, they clunked it off the rim, over and over.

I looked down the bench at Coach Benington. He leaned forward, elbows on his knees, chin resting in his palms. Periodically he shouted instructions: "Run your routes." "Watch the spacing." "Get in position." I realized that his input was meant to fine-tune the mechanics, not to create new ways to free his players to excel.

My frustration mounted. An urge welled up inside me to walk down to him and shout, "Put me in! I can make those shots." Two or three times I started to lift myself off the bench, but I sat back down and concentrated on encouraging my teammates. That was the first time the thought formed full-blown in my mind, *I've got to get out of this place.*

Two weeks later, after our season ended, Gil Beckemeier, Jerry Strange, and I drove to Evansville to watch my brother Gary's Bosse High team contend for the Southern Indiana Semistate Championship. If Bosse won its two games, they'd move on to Indianapolis the next weekend for the state's Final Four.

When we motored to Division Street, I saw the stadium for the first time in two years. It stood in the center of a big, open expanse, surrounded on all sides by row upon row of cars. Unlike Kiel Auditorium, Roberts hugged low to the ground, its playing floor recessed two stories below street level. It had a slightly curved roof and reddish-orange decorative girders, all suggesting adventure and playfulness. I felt my heart quicken and my excitement rise.

"This is where you played high school ball?" Jerry asked.

"Yep," I said, louder than necessary.

"Unbelievable," Gil said.

We walked inside the stadium to find over ten thousand people packed into the stands. The colors of the four competing schools filled the stands—Bosse, red; Jasper, black; Seymour, green; Eminence, yellow. Four sets of cheerleaders danced and twirled courtside, and thousands of students filled the air with chants and cheers. The fans seemed to quiver like thousands of bees around a honeycomb.

The Bosse game started. Both teams looked to be fueled by high-octane gasoline, one pushing the ball up the court as fast as it could, the other retaliating in the opposite direction just as swiftly. Centers and forwards led the fast breaks, and guards posted up under the basket. It looked to me like everyone on the court had license to create his own shot. I pictured myself out there, on this very same court, only two years before, playing as free and unencumbered as they.

During a time-out, Gil leaned across Jerry's lap and said, "I'm stoked."

"You're stoked?" I said, feeling something change inside me.

A week later I hitched a ride to Indianapolis to watch Bosse win the Indiana Basketball State Championship. Similar to the week before, I watched the Bulldogs play with spontaneity and freedom. They had structure to their game but weren't ruled by it. I loved every minute of action and felt at home.

Celebrations spilled into every hallway of the Holiday Inn after the game. Room doors stood open, people coming and going at will. I partied with ex-classmates, former teachers, and current students. I finally made my way to my parents' room sometime after midnight, crowded with relatives and well-wishers. Mom gave me a hug and said, "You should have had this too."

"Aw, Mom," I said. "Gary's winning is the next best thing to me winning."

"I know," she said, "but it's not fair."

"Well," I said, "it's not over for me yet."

Mom, Dad, and I drove from Indianapolis to Evansville the next morning in a mile-long caravan that trailed the Greyhound bus carrying the Bosse team. Mom sat in the backseat, and I rode shotgun next to Dad. The sun shone brilliantly in a cloudless blue sky. People stood on lawns alongside the two-lane highway, many holding up celebratory signs. Small-town movie marquises displayed "Go Bosse," "Our Heroes," and other congratulatory messages. High school bands played the Bulldog fight song in intersections as we passed through several small hamlets. I looked over at Dad and saw tears streaming down his face. "Look at your old dad," he said, laughing at his own sentimentality.

We rode in silence for a few miles, each of us lost in our own thoughts, me remembering the thrills of playing basketball in my days at Bosse. Right then I decided that I had to leave St. Louis University and try to transfer to Evansville College. I had made a decision, a decision perhaps driven by desperation and hatched out of the emotion of the moment, but a decision I knew I had to act upon. I knew as surely as I knew anything that I must make this move in order to be spared a life of "what-ifs," regrets, and self-recriminations.

I steeled myself and said, "Dad, can I talk to you?"

"Sure."

"I think I want to transfer back to Evansville College, if they'll still have me."

He glanced at me, then back to the road. "Aren't you happy at St. Louis?" The hum of the tires on the pavement filled the car.

"I am with St. Louis, but not with basketball. I might not be good enough to play college ball, I don't know, but these last two weekends have hit with me how much I still want to play."

"You know you'll have to sit out a year as a redshirt if you transfer, don't you?"

"I know," I said, "but if I don't make a move now, I never will. I'll feel like I've given up. I'd regret it forever."

"Okay," he said, patting my leg. "If that's what you want, you know your mom and I'll stand behind you. How about we figure out what we need to do when we get home tonight?"

A month later, I sat in Coach Arad McCutchan's living room on Boeke Avenue in Evansville. I told him I wanted to play basketball for Evansville College, if he'd have me.

Without hesitation, he said, "Glad you finally recognized your mistake. Welcome home."

We shook hands and I took my leave. Sitting in my car in front of his house, I let out a long sigh. *It's done,* I thought. I felt relieved but also scared. The aphorism my dad had preached to me when I was a child crossed my mind: "Be careful what you wish for, because it might come true." Now I'd have to start all over and lay it all on the line once again.

• • •

A CLEAR BLUE SKY CANOPIED the Evansville College campus on the third day of September 1962. The two- and three-story limestone buildings reflected the piercing sunlight and made me squint. I meandered under giant oaks and passed students sitting on concrete benches or lounging Indian style in small groups on the giant lawn. The color green—the grass below, the evergreens hugging the buildings, the leaves above—dominated the landscape. I smelled the freshly cut grass and felt energized and renewed.

That afternoon, after classes, I made my way to the National Guard Armory for my first preseason workout with the Aces. I hadn't anticipated the emotions it would arouse. I walked up the same concrete steps I had as a child alongside my parents and felt a surge of adrenaline shoot through me. When I pulled open the heavy metal entry doors and heard the sound of basketballs bouncing on wood, I felt the knots that always filled my gut before tip-off. I walked between the bleachers that had been rolled out from the walls to courtside and saw my Aces teammates, some of whom I had played against in high school and others I knew only by sight. Fear trumped everything as I saw the guys who would be my teammates and competitors.

I must have stood there for some time, because a voice snapped me awake. "Are you going to come out here and join us, Russ Grieger, or are you going to just stand there and gawk?"

The voice belonged to Wayne Boultinghouse, a boy I had befriended when we were teammates on an all-star team after our senior season in high school. He bounced a basketball to me as I walked onto the court toward him and introduced me to the Aces—Buster Briley, my old adversary from Madison; Ed Zausch, Jim Smith, and Paul Bullard; blue-chip freshmen Larry Humes and Sam Watkins; and Jerry Sloan, yet to play an Aces varsity game but already touted to be the best ever to wear an Aces uniform.

Once finished with the introductions, Sloan said, "Okay, now that we've got that shit out of the way, let's play us some basketball."

Right off, I knew this was an Indiana gym. We divided into teams—shirts and skins—and ran full court like schoolkids let out for recess. Buster Briley jacked up long-range bombs without hesitation. Jerry Sloan roamed the floor as if there were no rules except the ones he wrote. Larry Humes lofted hook shots so far from the basket I thought his follow-through would carry him out of bounds. It was not that there was no order or discipline, but that there was no "Slow it down to get the ball into the Bigs," no "Know your role and stick to it," no "Play for the percentage shot." Military cadence gave way to the beat of rock-and-roll.

Scrimmaging with the Aces took me to the very crossroads where my passion for basketball intersected with my battered self-esteem. These guys were all good, each of them the star of their high school team, each schooled to play basketball as an act of creativity, not proficiency. Though I'd been estranged from this style for two long years, this was the type of basketball that had been imprinted on my soul. I knew this was my last chance, that I had no excuses should I fail.

I tried my best to ignore these thoughts and focus on working the rust out of my game. I forced myself to take my shots without contemplation or hesitation, to attack the basket whenever I saw an opening, to try daring passes that would earn "all rights" if successful and "nice tries" if not. I wanted to find my Bosse spirit again, and I hoped, by acting like I had that spirit on the outside, I would find it inside.

During one scrimmage, I found myself guarding Buster Briley. He was six foot four and a free spirit, and he played with the innocence and abandon of a fifth-grader. He was not the fastest runner or the highest jumper, but he could sure shoot the basketball. And he did, from every angle, from any distance, with joy and confidence, no matter what the circumstance. His idea of heaven was surely a place where he could shoot jumpers that touched nothing but net, night and day, never getting tired or having to stop.

I couldn't help but like Buster, though I knew he might be a future rival. On that particular day, I summoned my two years of St. Louis University defensive skills. On successive possessions, I swiped the ball from him off the dribble, partially deflected one of his jump shots, and flipped the ball up from underneath as he held it in front of him so that it hit him in the chin and bounced free.

As we fought for the loose ball, he shouted "Dammit!" and lunged to wrestle me to the ground instead of retrieving the ball.

"Hey!" I said as we both scrambled to our feet, ready to square off. Several of the guys hustled between us to head off an escalation.

*Now it's for real,* I thought.

September slid into October, October into November, and November began the 1962–1963 basketball season. Before then, I'd competed with these guys as an equal, an Ace. Now I became a "redshirt," an athlete who had transferred from another school and so was ineligible for varsity competition for one year. Week after week I played on the "dummy team" at practice, playing defense against the first team as they practiced their offense and running the next opponent's offense so they could hone their defensive strategies. Week after week I sat at the end of the bench, in my street clothes, and watched the games as a spectator. I watched how they got into their opponents' faces on defense, imposing their will. I watched how smoothly they executed their offense, as smooth as silk, as graceful as a ballet. I watched as they made jumpers, layups, hooks, each and every time arousing in the stadium's adoring fans a burst of ecstasy. I watched Coach McCutchan shout "Hit it!" "Push it!" and "All right!" as the action unfurled in front of him. And I watched how the Aces kept up their chatter on the court, encouraging each other with "Good hustle" and "Good shot," how they helped each other up when they'd been knocked down, adding a slap to the backside for good measure. As I watched all that, I felt irrelevant and uncertain if I would ever play. I longed to be out there.

Thank God for the Tri-State Basketball League, a league comprised of former high school and college players from a three-state area surrounding Evansville— Kentucky, Illinois, and Indiana. The down-home names of the teams—Beck's Bar, Carmi Oilers, North Side Radiator—didn't do justice to the quality of the talent, the feistiness, the determination to win. And each match was played on the very same Agoga Tabernacle court where my eighth-grade Christ the King team had played.

My team, Lloyd's Barbershop, was made up of former Aces, men I had watched play when I was in high school, men who played with a rare combination of poise and abandon. I ran alongside All-American Hugh Ahlering as he barreled to the basket whenever he saw an opening. I zipped passes to Harold Cox, Ahlering's running mate, who mastered the art of stopping on a dime, leaping high into the air, and burying one long jumper after another. I positioned myself for the outlet passes that Dale Wise, the Aces all-time rebound leader, would inevitably deliver after ripping an errant shot off the boards.

When I ran the court with these men, I felt like an Evansville College Purple Ace. I felt it when we executed our tip-off play. I felt it when we ran the same offense Jerry Clayton had run for Coach McCutchan back in the Armory days, the one my Lloyd's teammates ran in their heyday, the one the 1962–1963 Aces now ran. I felt it when we filled the lanes and stormed down the court on fast breaks. Though Lloyd's was a pickup team, I felt part of a long-standing Aces culture that would stretch forever into the future.

Best of all, I rediscovered my feel for the game, scoring in double digits each game. I remember one play above all others. It was a Sunday afternoon. Sun shone through the windows and sliced across the court. Fewer than a thousand people sat in the stands, but this gymnasium, with its worn, yellowed floor, shabby grandstands, and musky smell, felt to me like the center of the universe. Sometime deep into the first half, I batted an inlet pass, intended for our opponent's center, to my running mate, Hugh Ahlering. Off we raced up court, on a two-on-one fast break, he on the right, me on the left. We passed the ball back and forth as we ran, neither of us dribbling, until Hugh got the ball to me at the top of the key. I dribbled with my left hand hard to the goal. Closing in on the basket, I feigned a two-handed chest pass to Ahlering on my right. When the defender took my fake, I switched the ball to my left hand and laid it off the glass and into the basket unmolested.

Nothing could have been sweeter than to hear Ahlering shout, "All-American move."

The topper came on the night of February 4, 1963, when I walked onto the Agoga court to play South 41 Furniture. A chill hung in the air. Every time someone entered the building, a wave of cold air wafted across the court. Just after our team finished their layup drill, I absentmindedly glanced down court. There, with his close-cropped hair and sloped shoulders, stood my grade-school hero, Jerry Clayton, shooting his unmistakable jump shot.

"Oh my God," I said to no one in particular.

I stood still for a minute, staring, trying to decide whether to play it cool or do the fan thing. I finally thought, *The hell with it,* and dribbled the ball across the centerline and right next to Clayton. As he settled onto the hardwood after releasing the ball at the top of his jump, I said, "Excuse me, Jerry, I just want to say hello. You've been my hero since I was a kid."

I startled when he said, "Russ Grieger, I know who you are."

I stood there a moment, not knowing what to say. Finally I said, "I can't believe I'm actually going to play against you tonight."

"Well, you are. How about that? Let's say we both have ourselves a great game."

And we did. He and I both scored twenty points. Lloyd's won 86–64, but that didn't matter. Being on the same court with Jerry Clayton, playing against him as a peer, meant everything to me. My basketball career had been bookended, and I now felt like I was exactly where I needed to be.

• • •

LLOYD'S BARBERSHOP ROMPED THROUGH THE Tri-State Basketball League undefeated, beating each of the other nine teams twice, for an 18–0 record. We topped that by winning the postseason tournament to finish a sparkling 21–0.

The Aces did almost as well as Lloyd's. They posted a solid 19–5 record, playing the running style of basketball that delighted both the fans and the players. In the process, they accomplished two of Arad McCutchan's three goals: one, to win their own holiday tournament; two, to win the conference championship. In tournament play, they won their NCAA regional but lost their opening NCAA finals game to the Southern Illinois Salukis. It was a devastating loss given that the Aces had beaten SIU by eighteen points earlier in the season.

The Evansville community grieved, but by summer they started looking forward to the 1963–1964 season, and with good reason. Four starters returned, along with supersubs Paul Bullard and Wayne Boultinghouse. Moving up to the varsity were Larry Humes, Sam Watkins, and me.

"We're going to have more depth than we've had in years," Coach McCutchan told the media.

Not a week went by without somebody stopping me on the street, in a restaurant, or at one of my favorite watering holes. "How're we going to do next year?" they asked.

"Just fine," I said. I wished I could speak with as much assurance about my own prospects.

# 10

## A DREAM COMES TRUE—ALMOST

I FELT A BITE IN THE air as I drove to Evansville College the morning of October 15, the first day of basketball practice for the 1963–1964 season. I glanced out my car window and sent a silent prayer over the treetops into the endless blue sky. I asked God to nudge this basketball season my way, to make it a season I could take pride in, a season without shame or regret. I reminded him how little it would take for him to blink that into existence, but how awfully much it meant to me.

On this day, at exactly three o'clock, Coach McCutchan blew his whistle to gather the Aces around him at center court. We stood in our practice gear, looking eager, as if we were about to break the huddle to start a real game. No one shuffled his feet, bounced a basketball, or even coughed. I stole a glance at the basketball talent all around me and thought, *How in the world will I ever break into the starting lineup?*

McCutchan got right down to the point. "Boys," he said, "I expect a lot out of you this season." He paused and glanced around. "Here's our goals: Win the conference championship. Beat Iowa, Purdue, and Notre Dame. Win the NCAA Championship."

*Is that all?* I thought.

He worked us hard that first day, as he did every day thereafter. In addition to laps around East Side Park and sprints up and down the Armory steps, he set up five drills that he ran in succession, punctuated by a sharp blast of his whistle to signal us to move on to the next. Two-on-two. *Bleat.* Three-on-three. *Bleat.* Rebounding. *Bleat.* Fast breaks. *Bleat.* Free throws. Then, in November, he began devoting the bulk of practice to five-on-fives and full-court scrimmages. I had never played basketball so intensely for such extended periods of time. I cut to the basket as hard as I could, filled the fast-break lane with all the speed I could muster, and guarded my man with the tenacity of a leech. I felt that every second mattered, every move counted.

As if to intentionally drive us mad, McCutchan experimented with different lineups. No one, except Sloan, knew where he stood. One uncertain day fed into another. The voices of self-doubt escalated in my head. I started waking up early with a dread that unsettled my stomach. I became irritable with my parents, disinterested in my schoolwork.

On the Monday before Thanksgiving, the day of President Kennedy's burial, Coach McCutchan stuck his head into the locker room and told me to meet him in his office. Being summoned to Coach's office was never a good thing. My insides went numb and an *Oh, no!* formed in my mind.

I laced up my sneakers, pulled on my practice jersey, and made my way to his office.

When I appeared at McCutchan's open doorway, he was holding a phone to his ear and motioned me to sit on the wooden chair to the right of his desk. I looked out the window behind him toward Walnut Street as he talked. The sky was gray and the grass a bland autumn tan. Three crows stood in the gutter, their heads bobbing up and down, pecking away at the carcass of a dead squirrel. They flew away when a vehicle approached, but returned to continue eviscerating their prey once the car passed.

I looked at Coach McCutchan, my mind a blank. He jotted notes on a piece of paper while uttering intermittent "uh-huhs" into the telephone. I noted his receding hairline and the gray stubble on his face. I studied his brown eyes framed by dark horn-rimmed glasses. I tried to penetrate his mind and divine what he had in store for me, but I could fathom nothing.

Coach hung up the phone, cleared his throat, and turned to me. "Well, Russ," he said, leaning back in his chair and putting his hands behind his head, "you've really put out tremendous effort this fall, haven't you?"

"I've tried," I said, barely breathing.

"I know you have, and I appreciate it. I just wanted to let you know that I've got a dilemma on my hands, and I'm not sure what to do about it. We've got nine guys who could easily start, you included, but only five spots."

I didn't like the direction he was heading and wanted to shout, "Get to the point!" but contained myself. "We sure are blessed with tons of talent," I said instead.

"We are, indeed. I haven't made a decision how to handle it quite yet—sit four of you, run a platoon system, I don't know. I just want you to keep hustling like you've been doing. No matter what I decide, I want you to know that you'll see lots of playing time."

I did not know what to say, so I said nothing.

"Okay then, get out there and warm up. I'll see you on the court in a few minutes."

I walked back to the practice gym feeling confused. My mind raced. *What was he trying to tell me? Was he preparing me for the bench? Was this a warning?* I felt like that dead squirrel on Walnut Street, being pecked to death.

I failed to distinguish myself the rest of the week and felt less and less hopeful that I'd be one of the starters. As my hope descended, my anxiety mounted. I felt a burning in the center of my chest. My stomach knotted as I felt plagued by thoughts of self-doubt. I couldn't shake it, feeling exposed and judged by everyone I passed on campus.

I slunk into Dr. Paul Grabill's Shakespeare seminar the following Monday and slouched in my chair, neither paying attention nor participating. I could've cared less about Othello, Iago, or Desdemona, so absorbed was I in my own self-pity. I didn't want to be there, but I couldn't think of anywhere else I could go to feel better.

On my way out after class, Dr. Grabill's booming voice stopped me. "Mr. Grieger, if you've got a minute, let's chat in my office."

I had first met Paul Grabill in the first week of the quarter, in early September. I sat in a one-story wooden building that looked like an army barracks. Ninety-degree temperatures and major-league humidity left me dripping with sweat. Sitting next to one of the open windows, I watched men wearing blue work pants and short-sleeved shirts manicure the Evansville College lawns. Squirrels cut back and forth under trees while birds and butterflies whirled lazily overhead. I chuckled when I looked down at my one-armed chair and saw carved on it "Jimmy Loves Sharon." Next to that read, "Who cares."

A minute before eleven o'clock, a short pixie of a man hobbled into the class-room, steadying himself with a cane and carrying a thick book against his chest. He wore a sport coat that hung too low on his body. He had a ruddy complexion, curly red hair, and a well-manicured goatee. The sparkle in his eyes contrasted with his weakened, shrunken body, the result of rheumatoid arthritis.

Dr. Grabill shuffled sideways behind his desk and dropped down into a wooden chair. With a deep sigh, he laid his textbook down in front of him with both hands like a priest placing an opened Bible on an altar. In a rich baritone voice that he projected to the back of the room, he spoke of William Shakespeare without notes and with a reverence that lent elegance to his words. He described Shakespeare as the greatest dramatist the world had ever known. When he read from Hamlet, Othello, Macbeth, and Lear, I closed my eyes and saw flesh-and-blood people uttering the words he spoke.

At the end of class, Dr. Grabill tapped his cane on the floor as I filed past his desk to leave. "May I have a word with you?"

I followed him as he labored to his office. Papers littered his desk and books and folders piled high on the floor. In a bookshelf sat a basketball that had been autographed by the members of the Aces 1960 NCAA Championship team.

"Well, Mr. Grieger," he said, "I must admit I was surprised to see one of you jocks in my Shakespeare class."

"It was either Shakespeare or basket weaving," I joked.

He laughed. "Seriously, what brought you to me?"

"I've almost completed my psychology major. I still have two years' eligibility, and I've been thinking of taking a second major. I thought maybe English literature."

Dr. Grabill tilted his head to the side, as if studying me. He joined the fingers of his two hands together, pointing upward as if praying, holding them to his chin. "Okay then, I've got a proposition for you."

"Okay?"

"How about you do take that second major in English literature and I'll be your advisor."

"You'd do that? Why?"

"Selfishness, Mr. Grieger, pure selfishness. For one, my faith in higher education will be restored, if, that is, you're not an athletic stereotype." He chuckled. "Two, I'm an Aces fan. You can keep me posted on the inner goings-on of the team." He paused. "So, what do you say?"

"I say 'great!' I'm in."

I met with Dr. Grabill each week thereafter. I cherished my time with him. He always offered me pearls of wisdom about the nature of being human, answers to intriguing mysteries of the universe, principles with which to base a life of meaning and character.

On this cold November morning, in my junior year, I needed something from him more than ever. He settled into his black swivel chair and let out a long sigh. So did I. It gave me comfort to be here.

"Well, I take it things are not going so well in Aces land?"

I told him about my conversation with Arad McCutchan and began to explain the coach's nine-man dilemma. Midway through, though, my emotions overcame me and I poured out all the insecurities and self-doubts I had carried for a decade. I had never shared these thoughts with anyone before. I felt naked, embarrassed by my vulnerability.

Dr. Grabill listened without speaking. When I finished, he sat silently for a long time. Then he said, "Can I tell you a story?"

I nodded.

"My roommate at the University of Illinois, an All-Big Ten football first-teamer his sophomore year, returned to school his junior year and flat-out quit the team. When I asked him why, he told me, 'It's just a game. It's not that important.'"

Dr. Grabill paused and looked at me, seeming to gather his thoughts.

Then, with his strong voice, too powerful for this cramped office, he went on: "Russ, he was right. Like football, basketball is just a game. You're making it almost life and death. You sound like you think you'll cease to exist if you're not out there on the stadium court."

His voice penetrated my mind like a knife. I could hardly breathe as I listened to my own thoughts come out of his mouth. "But that's how I feel," I said.

"I know you do. But the truth is that there's so much more to you than basketball. You're a student, a son, God knows what else. You're all those and more, no matter what happens on the court. Lighten up. You're too hard on yourself. If you never play a minute this year, you're still smart, you have friends, a family that loves you. You're still you. Do you follow me?"

"I do, but I've never thought that way, not once in my life."

"Not yet, maybe. But you can. Do you think Shakespeare was Shakespeare when he was your age? You weren't born with that pretty jump shot of yours, were you? You may not understand this, but you and basketball are two separate vessels. You need to pry the two apart. Just like shooting a basketball, you've got to train yourself to think this way. I don't know how long it'll take, my young friend, but I know you're worth the effort. The only question is, do you?"

I sat there, too overwhelmed to speak. He too sat silently, watching me. Finally I said, "Forget Shakespeare, Dr. Grabill, that's the greatest psychotherapy session ever."

He smiled, which I took as his blessing. "Okay then, get out of here. I've got papers to grade."

I left Dr. Grabill's office and strolled along the concrete paths of the Evansville College campus, past the library, to the student union. I felt the cold, but I noticed for the first time in weeks how brilliant the sun shone, how bright the sky seemed. I felt lighthearted and wanted to break into a jog. An image of French fries piled alongside a hamburger formed in my mind. I felt starved.

• • •

SOMEONE ONCE SAID THAT LEARNING is a gift, even when pain is your teacher. I didn't see it that way on December 7, 1963, the night of the Aces' home opener against the University of Iowa. On that night, I stood on the sidelines, wearing my white short-sleeved warm-up jacket, and watched the Aces starting five trot one by one to center court after being introduced by the public address announcer. Despite my best efforts to think otherwise, I heard the thunderclap of each of their names as a guilty verdict blasted at me from a jury foreman: Loser! Loser! Loser! Loser! Loser!

I settled on the bench and watched the referee toss the ball upward to start the game. The pace was furious and the contact brutal. At one point, Jerry Sloan and Iowa's Dave Roach got into a rebounding scuffle and Roach came away with a bloody nose. A bit later, Larry Humes decked Hawkeye Dennis Pauling with a forearm smash to the chin.

I sat two seats to the right of Coach McCutchan and took in the same play as he did. The Aces botched passes they'd normally complete, clanged shots off the rim they could make in their sleep, committed silly fouls like from their high school days. I had no doubt I'd hear Coach McCutchan call my name before too long, just as he had in our opening games against New Mexico State and the University of Arizona.

The game clock blinked forward five minutes, ten, then fifteen, and finally to halftime. I saw no action. In the locker room, those who'd played sat in uniforms soaked with sweat. My uniform was dry and unwrinkled, an unmistakable sign that I was a benchwarmer, a nobody, a failure. If I could have stayed hidden in the locker room after halftime, I would have.

I jogged out for the second half and dutifully took my place on the bench. Even in my darkened mood, I was able to appreciate the artistry Buster Briley displayed during the first ten minutes of action. From distances that defied logic, he lofted nine shots into the air that seemed to take an eternity to get to the basket, swishing five of them. Each shot elicited a gasp of anticipation from the crowd as it hung in the air and an explosion of exultation when it found the net. I couldn't help but remember when he and I had traded baskets four years earlier when Bosse High played his team in Madison, Indiana. The disparity now between him being on the court and me on the bench tore my self-esteem to shreds.

The Aces fought hard but continued to struggle before finally succumbing to the Hawkeyes, 75–72. I saw not one second of action. As I walked off the court, I glanced up and saw Dr. Grabill. He looked at me, tapped his temple, and nodded, signaling for me to remember what he'd told me just weeks before. I nodded in assent but knew there was nothing I could do that night to quell the humiliation and self-loathing I felt. In the locker room, I felt shame for the bitter delight I harbored in our defeat. I couldn't wait to get out of the locker room and meet up with my fraternity brothers for pitchers of ice-cold beer—anything to deaden the pain.

Over the next few weeks, I tried hard to think the way Dr. Grabill had coached me, but with little success. My embarrassment remained. I went to my classes but barely paid attention. I avoided socializing. I even dreaded going to basketball practice. Despite meeting Dr. Grabill for what he called his "weekly booster shot," I seemed to grasp only air every time I tried to take hold of a solid sense of myself beyond basketball. But I tried.

Two weeks before Christmas, the Purdue Boilermakers came to Roberts Stadium to take on the Aces. It didn't register at the time as anything special, but, while warming up before the game, I noticed feeling a bit lighter, crisper, as if my senses were more alive.

When Purdue unexpectedly started the game by defending with a two-three zone, I sat and watched something of exceptional beauty unfold that only a basketball aficionado could appreciate. The five Aces on the court immediately realized the Boilermakers' tactic and, without prompting from Coach McCutchan, organized themselves into a one-three-one zone offense. One Ace moved out to the point a few feet from the top of the circle while another stationed himself near the basket. The other three formed a horizontal line between those two Aces, with one stationed at about the free-throw line and the other two off to either of his sides on the wings.

The Aces poked and probed around the perimeter, trying to get the ball past the top two Boilermaker defenders to the Ace on the free-throw line. They did this repeatedly, creating a four-on-three offensive advantage: sometimes the Ace at the free-throw line found himself open and popped an easy jumper; then, when one of the three Purdue defenders challenged him, he zipped the ball to one of his three open teammates for an uncontested shot. Despite wanting to be out there doing what they were doing, I felt great pride in my teammates as they executed their offense to perfection.

Midway through the first half, Arad McCutchan looked to his right and said, "You four, get in there," meaning me, Wayne Boultinghouse, Paul Bullard, and Jim Smith to replace everyone but Sloan.

We jumped up as one. Again I noticed the brightness of the lights, the intensity of the sound, the rabidity of the crowd. I promptly nailed a twenty-five-footer from the wing that I knew to be true the moment it left my hand. A moment later, I sank a fifteen-footer, and not long after that I added another from the outer precincts that rattled the rims before falling through. I felt focused, lost in the game, masterful. By halftime, we had padded a single-digit lead to a whopping twenty-two points, 56–34.

In the second half, we repeated the same scenario as the first. The first team kept control of the game and surrendered the court to the four of us after eight minutes of smooth, fluid work. I felt comfortable and in the groove alongside my teammates. I loved every second of action and, for the first time since my Bosse days, felt fully in control of myself.

The fans loved it too, screaming as if it were a Beach Boys concert. My signature moment came at exactly 9:15 p.m. Wayne Boultinghouse dogged his man near half-court while I dropped off mine to protect the middle. In a desperate attempt to advance the ball, the Purdue guard bounced an unadvised pass toward a teammate atop the free-throw circle. I stretched to my left, almost doing the splits, and intercepted the ball.

"Wayne!" I yelled to alert him as I streaked up the court on the dribble, he sprinting alongside me on my left. One Boilermaker stood between us and the basket. Reaching the top of the key, I lowered my head and drove hard to the basket. I knew that if he lagged I'd have an easy layup, but if he challenged me I could pass the ball to Boultinghouse for his score. The defender chose to attack me and, as I neared the basket, I whipped a right-handed, behind-the-back pass off my dribble to Wayne, who laid it in for an easy two points.

The stadium erupted. Purdue called time-out. When we gathered in front of the bench, McCutchan yelled, "Grieger!" I knew he deplored razzle-dazzle, so I hung on the outskirts of the huddle until Sloan grabbed me by my shirt and pulled me in. "Get in here and face the music," he said with a smile on his face. Even Coach laughed.

After the game, the fans crammed into the steamy dressing room filled with so much noise that it was difficult to converse. People tousled my hair and slapped me on the back. After the gloom of the last few weeks, I felt reborn.

The ego strokes started the very next day and, like fool's gold, invited me to continue to play the game of feeling good about myself based on my basketball success. First, scribe Bill Robertson wrote:

Russ Grieger stepped into the fury as though born to the storm and added flashes of class. He hit seven of nine shots from the field, set up four other baskets, and harassed the enemy with such skill that the Boilermakers must have wished he stayed in St. Louis.

Then, the day after Christmas, the *Sterling Brewers Roundball Review* named me the player of the week, saying:

This might easily have been the finest game of Evansville's long basketball history . . . The starting five was spectacular but the honor for the night must go to the Firehouse Five. When Coach McCutchan substituted in the first half, he sent in Russ Grieger, Wayne Boultinghouse, David Bullard and Jim Smith, leaving Jerry Sloan in the game. Grieger and Boultinghouse led a horse race charge that literally wiped out any chance Purdue might have had for a comeback. Russ and Wayne pair perfectly and, with their good speed and unusual size, they made it most difficult for a defender to stop the fastbreak. The Firehouse Five is on a par with the starting five and what more could a coach ask.

Russ Grieger came to the Aces from St. Louis with fine credentials as a ballhandler and shooter. Russ has now shown that his abilities also include a glue-like defense and real zip on the fast break. It was Grieger who started the Firehouse Five rolling by knocking in two straight from around the circle and then pairing with Boultinghouse to keep the fast break rolling. There is no better guard on the squad.

And then there was still more. Before our game against Indiana State, Craig Brosius, sports editor of Terre Haute's *The Indiana Statesman*, wrote:

Jerry Sloan and Larry Humes are offensive threats while big Ed Zausch is a very good boardsman and occasionally a good scorer. Sam Watkins is a very good boardsman and occasionally a good shooter, but the real fifth man is Russ Grieger. Grieger is a good shot, a solid playmaker, and a real hustler.

Reading all this, I could feel the pull of something that was always there, always present in the back of my mind: the belief that there was something more at stake for me than just playing time and newspaper ink and public recognition. Basketball took me to the very core of being human, and then it took me past that place to something vile and ugly. It took me to that place where the only thing that existed in the world to me was whether or not I proved to be worthy. But, for the first time, I saw what I was doing to myself and fought it. The problem, though, was that the thought that my worth depended on how well I played basketball was too strong to resist.

· · ·

THE PURDUE GAME GAVE BIRTH to the Aces' platoon system, which obliterated the concept of a starting five and rescued my deflated self-esteem. Coach McCutchan spoke of it as a wheel: Jerry Sloan occupied the hub, with two sets of four spokes extending out from him. One foursome—Buster Briley, Ed Zausch, Larry Humes, Sam Watkins—started the game; a second foursome—Boultinghouse, Bullard, Smith, and me—joined Sloan for substantial periods of the first and second half.

The platoon strategy paid off. It guaranteed that the Aces ran on fresher legs than our opponents. We played fast and relentless on offense, pushing the ball up the court, shooting with daring, and fast breaking at every opportunity. On defense, we played aggressive, attacking, attacking, attacking. We took control of the tempo at the beginning of the game and never let up. In this way, Coach kept nine high-octane athletes happy and ego-fed. And this was true of me more than anyone.

· · ·

TWO WEEKS BEFORE OUR TWENTIETH GAME of the season against the St. Joseph's Pumas, I sat in a corner booth in The Indian. My buddy Gene lounged across from me. We bounced in rhythm as we sang along with the Beatles' "I Want to Hold Your Hand."

As the song finished, Joyce walked in with two of her Alpha Omega Pi sorority sisters. Gene and I slid over as they scooted across the burgundy vinyl upholstery, Joyce next to me, the other two alongside Gene. The smell of Shalimar filled the booth.

"Well, hello, ladies," Gene said in a sultry tone.

Joyce looked at him and rolled her pale blue eyes, then turned to me and said, "We've got a proposition for you."

"I think that's what Gene was about to suggest," I said.

"Just listen," she said, jabbing me in the ribs with her elbow. She then told me that the AOPi sorority wanted me to represent them in that year's Bachelor of the Year contest. She explained that each of the sororities would put up a candidate. Only the campus females could vote, and the winner would be crowned by the Basketball Queen at halftime of the St. Joseph's game.

"Well?" She looked at me with pleading eyes.

"I don't know," I said, not sure what I was getting into.

"Do it, frater," Gene said. "I'll get the guys to dress like girls and vote for you."

"Please, pretty please, please with cream and sugar," Joyce said, holding her hands together prayer style.

"Okay, I'll do it. But make sure your sisters vote so I don't end up embarrassed."

The day before the St. Joseph's game, I stood in the foyer outside The Indian along with my five opponents. We all wore dark suits and were surrounded by girls from the sorority we represented. With a large red corsage in my lapel, I went into my competitive mode, offering smiles, handshakes, friendly flirtatious comments, doing whatever I could to win.

That evening, the Aces had all but put St. Joseph's away by halftime, leading 53–26, when the six of us vying for Bachelor of the Year strode to center court to find out our fate. Basketball Queen Pam Miller stood waiting for us. She looked trim and curvaceous in a black skirt and lime-green sweater. Her light brown hair was coiffed into a French twist that glistened under the overhead lights.

I stood in line alongside my fellow contestants, me in my Aces warm-ups, they in street clothes, feeling the same tension as I had before the game. I glanced into the student section and located my fraternity brothers. They all stood looking at me with sappy expressions, holding their hands clasped over their hearts. When introduced, I stepped forward and waved to the crowd. When the others were introduced, I rehearsed in my mind how to react should I end up losing.

The time came for the announcement, and I looked down at the floor to steel myself. When the public address announcer intoned my name, I threw my hands up in the air like a triumphant quarterback who had just thrown the winning touchdown pass. I stepped toward a smiling Pam, who placed a cardboard crown on my head, kissed me on my cheek, and presented me with my prize—a one-year subscription to *Playboy* magazine.

I accepted the subscription, plus the warm applause, and then walked off the court to rejoin my teammates in the locker room.

I felt happy and proud. But, had I been more aware, I would have noticed the lightning-quick release of tension from my body once I heard my name called. But I didn't. Had I been more astute, I would have recognized that, like with basketball, I had wrapped my fragile sense of self up with being the Evansville

College Bachelor of the Year. But I didn't. Had I been forward thinking, I would have determined to use this Bachelor of the Year experience to prepare myself for the mental battles I would face the rest of this season and thereafter. But I didn't.

• • •

THE ACES PILED ONE WIN on top of another. We finished the regular season 21–3 and then romped through five straight opponents to win Evansville College's third NCAA Championship. We barely broke a sweat in the tournament, beating these teams by an average of sixteen and a half points.

Joyce waited for me outside the dressing room after the championship game. We drove to Art and Helen's to meet up with my fraternity brothers in the back room, where a band was playing. They greeted me with cheers, hugs, and more beer than I could drink.

I dropped Joyce off at her house after one o'clock in the morning and cruised slowly through the deserted streets of Evansville, grateful to finally be alone. I drifted along Washington Avenue past Bosse High School, its Gothic structure illuminated in the moonlight, where, eight years ago, it all began. I kept going till I turned left on Weinbach Avenue and then left again on Lincoln Avenue, where I coasted in front of Evansville College, now empty and quiet under a canopy of oak trees. I inched past Carson Center, dark except for the entry hall, where the trophy case stood, bathed by soft overhead lights. Our latest prize would be there soon. Then I drove to Division Street, where Roberts Stadium sat, flat and majestic, alone in the center of its empty parking lot, seeming to communicate that it was eternal, though players and fans would all come and go.

As I drove from the stadium toward home on Chandler Avenue, I thought about these last two years at Evansville College. I had accomplished much. I had helped resurrect a fraternity. I'd served as junior class vice-president and senior class treasurer (although athletically I was a sophomore and a junior). I'd pursued a double major—one in psychology, the other in English literature. I had all the friends anyone could want.

But I knew that basketball was the glue that held everything together. For four long years—two at St. Louis, two at Evansville College—I had lived in a basketball wilderness. Now I was back.

I pulled into my driveway, crept along the side of the house so as not to wake my parents, and turned off the motor before pulling into the garage. I stared through the windshield at the basketball goal that stood erect in the moonlight, strong and noble, like the sentry who guarded the Tomb of the Unknown Soldier. I realized that, as glorious as this 1963–1964 basketball season had been, I still felt unfulfilled. I was a platoon player. I embraced the honor of being an Evansville College Purple Ace, but I still craved the status of being one of five, not one of nine. I loved the thrill of the on-court parries and thrusts, but I wanted to be part of it at the beginning, in the middle, and at the end of games. The next season would be my last. Could I make this happen?

Come October 15, 1964, I'd find out.

The 1964–1965 Evansville College Purple Aces. First row: Jim Rubush, Gary McClary, Russ Grieger, Bill Simpson, Terry Atwater, Ron Eberhard. Second row: Jim Forman, Ron Johnson, Rick Kingston, Early McCurdy, Don Jordon. Third row: Herb Williams, Sam Watkins, Jerry Sloan, Larry Denton, Larry Humes, John O'Neal. Reprinted with permission from the University of Evansville.

Assistant coach Tom O'Brien and Coach Arad McCutchan hugging after clinching the NCAA Championship. Reprinted with permission from the University of Evansville.

All-American Jerry Sloan scoring two points against Iowa.
Reprinted with permission from the University of Evansville.

Jerry Sloan capturing a rebound against Southern Illinois during the NCAA
Championship game. Courtesy of *The Evansville Courier and Press.*

Herb Williams snares another rebound. Reprinted
with permission from the University of Evansville.

Herb Williams following through
after a slam dunk against Southern
Illinois University. Courtesy of
*The Evansville Courier and Press.*

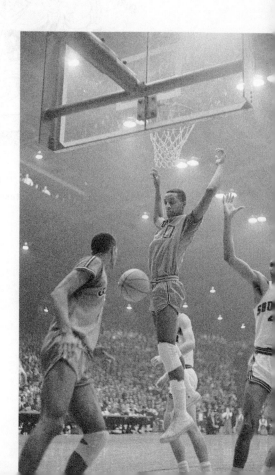

Ace Purple, Evansville College mascot, captured by sketch artist Larry Hill before the Holiday Tournament. Courtesy of *The Evansville Courier and Press*, drawing by Larry Hill.

Larry Humes eludes his defender for another score. Reprinted with permission from the University of Evansville.

Larry Humes about to leap for one of his balletic scoring shots. Courtesy of *The Evansville Courier and Press.*

Russ Grieger leaps high to defend against a shot by Southern Illinois
University's Walt Frazier. Reprinted with permission from the University of
Evansville.

Russ Grieger crowds Iowa
Hawkeye. Courtesy of *The
Evansville Courier and Press.*

Sam Watkins scores another basket against LSU in the Holiday Tournament. Reprinted with permission from the University of Evansville.

Sam Watkins fights for a rebound against Southern Illinois University in the NCAA Championship. Courtesy of *The Evansville Courier and Press.*

# NCAA—Aces All the Way . . . Again!

MOST VALUABLE PLAYER SPEAKS—Jerry Sloan, Evansville College All-American, accepting the College-Division Tournament most-valuable-player award for the second year in a row, paused to thank the Evansville fans for his four years here.

HAPPINESS MOMENT—Russ Grieger hugs Jerry Sloan after both had played the full 40 minutes in Evansville's overtime win over Southern Illinois last night at the Sta-

dium. Smiling in the rear (right) is Deva Patterson, SIU scout.

POETRY IN MOTION—Larry Humes, who has a thirst for every occasion, shows how it's done backward and forehand in this picture from last night's championship game against Southern Illinois. It was one of 10 baskets the Evansville junior hit in the Aces' sensational 85-82 triumph over the Salukis to bring them their fourth NCAA title. At left (44) is SIU's Boyd O'Neal. In center is Walt Frazier and at right is Joe Ramsey of SIU.

## SOUTHERN ILLINOIS FALLS IN OVERTIME THRILLER, 85-82—

# Invincible Aces Still Rule Basketball World

### A Fitting Farewell

## 'Good Lord Was With Us'

### A Time for Laughter, a Time for Tears . . .

### Didn't Believe in Losing

## Providence Expels St. Joe

### Michigan, Vanderbilt in NCAA Regional Showdown

LOOK WHAT DADDY WON—Mrs. Jerry Sloan shows her six-month-old daughter, Kathy Lynn, the prize her father won for helping Evansville College win the national college division championship last night. The prize — A watch, presented by the NCAA to each member of the Evansville team.

*The Evansville Press* headlines following the NCAA Championship game. Sloan in left picture, Grieger and Sloan in the middle, Humes is on the right. Courtesy of *The Evansville Courier and Press*.

The bench after the NCAA Championship game. Front row: Bill Simpson, Ron Eberhard, Larry Humes. Second row: Jim Rubush, Russ Grieger, Sam Watkins, Jerry Sloan, Herb Williams. Courtesy of *The Evansville Courier and Press.*

Ace Purple stuffing the trophy case after the
NCAA Championship. Courtesy of *The Evansville
Courier and Press*, drawing by Larry Hill.

# Part Three

## The Aces Succeed

It is not the critic who counts, or how the strong man stumbled and fell, or where the doer of deeds could have done them better. The credit belongs to the man who is actually in the arena, whose face is marred by dust and sweat and blood, who strives valiantly, who errs and comes short again and again, who knows the great enthusiasms, the great devotion, and spends himself in a worthy cause; and if he fails, at least fails while daring greatly, so that he'll never be with those cold and timid souls who neither know victory nor defeat.
—Theodore Roosevelt

# Part Three

## The Aces Succeed

# 11

## NORTHWESTERN

W E WON OUR SEASON OPENER against the Iowa Hawkeyes, no thanks to me. It was not that I embarrassed myself with amateurish air balls, ill-conceived passes, or club-fisted ball handling. It was just that my play made little impact one way or another.

I knew I had to pick up my performance. At two o'clock on the Monday after the Iowa game, I hustled to Carson Center to put in extra work before we practiced for our Wednesday-night game against the Northwestern Wildcats. There I found my running mate, Sam Watkins, shooting alone.

"Hey," I said.

"Hey," he replied and kept up his drill, the only sound the bouncing of the ball against the floor. He shot, retrieved the ball, lobbed it out to a spot on the court, ran to it, and shot it again. Then he repeated the cycle.

The nickname Silent Sam fit him well. He carried himself with a poker face, tight-lipped under a pencil-thin mustache, expressionless and inscrutable. He said little and, when he did, it was said very quietly, his lips barely moving, always getting straight to the point.

Still in my street clothes, I walked under the basket and rebounded for Sam. "Why're you here so early?" I asked.

"Ain't nobody going to get me better but me."

"But you had a great second half against Iowa."

"Not good enough." He kept shooting.

I shoveled him the ball. He shot from each of seven spots around an arc fifteen feet from the basket, starting in one corner and ending in the other. Neither of us said a word. *Thump, thump, scratch . . . Thump, thump, scratch . . . Thump, thump, scratch.*

As I continued to feed the ball to him, neither of us speaking, I wondered what it was that fueled his icy, dogged determination. I knew that his parents and seven siblings had moved from Alabama to Louisville when he was six years old. I knew that neither of Sam's parents had gone past high school, that he was the first in his family to go to college, and that his parents watched his grades more closely than they did his points per game. I knew that, having attended mostly segregated, all-black schools, he had suffered racial indignities since matriculating to Evansville. Did he carry a seriousness of purpose such that basketball was a mere stepping-stone? Could he be fired by a keen sense of racial injustice, finding it hypocritical to be the recipient of adulation in his Aces uniform but disrespected when in his street clothes? I had no idea, but I longed to possess the singular dedication he did, uncontaminated by my neurotic fears and petty insecurities.

I glanced at the wall clock; it read 2:20 p.m. "Hey, I'd better get dressed. I need this more than you."

"Hustle out," Sam said. "I owe you a few rebounds."

◆  ◆  ◆

WEDNESDAY NIGHT, DECEMBER 9, THE referee walked to the centerline at exactly eight o'clock, toting the ball under his arm. There stood Herb Williams and Northwestern's Jim Pitts, shuffling their feet and flaring their nostrils.

From the Big Ten, the Northwestern Wildcats were tall and brawny, flooring six-foot-five Don Jackson and six-foot-six Walt Kozlicki at forward and six-foot-eight Jim Pitts at center. Even hotshot guard Jim Burns, who starred at Jerry Sloan's Macleansboro High in southern Illinois, stood six foot four.

"We can't hope to match them in size and physical strength," Coach McCutchan said to reporters before the same, "so we're going to have to do something different or get beat. We have to go out after them."

The referee tossed the ball toward the overhanging scoreboard. Herb tipped it forward to Sloan and the game began. We attacked the Wildcats with everything we had. Every possession took on the feel of hand-to-hand combat. Every rebound became a battle, sending two and sometimes three bodies flying before one lone survivor claimed the ball.

Five minutes into the game, forward Walt Kozlicki wrestled Larry Humes for the ball, all the way from under the basket to the Northwestern bench. Both teams jumped up and twenty-five players bordered on a riot, shoving and pushing and trash talking. Referees and coaches separated the teams and the game continued.

I was so eager to assert myself that this game resembled the one against Iowa. Instead of gliding in that magical zone between relaxation and fury, I lurched from spot to spot, making every cut with my body tensed and dogging my man as if he were the most dangerous person on earth. Not long into the game, I gasped for air. I desperately wanted to run the court coordinated and rhythmic as I once had, but I didn't know how.

My teammates must have felt much as I did, because we played as raggedly as a YMCA team made up of thirty-year-olds. I bounced a pass to Humes under the basket too low for him to handle, the ball hitting his shin and rebounded into a Wildcat's hands. Williams grabbed a rebound and sailed an outlet pass over Sloan's head out of bounds. Watkins accidentally kicked the ball while making a cross-over dribble on the way to the basket. During that first half, our performance dropped, but not our shots; our errors mounted, but not our points. Had it not been for Humes's fifteen points, our halftime deficit of 49–40 could have been much worse.

I slumped on a chair in the locker room, my legs outstretched and my arms hanging loose at my sides. Sweat streamed down my face and dripped off my arms. The others slouched like me. I wondered if they felt as inadequate as I did.

No one said a word until Herb Williams slapped his towel to the floor between his legs. "We sucked."

"Hey," Watkins said, without raising his voice, "just because we sucked in the first half doesn't mean we have to suck the rest of the game."

We all looked at Sam. His words hung in the air, as much a challenge as a truth. Sloan said, "That's right!" I nodded, startled by the power of his words.

At that moment, Coach McCutchan walked in. A less wise coach would have blistered us with a series of profane epitaphs and questioned our manhood. But not him. With his tie still neat at his neck and his sport coat wrinkle free, he studied the stat sheet while rubbing his hand from his forehead back over his close-cropped hair. Noting our poor shooting, he simply said, "Keep working the offense and they'll start to fall." Looking farther down the sheet, he added, "We're holding our own on the boards, boys, so keep battling." Finally, "Don't let up on your aggressiveness, but be careful not to make foolish fouls. Every possession will count this next half for us to catch up."

He stuffed the stat sheet into his coat pocket and looked around the room. "Boys, we're better than that team. Let's go out and prove it."

Again the referee tossed the ball into the air, and within seconds Humes laid it into the basket from a pass from Watkins. Sloan then converted a three-point play. When Williams barreled to the basket on a two-on-one fast break, we had closed the gap to 62–60. The somnolent crowd rose to their feet and cheered.

Somewhere in the middle of all this, I relaxed and caught my wind. I could run without gasping for each breath. My moves flowed. I hit a twenty-foot jump shot from behind the free-throw arc that scratched nothing but net. A few possessions later, I banked a short jumper off the glass and into the basket. My playing felt effortless and smooth again.

But the Northwestern Wildcats didn't care about my resurrection, rallying to once again open up another seven-point lead, 69–62. This sent the crowd back into their seats. It was at that point that Sam Watkins played what had to be the best ten minutes of his life. With narrowed eyes, he canned two free throws after being fouled, putting the score at 69–64. After Sloan hit a short jumper on the tail end of a fast break, Watkins then drilled a jumper, 69–68, and then another, putting us ahead for the first time since early in the game, 70–69. The lead went back and forth. With the clock reading 6:31, Sam gave us the lead again, 74–73, by dropping a fifteen-footer from his favorite spot, left of the basket, just beyond the foul lane. Moments later, he scored again from the baseline off a pass from Sloan, increasing our lead to 76–73. The crowd erupted every time we made a defensive stop, after every hard-won rebound, following every basket.

Northwestern immediately cut our lead to one, 76–75. A low murmur floated through the stadium. I dribbled up court to start the offense. Coach McCutchan stood at the sideline and yelled, "Slow it down!," pumping both palms toward the floor. He wanted us to run time off the clock and only take high-percentage shots.

"Ugh," I grunted. Ball handling had never been my strength. Northwestern immediately understood our strategy and each Wildcat closed in on us tight. I dribbled with my left hand close to the centerline, my defender riding my right hip so close I could feel his breath on my shoulder. He took a swipe at the ball, missed, but caused me to almost lose control. I gathered in the ball, dribbled out of danger, and delivered it into Watkins's safe hands.

"You're gonna blow it, shithead," my defender said.

"Fuck you," I said, careful not to let self-doubt register on my face.

At that moment, Watkins made the defining play of the game. While trying to pass the ball to Sloan on the sideline by our bench, Jim Burns knocked the ball loose from Sam's hands and dribbled toward the basket for the go-ahead score. Sam rocketed after him and fouled him hard just before he could rise up and stuff the ball through the hoop.

Coach McCutchan later said he thought Burns would can both of his free throws and started figuring out how we could get those two points back. But Burns missed the front end of his one-and-one. Larry Humes snatched the rebound, was fouled, and dropped his two foul shots for a 78–75 margin. With thirty-eight seconds left, I made my free throw after being mugged by my defender, who was trying to snatch the ball from my hands. That made the score 79–75, Aces, and the game was all but over. A tip-in and a short jumper by Humes gave us our 83–75 victory.

At the sound of the game-ending buzzer, the crowd roared. The excitement proved too much for one frenzied fan, who passed out.

Fans packed into our locker room. There was little room to walk, certainly no privacy. Well-wishers tripped over each other to pat our shoulders and offer congratulations. Next to me, Jerry Sloan said to sports writer Al Dunning, "We really went after them, didn't we?"

I left the locker room feeling drained. I knew I needed to get a good night's sleep for my next morning's classes. But, instead of heading home, I drove west on Division Street past Harold's Stadium Inn and the Forget-Me-Not, both favorite watering holes of Aces fans. Cars jammed their parking lots. Through windows, I saw red-shirted patrons standing shoulder to shoulder, holding glasses of beer and laughing. I made my way to East Side Park, just behind Carson Center, a grassy, tree-cluttered expanse where I had played Little League and Pony League baseball as a young adolescent. I occasionally visited this park to gather my sanity when I needed to get away from basketball.

I parked and, with my coat collar turned up and fastened at the neck, walked the bases of the Pony League diamond, starting at home plate, on to first base, around second and third, then to home plate, finally heading to the dugout. I sat there, protected from the wind, sitting on my hands to keep them warm. I looked up at the sky, inky black except for the twinkling stars whose light had traveled the heavens for thousands of years to get to my eyes. I thought about the season so far, only two games in, happy for our wins but discouraged by my lackluster playing. I sent out a prayer over the centerfield fence, up to the heavens, asking for help in this, my last basketball season.

Then I remembered that the next night I was supposed to accompany Dr. Grabill, who was to give a reading at the Rotary Club in downtown Evansville.

*He'll help me figure this out,* I reassured myself.

Relieved, I walked to the pitcher's mound and put my right foot on the rubber, as I had done hundreds of times in summers past. I bent forward and imagined the catcher giving me a signal. A fast ball, low and away. I wound up, raised my left leg into the air, and blazed the ball to the batter with a perfect follow-through. The ball exploded into the catcher's mitt. I smiled, walked back to my car, and drove home.

◆ ◆ ◆

I WORE A DARK-BLUE sport coat, gray slacks, and a button-down white oxford the next evening as I waited in my parents' living room for Dr. Grabill to pick me up. These get-togethers had proved invaluable ever since I'd first sat knee to knee with him the year before and poured out my basketball worries. I had come to depend on them to help me manage my insecurities, not to mention the many mysteries of the universe he discussed with me.

When I heard his horn, I hustled outside to find him sitting low behind the wheel, his body diminished by the ravages of his degenerative disease. He too was dressed in a dark-blue blazer over a red plaid vest that looked cut from a Scottish kilt. He had neatly combed his receding hair as well as his red mustache and goatee. The twinkle in his eyes seemed more sparkling than usual, communicating, I thought, his eagerness for tonight's performance.

"I'd offer to drive," I said, sliding into the passenger seat, "but I have no idea how to run this contraption." Several devices surrounding the steering wheel allowed him to operate the car without using his legs.

He laughed. "That's all right, I think I can manage to get us downtown."

After dry roast beef and even drier announcements, the Rotarians turned the floor over to Dr. Grabill. He stood, hunched and stooped, supported by a cane. He slowly surveyed the room, then, in that booming yet melodious voice I had heard many times in his classroom, he read a fictionalized version of Jesus' Last Supper. As he read, his eyes blazed, his shoulders squared, and his spine straightened. When he finished, he stood stock-still for a moment before the crowd erupted into a thunderous ovation. He glanced at me and winked.

*Unbelievable,* I thought. The fact that this man could arouse such passion without leading a fast break, sinking a jumper, or snaring a rebound was not lost on me.

On the way out, the Rotarians gave Dr. Grabill respectful praise, while giving me more raucous "Go Aces!" Then we slowly walked to his car, threaded our way through stop-and-go downtown traffic, and finally motored to my house. When we arrived, he shut off the engine, a signal of his availability for another tutorial. He relaxed his body, rested his head against the back of the seat, and shot me a sly look. "Well, tell me about the game last night."

I did. I told him about our pregame strategies. I told him about what Coach had said to us at halftime when we were down by nine points. I told him what Watkins had said and how impressed I was with his second-half heroics.

Dr. Grabill listened, glancing at me now and then, absorbing the inside story of the Aces with what looked to me to be the same pleasure he would get from a production of *Macbeth.* That's when I poured out my doubts about my relevance to this team.

He sat still for a moment, holding his hands together chest high with his fingertips touching. I waited. He finally looked at me and asked, "What did you think about my presentation tonight?"

I cleared my throat, wondering about the significance of his question. "It was great," I said. "I think they really liked it."

"Thanks, but did you notice anything out of the ordinary about the people there tonight?"

I thought for a minute. "Not really. They looked pretty much like those at all the Aces functions I have to attend."

"Exactly. There was nothing special about that group—no Nobel laureates, no Pulitzer Prize recipients, not even college All-Americans. Just a group of regular people, right?" He looked at me and smiled.

I nodded. "Right."

"So, here's my question. Should those people have mattered to me at all?"

I squirmed in my seat, sensing a trap. "Well, they're human beings. Shouldn't they matter?"

"Yes, indeed they should, Russ. Those Rotarians did matter. I agreed to give them a reading, and I had a responsibility to deliver my very best. I was there for them, whether or not they had any appreciation of what I had to offer." He paused and pointed a gnarled finger at me. "But, you know what? They were also there for me. I took advantage of them. I used them." He chuckled.

"Are you serious? How so?"

"That's right." He nodded. "You see, I have this passion for expressing my deepest thoughts through the most elegant words I know. Those people tonight provided me an opportunity to do just that—to express my passion."

I sat silently.

"I was there for them, to be sure. But, more importantly, they were there for me. They just didn't know it." He paused. "Do you understand what I'm saying?"

"I think so. But what's that got to do with me?"

"Well, you could do the same with basketball, you know. You forget I've been around this town a long while. I watched you play ball at Bosse years ago. I remember your senior year. It looked to me like you played that whole season to express yourself. It looked to me that back then you weren't an athlete but a poet."

I sat stunned. The truth of what he'd said bore into me. I flashed back on those strange and mysterious out-of-body experiences I'd had that year. I realized that I'd lost something precious since then, and I hadn't even known I'd lost it.

"So what do I do?" I finally asked.

"It's simple, Russ, but it won't be easy. Your passion's still there, or you wouldn't be so tied up in knots. It's more about perspective than anything else."

"Perspective?"

"Yes! You've got to remember why you used to play basketball. It was to express what's inside of you. Listen, you don't need to be a star, to grab headlines, or even to play well. You need to be self-absorbed, selfish in fact, playing the game for you, in order to express yourself—good, bad, or indifferent."

I sighed. "I haven't really done that for a long time. I don't even know if I can do that again."

"Maybe not." He patted my leg. "But you can begin to work on it tomorrow at practice and then Saturday during the Notre Dame game. Who knows, it may come back faster than you think."

I wished Dr. Grabill a good night and stepped out of the car, watching for a moment as his car's taillights receded into the distance. Then I turned and walked into the house to find Mom and Dad watching TV. Dad wore his plaid terry-cloth robe cinched at the waist. Mom sat in her blue silk robe, her hair wrapped in a hair net to protect the setting she'd gotten that afternoon.

"Hi, dearie," Mom said. "Have a good time?"

"Yeah." I walked over to kiss her on the cheek, patting Dad on the shoulder as I passed by.

I went to my bedroom and sat down at my desk. I felt like both laughing and crying, I didn't know which. The season so far had been a struggle, but I had a direction. I had hope.

# 12

## NOTRE DAME

**M**Y TEAM WAS 2–0 AND scheduled to play Notre Dame Saturday night, December 12. When I heard the words "Notre Dame," I pictured golden football helmets, the face of Jesus gazing down on the gridiron from the wall of the campus library, and the dying words of George Gipp imploring Knute Rockne to "win one for the Gipper."

Most famous for football, Notre Dame's basketball team didn't exactly play in the same league as the Little Sisters of the Poor. They had already won their first four games this season, and their 105.5 scoring average demonstrated an ability to score quick, often, and without mercy. Their six-foot-ten center, Walt Sahm, took care of the muscular work under the basket, while flashy guard Larry Sheffield strutted his magic from the frontcourt. He previewed what he had in store for us by scoring forty-seven points against Michigan State the same night we struggled to defeat Northwestern. According to sportswriter Bill Robertson, a respectable loss, in the ten-point range, would be acceptable, as long as we played well.

The day before the Notre Dame game dawned cold and biting. I wore my Aces letter jacket to school, intending for it to spark me to play basketball with the same joy and daring as I once had at Bosse. Sliding behind the wheel of my car, I determined to put into practice Dr. Grabill's lessons from the night before—to play for my own pleasure, as an expression of whatever poetry I had in my soul, not to try to prove anything to anyone, including myself.

I hustled across campus, my hands deep in my pockets, my shoulders hunched forward against the cold. Thin, wispy clouds gave the sky a whitish complexion but did not block a weak, hazy glare from the sun. Clusters of birds swirled from one branch to another. Only an occasional student walked past me, giving the campus the desolate feel of a cemetery.

Inside The Indian the silence outside gave way to the sounds of boisterous rock-and-roll, dozens of conversations, and the sizzle of cooking hamburgers and hot dogs. I snapped open my coat and, blowing into my fists, spotted my fraternity brothers—Gene, Klee, and Terry—sitting at a booth in the back.

"Hey, frater," Terry said as I slid in beside him, his Southside Chicago accent standing out amid the Indiana twang of the rest of us.

"Hey," I said back, nodding to everyone.

"Here," Gene said, sliding a chocolate-covered donut in front of me. "You'll need the energy for Notre Dame tomorrow night."

"Yeah," said Klee, "you're going to need all you've got. Those mothers are beasts."

"Sounds like you all don't think we should even show up."

"It's not you, frater," Gene said. "Those tuna eaters got the Pope on their side."

"But can the Pope dunk?"

"Starting at guard, standing an even six feet, solid as a rock, St. Peter," Klee said, mimicking a courtside announcer.

"Hey, guys, here's an idea," Terry said. "How about we get a priest to lead us in prayer before the game?" He pretended to dip his fingers into holy water and make the sign of the cross.

"I don't know about the game, but I do know one thing," I said. "You guys are going to roast in hell."

We laughed. I ate the donut, plus two more, and then headed outside to battle the wintery cold on my way to my eleven o'clock class. I felt heartened. I had held on to my new attitude without lapsing into my usual fear or doubt. None of my fraternity brothers noticed, but I did.

Walking into Carson Center after class, I ran into our scout, Dave Fulkerson, as he double-timed past the trophy case to our meeting room down the Hall of Champions. Left-handed and six foot three, he had been on the team a few seasons before, but he'd realized he had a limited future as a player and took on the role of scouting future opponents for Coach McCutchan. With bulging eyes and a wide grin, he grabbed me hard by the shoulders and practically shouted, "We can beat these guys!"

"Which guys?" I asked, knowing full well he meant Notre Dame. I thought, but didn't add, "You're about the only one who thinks so."

"I watched Notre Dame beat Michigan State Wednesday night. We can take them," he said before hustling off.

I made my way into the dressing room, the familiar scent of sweat, rubbing alcohol, and talcum powder filling my nostrils. I noticed once again the sign over the shower entrance. It read, "It's an honor and a privilege to wear an Aces uniform." The sound of basketballs bouncing from the court played like background music. A few teammates sat in front of their lockers, undressing.

"Looking ravishing, guys," I said.

"You too, Grieger," Jim Forman replied, extending his middle finger.

I changed into my practice shorts and shirt, feeling warm and smelling fresh as if they had just come out of the dryer. I carried my socks and shoes into the training room to get my ankles taped. There sat Jerry Sloan and Herb Williams, each leaning back on a long table, their legs dangling over the end as their ankles were trussed by student managers.

"Welcome," Bill Mantraselle, our team trainer, said. Dark-haired, round-faced, and soft-featured, he was a devout Catholic with a slight Irish lilt to his voice.

I slid onto the empty table beside Herb Williams. Bill grabbed a roll of tape to start on my left ankle. No one said a word.

"I ran into Fulkerson outside," I finally said to no one in particular. "He swears we can beat Notre Dame."

"Fulkerson always thinks we can win," Jerry said from the other side of Herb.

"You don't think we can?" asked Herb.

"I'll tell you one thing—" Jerry squeezed his ankles with both hands to secure the tape job "—they'd better come ready to play, cause I ain't backing down."

"I'll tell you another thing," I said, winking at Bill, my inner smart-ass getting the better of me. "We'd better bring our A game, leave our blood on the court, and remember that they too put their pants on one leg at a time."

"I knew we'd never get through this conversation without Grieger throwing out some of his psychology talk," Jerry said, walking out of the room, Herb right behind him.

Bill finished my left ankle and started on my right. "What do you think?" I asked, letting my guard down now that I was alone with him. "Think we can win?"

"You guys have already beaten two pretty good teams, and you haven't even put a whole game together yet."

"I don't know," I said, pulling on my socks and tying my shoelaces.

"Well, better get out there before Mac comes in here after you," Bill said. "It'll be okay. You'll see."

Coach McCutchan led us from the practice court to our team meeting room to enlighten us about his plan to defeat Notre Dame. I picked up a ball and dribbled as we walked, thumping a drumbeat to our march.

We settled into the classroom chairs, a movie projector mounted on a four-wheeled metal table sitting at the back wall. Dim sunlight filtered into the room, requiring Coach to flip on the overhead florescent lights. On the blackboard, spread across the entire wall, he had written our defensive assignments in bold white chalk. I thought, *Oh, shit,* when I saw third down the list, "Grieger–Sheffield."

"Okay, boys, listen up." McCutchan's voice was steady and authoritative, the same voice that he used, I was sure, when he taught his mathematics class. "Here is how we're going to beat Notre Dame. First, they don't play disciplined defense, so we'll be able to score. Run the offense and take your shots. If one doesn't fall, there'll be another chance. Okay?"

We nodded.

"Now, you'll need to use your heads." He tapped his temple with his forefinger. "Their tall frontline will get some offensive rebounds, and they'll want to stuff the ball right back into the basket. When they do, either foul them hard so they don't score, or just let them score. We don't want to dig a hole by giving them three points when two will do just fine. Got it?"

We nodded again.

"Third, Grieger's going to be all over Sheffield. But we need everybody to be ready to help out. If we hold him down, we win."

More nods. I sighed but reminded myself, without moving my lips, *You can take him!*

"Now, boys, Dave's going to diagram their offensive plays, and then I'll show you exactly what we're going to do to defeat them. Pay attention."

After Dave did, McCutchan took over, alternatively working the blackboard and emphasizing his points by thrusting the chalk in his hand at us. He slashed lines from one spot on the board to another, emphasizing paths he wanted us to take, scratched dashes to indicate where he wanted us to stop an opponent dead in his tracks, drew circles round and round to emphasize a position never to be relinquished. I noticed how methodical and authoritative he was, as if he were a surgeon lecturing a classroom full of fledgling doctors on the sequence of procedures to repair a patient's defective heart. I glanced around at my teammates, seeing that each of them listened with rapt attention, totally focused on absorbing exactly what Coach wanted us to do. The thought crossed my mind that no one in this room considered the prospect of either winning or losing. They seemed only interested in executing their job, playing their game.

Once finished, McCutchan walked us back to the practice court. I bounced the basketball on the way, consciously absorbing the feel of its texture, the rhythm of it leaving my hand and rebounding from the floor back to me again, all in an attempt to pound my new perspective into my head. The third team waited for us there, ready to run Notre Dame's offense so we could rehearse what McCutchan had just showed us. What remained was the game itself, the following night.

•  •  •

A STANDING-ROOM-ONLY CROWD of 12,807 greeted us with a thunderous roar when we trotted onto the court. I scanned the student section and spotted Gene, Klee, and Terry, standing and talking, cups in their hands, like they were drinking beer at a party.

While warming up, I practiced my positive thinking as much as I did my shooting. I repeated to myself, "Just play!" When we exited the court for our last-minute instructions, I made eye contact with Dr. Grabill sitting in the bleachers. He nodded as if vibing me with our little secret.

As we gathered around Coach McCutchan prior to the player introductions, I glanced behind the bench and saw Mom and Dad two-thirds of the way up toward the bleachers. Mom wore her red skirt and red blouse, Dad his red V-neck sweater that covered a white-collared shirt. I caught their eyes and gave a slight nod. Mom smiled and waved. Dad raised his hand as if taking an oath, then gave a victory sign, and finally made a fist. I grinned.

Standing at the centerline to face off against the six-foot-ten Walt Sahm, Herb Williams told the referee, "I might look little, but throw the ball high so I can get it." The referee did, and Herb tipped the ball back to me. I threw it baseball style to Sloan, who was streaking down the right side in front of our bench. He dropped a fifteen-foot jumper from the baseline: 2–0 Aces.

Both teams played up-tempo basketball, sprinting up and down the court at every opportunity. I relaxed into the rhythm of the game and felt alive and energetic. *Thank God*, I thought.

This fast-paced style opened up the court for Larry Humes. Lean and limber at six foot four, he slipped through the smallest space, contorting his body like he had no spine, creating shots he invented on the spot. We built that early 2–0 margin to 29–17 with 9:07 still left in the half. But, then, as if the basketball gods had sealed a lid on the basket, our jumpers began to clang and clunk off the rim with maddening regularity. Even Humes lost his magic touch as his layups and hooks rolled around the rim and dropped away. We missed thirteen shots in a row over a five-and-a-half-minute span before we made our next basket.

Thirty-three seconds before halftime, big Walt Sahm made a free throw and then a layup for the Irish to take a 43–39 advantage with them into the locker room. A low murmur floated down upon us as we walked off the court.

We sat around the perimeter of the locker room with our legs splayed in front of us. Our white jerseys, wet with sweat, clung to our torsos. Student managers passed out towels and cups of Coke and water. We wiped our faces and sipped our drinks, sitting silently.

As usual, Coach McCutchan focused on strategy rather than emotion. The main adjustment he made startled me as much as if he'd slapped my face. He told me to take Humes's position under the basket and had Larry take mine at guard. "With Sheffield down under to defend Russ, we'll have an edge there," he explained.

I glanced at my teammates over the rim of my cup as I sipped my Coke. Not one of them raised an eyebrow or exchanged a glance. I caught myself thinking, *I can't let them down*, then quickly changed the thought to a forceful, *Just play, like on the court behind your house.*

Herb Williams once more stood toe to toe with jumbo Walt Sahm at the centerline. The referee tossed up the ball, and we again secured possession to start the second half. Noticing Sheffield's absence on the court, I ran to Larry and told him to take his normal position close to the basket. Along with my teammates, I then proceeded to feed him the ball so he could work his magic.

On our first two possessions, Larry canned a free throw and then squirmed through two defenders for a twisting layup. After Herb Williams converted the front end of two free throws, we tied the score 43–43 only 1:15 into the half. But Notre Dame bounced right back to score six straight points to take a 49–43 lead.

Then Larry Sheffield checked into the game. *This is it*, I thought, and yelled at Humes, "I'll take it down low." I stationed myself where he usually played, while he moved to the periphery to take my spot.

With Sheffield guarding me, Sam bounced the ball to me along the right side of the free-throw lane. I pivoted my body around to face the basket, dribbled toward the baseline, pounded the ball to the floor hard one last time, jumped, and lofted a ten-foot jump shot over Sheffield's outstretched hands that caressed the nets for two points: 49–45, Notre Dame. On our next possession, Jerry fed me the ball on the baseline some ten feet from the basket. Sheffield laid off, fearful, I suppose, that I might dribble past him for an easy layup. Taking advantage of the space, I lofted another jumper without dribbling—*swish*: 49–47.

I trotted back to play defense as raucous cheering descended around me. I forced myself to stay focused. Sheffield dribbled the ball up the center of the court to start the Notre Dame offense, with me determined to keep him from advancing the ball. As he moved to my left, I shuffled my feet sideways to force him to the sidelines. He escalated his speed, trying to get the angle, but I anticipated this and beat him to the spot. He plowed right into my chest with his left shoulder, knocking me onto my backside in front of our bench. With a blast of his whistle, the referee called a charging foul on Sheffield and awarded me the ball out of bounds. Fans howled, my teammates cheered, and Coach yelled, "Atta boy!"

*God, this is fun*, I thought.

I inbounded the ball to Sam and hustled down the court to assume my position under the basket. As Watkins passed the ball to Humes on the right wing, I positioned myself so Sheffield was trapped behind me. With my bottom sticking out to distance him and one arm extended behind me to hold him in place, I signaled for the ball. Larry fed me a perfect inlet pass that I gathered in against my chest. I tucked the ball under my left arm while faking up and to my right with my right hand and shoulder. As Sheffield sailed into the air, I pivoted to my left and banked home an uncontested layup: 49–49.

Almost immediately Notre Dame called time-out. Pandemonium erupted, sweet to my ears. I walked to the huddle, where I was met with smiles and kudos from my teammates.

When we returned to the court, we found that Notre Dame had switched from a man-to-man to a zone defense. Although this ended my moment in the spotlight, I took it as a personal triumph. I felt more pleasure during those last few minutes than I had in years.

The Aces and the Irish traded baskets for the next few minutes when, tied at 63–63, I hit another jumper from the right side, Watkins laid the ball in on a fast-break pass from Sloan, and then Humes hit a jumper from near the foul circle. We led 69–63 and, then, mere minutes later, 75–65. We outscored the vaunted Notre Dame juggernaut 12–2 over a three-and-a-half-minute stretch. Even St. Patrick couldn't have saved the Irish at this point. They threatened one last time by closing the gap to 85–81, but we responded with an avalanche of free throws for a final 89–82 victory.

The Aces fans stood and stomped and cheered as we left the floor. We could still hear them even after we got to the dressing room, as if they had just seen The Beatles and were waiting for an encore.

For the third game in a row, our postgame dressing room filled to capacity. Sportswriters clawed for our comments. Fans jockeyed for our autographs. In the end, Humes had scored thirty-seven points, Sloan sixteen, Watkins fourteen (all in the second half), and I'd scored thirteen. Williams had corralled eleven rebounds, as had Sloan. Even the normally self-contained Arad McCutchan gushed to a group of reporters, "This has to rank as one of my great thrills in coaching. I'm speaking of this win right behind the victories over Iowa and Northwestern. We might just quit right now."

As I absorbed the heady mixture of exuberance and adoration, I felt happy. For the first time this season I felt that I belonged on the starting team.

• • •

MY GIRLFRIEND, JOYCE, WAITED FOR me outside the locker room. Blond and fair, smiling in that understated way I found beguiling, she said, "You must be full of yourself tonight."

"I am," I said and took her arm to guide her to the exit.

"So, what do you want to do?"

I thought for a minute. "You know what? I think I want to go home and be with my family. How about it?"

"Let's do it."

Joyce and I could hear the happy sounds of celebrating inside my parents' house the moment we reached the front door. I peeked in and saw Mom and Dad; my cousin Beverly and her husband, Bill; my uncle Doc and aunt Wilma; and my widowed aunts, Margaret, Mill, and Rose Lee. They sat around the dining-room table, a postgame ritual that had started at the beginning of my high school career. All wore red.

Bill spotted me and said, "Russell!"

I walked in, Joyce trailing behind. We squeezed in at the table. Jutting his jaw out, as was his habit, Uncle Doc said, "Russ, you better promise that you and Joyce won't run off and get married. The Aces would never win another game without you."

Joyce and I glanced at each other. Mom said, "Oh, Doc, you fool."

"Don't you worry about the Aces, Doc," I said. "The Aces would do just fine without me."

But, the truth was, I didn't want the Aces to do just fine without me. I wanted to be indispensable, crucial to the Aces' success. I didn't say that, but what I did say was, "Did you notice that Coach McCutchan didn't substitute for any of the starters even once during the entire second half?"

# 13

## A HOLIDAY FEAST

WE BUTTONED OUR COATS AND climbed into our Ford Galaxie, its heater whirring hard to take the edge off temperatures that hovered in the midtwenties. With gloved hands, Dad adjusted the review mirror. Mom settled into the passenger seat and arranged a carefully folded map to guide us to the lands of reindeer, the baby Jesus, and Santa Claus. Joyce and I huddled close together behind Mom, trying to keep ourselves warm.

Dad backed the car out of the driveway and sped from one neighborhood to the next, slowing to a crawl in front of homes worthy of our "oohs" and "ahhs." We found a house that displayed a plump, floor-to-ceiling fir, all its bulbs and ornaments glowing a brilliant blue. Another house exhibited a tree flocked thick with artificial snow, twinkling hundreds of miniature lights the color of ice.

We sat wordlessly, absorbed in the splendor. I felt a glow that matched what I saw through the car's window, thinking how lucky I was to be in that car, with my loved ones, cocooned within the greater Evansville community, a community that had so embraced me and my teammates.

Only that Sunday morning, after our win over Notre Dame, sportswriter Bill Fluty had written in the *Evansville Courier and Press*:

Right now the Aces have beaten three pretty good ball clubs and it must give Jerry Sloan, Larry Humes, Sam Watkins, Russ Grieger, and Herb Williams a sense of personal satisfaction to know they can play with the big boys.

Further down the column, he singled me out with an early Christmas present:

Humes has certainly lived up to the "most improved" tag put on him before the first shot was fired. But the Aces have another player who improves with every game—the old "Gringo" himself, Russ Grieger. Although he hasn't shown up strong in the scoring column, he has turned in three steady games and took charge of controlling the ball while the Aces were in the process of protecting their lead in the last few minutes against Notre Dame. Russ is also showing signs of regaining the superb shooting touch he displayed at Bosse. Grieger has been around in this game and gives the Aces another cool head in the heat.

I read this article twice and felt something I couldn't immediately put into words. It was the sense of being legitimate, as if I'd previously been a pledge and had now been initiated as an official fraternity member.

Dad woke me from my reverie. "Hey, how about we hit one more neighborhood before we go home for hot chocolate?"

We made our way east on Washington Avenue to an outlying subdivision called Arcadian Acres. The tan zoysia lawns sprawled lush and large, and the architecturally perfect shrubs hugged close to their houses. Giant oaks loomed in no discernible pattern. Their empty branches cast finger-shaped shadows across the landscape.

We motored at a snail's pace, our attention captured by one and then another show of brilliance. At the end of a cul-de-sac, near the back of the neighborhood, we hit the jackpot. The house was dark, except for a giant floor-to-ceiling Christmas tree that filled the whole of its large picture window. Flocked white, there were different colored lights that blinked on at five-second intervals—first red, then green, then yellow, then blue, and finally white. The sequence repeated over and over. With each change, the insides of the house and the front lawn glowed with that color.

We watched the show through three or four rotations, no one speaking until Mom said, "This makes me want Christmas to be tomorrow."

"Don't wish your life away, Florence," Dad said. "We've still got days before Santa comes."

"And two basketball games," I added.

"Right," Dad said. "Now let's go get that hot chocolate."

The following Wednesday, still in a Christmas glow, I hurried from my nine-o'clock class and drove downtown to purchase Christmas presents for both Mom and Joyce. Parking across the street from a jewelry store, I reluctantly left the relative warmth of the car and stood shivering at the intersection. Biting winds drove me to shove my hands into my pockets and contract within my coat. Looking to my left, I nodded at a street-corner Santa steadily jingling a bell held in a red-mittened hand.

Just when the traffic light turned green, I heard high-pitched squeals behind me. Turning, I saw three women in their midthirties smiling at me. One, a blond with a generous fur collar framing her face, said, "It's you!"

"It is," I said. "The one and only."

"We almost didn't recognize you with your clothes on," the brunette said. The women giggled.

I grinned, feeling a tingle of excitement. I wondered if I was on the brink of fulfilling a fantasy and quickly calculated how much time I had before practice. My purpose for being downtown vanished from my mind.

"Well, I don't know about you, girls," the third one said, "but I think I'd rather have a hug than an autograph."

"My pleasure," I said and gave each a hug, inhaling their sweet perfume one by one. The light changed and they said their goodbyes.

"Almost got yourself an early Christmas present, didn't you?" Santa said with a wink.

"Oh well." I spread my arms, palms facing up. "Easy come, easy go."

I crossed the street, feeling puffed up, not anticipating the crisis that lay ahead come that weekend at the stadium.

•   •   •

THAT WEDNESDAY AFTERNOON, WE BEGAN our preparations for Evansville College's ninth annual Holiday Tournament. If we defeated our first opponent on Friday night, the George Washington University Colonials, we'd then play the winner of the Louisiana State University–University of Denver tussle the next night.

I sat down in our team meeting room next to the window facing Walnut Street. On my left sat my Bosse High friend, Jim Forman. Cold air seeped in and sent a chill through me. The other Aces, all dressed in their practice outfits, slouched in their one-armed classroom chairs. Just when I was about to tell Forman about my downtown adventure, he elbowed me and said, "Hey, check it out," nodding toward the front of the room.

I looked up and saw scout Dave Fulkerson diagramming George Washington's offensive plays on the left side of the blackboard. To his right, he had scrawled our defensive assignments. I spotted, third down on the list, "Clark–Grieger." The euphoria that had filled me that morning quickly drained away. "No way!"

"You don't want to cover your old buddy?" Forman asked.

"Damn straight I do," I answered with a bravado I hoped would mask the threat I felt.

Mark Clark was a boy I barely knew and someone who had done nothing whatsoever to offend me. A graduate of Evansville Reitz High School, he'd led the city in scoring his senior year, one year after I'd done the same at Bosse. Like me, he'd made the All-City team and had the honor of being recruited by Coach McCutchan before he'd decided to accept a basketball scholarship at George Washington. The newspapers had played up his return to Evansville as a homecoming of sorts and an opportunity see how he matched up against the Aces.

I would never admit that I felt threatened by my match-up with Clark. But I did. My ability to keep my self-identity separate from basketball failed me. If he outplayed me, I thought, I'd be humiliated. While practicing hard that day and the next calmed my anxieties, I did my best to counter my ego-driven fears with the new thoughts Dr. Grabill had taught me: "You play basketball, but you're so much more than that." "This game is not life and death." "Nobody really cares who's the better basketball player but you, so quit the competition and just have fun." How I wished the saying of those words and the believing of them equaled each other.

On Friday night, Mark Clark hit the game's first basket. This aroused the ego demons in me, and I guarded him from that point on with extra determination and ferocity, bumping him with my hips and shoulders every chance I got. My message: "This isn't some touchy-feely celebration in your honor."

Clark and I stood next to each other behind the free-throw circle, barely ten minutes into the game. He stood about my height, though more slender. He had light-brown hair, bordering on blond, and a fair complexion that gave him a look of innocence. Just before the referee handed the ball to one of the Colonials to shoot his free throw, Clark said, "You play a lot more aggressive than you did at Bosse."

I glanced at him, about to say something cutting, when I spotted Dr. Grabill behind the backboard, his eyes intent on the action. I imagined him tapping his finger to his temple, as if to say: "Don't go there. Clark's not your enemy. Those nutty thoughts in your head are. Just play and enjoy."

I turned to Clark and smiled. "How does it feel to be back on this court after all these years?" I didn't care what his answer was. What mattered to me was that I'd responded to him in a noncombative manner.

George Washington stayed close to us for ten minutes, trailing only 21–16. But our relentless full-court press and constant offensive pressure wore them down and we broke loose. It started with Larry Humes scoring five straight points and then pulling off such a pure and simple piece of basketball artistry it could only be appreciated by someone right there beside him. He dribbled the ball full speed up the middle of the court on a three-on-one fast break. Watkins filled the left lane, I the right. At the free-throw line, Humes darted a quick look left toward Watkins, drawing his defender in that direction, and then dropped a soft bounce pass to me as I barreled toward the basket. I took the ball in full stride, lifted off my right leg, and gently laid it left-handed into the basket.

After that play, I forgot about myself. The sense of connection I experienced with Humes left me intoxicated. I knew I needed him to do what I did, and I knew he needed me to do what he did. I wanted to embrace him but settled for "Great pass."

I then watched in amazement as Humes hit three consecutive baskets, each a gem—a floating right-handed hook while crossing the lane on a lead pass from Sloan, a short jumper that brushed softly off the glass into the basket, and a twisting layup after slithering between two defenders. That flurry of baskets cracked the game wide open, and we took a 52–30 lead into the dressing room at halftime.

When we returned to the court for the second half, Coach McCutchan once again had me take my man down low to take advantage of my height advantage. In the first three minutes, I hit three baskets, two jump shots—one from the corner and another from close range—and a third, a sweeping left-handed hook off a drive down the free-throw lane that drew a roar from the crowd. I felt powerful and smiled as I trotted back to play defense.

Seconds later, leading 64–37, McCutchan substituted en masse. The stadium crowd stood and showered appreciation on us for a full minute. The five of us exchanged pats on the fanny and "Great jobs" before settling into our chairs to enjoy the mop-up.

Herbie Williams sat to my left, Dave Fulkerson to my right. Fulkerson said, "You played like a man possessed. What was it—the battle of the Evansville boys?"

"Not really," I replied, but I said nothing else, unwilling to share my secret inner battle with him.

"Well, you kicked ass anyway."

• • •

I FELT SURPRISINGLY AT EASE before the Louisiana State game. I had survived my emotional crisis the night before and was determined to play this game without ego, simply to enjoy the game, the team, and the pageantry.

That Saturday evening, I walked through the players' entrance and up the back staircase to the nosebleed seats. Wearing a purple hooded sweatshirt pulled loose over my head to hide my face, I watched the consolation game from the aisle high above. The court shone brightly, as if illuminated by a massive spotlight. The players looked small. The noise had not yet risen to the level where conversation was impossible, so I could hear the bouncing of the ball and the abrupt blasts of whistles above the buzz of the crowd.

I surveyed the stands and saw that the color red blazed everywhere except on the court. It was as if twelve thousand Santa Clauses surrounded the playing area to create a giant Christmas wreath. I noticed a man wearing a red flannel shirt that hung loose outside his trousers. Another wore a red sport coat over a white, open-collared pullover. A woman walked by wearing a red skirt and a shiny red blouse, her mouth decorated with red lipstick.

As I studied the people seated around me, a thought crossed my mind that was so new and mind-blowing my breath caught. *These are just people. They're here to support, not judge me.* Tension drained from my body, and I felt at ease.

Later, dressed for the game, I trotted with my teammates the length of the court to the far basket for warm-ups. The throng stood as one to greet us. Waiting my turn in the layup line, I looked up to where I'd stood in the bleachers and tried to pick out the people I'd seen earlier. I wanted to look them in the eye and thank them.

After completing our warm-ups, we retreated to the dressing room to review our game plan. Coach McCutchan stood erect at the center of the room, legs parted, hands balled into fists. With pursed lips and narrowed eyes, he resembled a stern parent facing down a teenager late for curfew.

He held that posture until we settled into chairs around the room's perimeter. He pulled off his black horn-rimmed glasses and rubbed his palm over his forehead then back through his close-cropped hair. In a voice louder than normal, he said, "Boys, it's come to my attention that the LSU coach bragged after last night's game, 'We'll kick their schoolboy asses.'"

I glanced at Watkins, across from me. He lowered his chin onto his chest and peered back, as if to say, "What the hell's coming now?"

"Okay, boys!" Coach stomped his right foot to the floor just like he did when protesting a referee's call. "Let's just see who kicks whose ass. If you've never kicked ass before, I want you to do it tonight."

Collectively, we rose and started clapping and hollering. I stifled a grin and thought, *Guess I'm not the only one with ego issues here.*

The ball went up and we unleashed thirteen points by the time LSU scored their third. The rout was on. With a stifling full-court press, we amassed a 48–32 lead at halftime behind Larry Humes's twenty-one points, a total that was almost halfway to the Evansville College's single-game scoring record of forty-seven, set by Aces great Ed Smallwood five seasons before.

I trotted back to the court after the break, relaxed. I knew the Holiday Tournament championship was in the bag, that we'd play the second half for fun. I searched the student section and spotted Joyce, who gave me a little wave. Next to her sat my buddy Gene. He cupped his hand as if holding a glass of beer and mimed taking a long drink. I gave him a nod to confirm our get-together after the game.

Larry Humes went crazy in the second half, playing with even more daring than he had in the first. He mixed classic jumpers with sweeping hooks and spine-contorting drives that he improvised on the spot. With twelve minutes remaining in the game, he had amassed thirty-nine points, only eight shy of the record.

I had seen Humes's masterpiece moves many times before. What struck me was what I saw on his face. His eyes kept pace with the action, but they did not seem to acknowledge or even recognize the teammates who ran at his side. He held his jaw tight, yet he carried a hint of a smile. I understood that he had risen to a realm separate from the rest of us. I flashed back to my senior year at Bosse High, when I'd inhabited the same rare heights he now occupied. I remembered feeling as if the other players on the court were pawns to use for my own joy. I remembered thinking, *No one blocks my way*, as I seemed to float over and around, even through them. I determined to do everything I could to help Humes stay in his zone.

At the 10:50 mark, Humes sprint-dribbled down the court alongside Watkins on a two-on-one fast break. He drove hard to the basket, drawing the defender toward him, only to flip the ball at the last second behind his head to Sam, who was streaking to the basket for an uncontested layup. He took a nasty tumble as he soared out of bounds and immediately left the game, holding his back.

With 7:28 on the clock, Humes returned to the loudest roar of the night. With the victory already assured, the crowd lusted after the scoring record. He immediately grabbed a rebound and laid the ball back in for two points. Then he sank two free throws after being bumped hard on a jump shot. He followed that with a breakaway layup after a steal by Jerry Sloan. He now had forty-five points, only three points shy of the record.

Then it happened. With the clock showing 6:46 and the Aces leading 85–56, Coach McCutchan pulled the five of us from the game. The crowd gave us a prolonged standing ovation. I had no doubt Larry would break the record once he returned. At the 6:05 mark, the crowd began to chant, "Humes! Humes! Humes!" When they received no satisfaction, they turned their wrath on Coach McCutchan, lambasting him with boos and catcalls.

I sat on the bench, sandwiched between McCutchan and Humes. Humes leaned back with his legs outstretched, his arms dangling over the back of his chair, shoulders slumped. "This sucks," he said, low, under his breath. Coach McCutchan leaned forward with his elbows on his knees, his chin resting on his hands. He gazed at the action on the court, stony-faced. *My God,* I thought, *he's not going to put Larry back in!*

The score read 90–70, with 1:15 left, when Humes bent forward and unlaced his shoes. This dejected surrender egged the crowd on to even greater levels of protest.

After the game, fans crowded the locker room, irate. Humes sat in a corner, leaning back against the wall, his shoes, socks, and shirt gathered on the floor in front of him. With silent nods and downcast eyes, he accepted congratulations for his great game and assurances that he'd one day break the record.

Coach McCutchan held court with the press corps outside the dressing room. He explained: "In the past, we've broken a record only when we needed the points, and I don't think we need to change now."

I showered and dressed, feeling confused and conflicted. Should I side with my coach, our leader, a man of impeccable character? Or should I support my teammate who ran the court with me every day, a brother and a soul mate? As much as I respected McCutchan, I couldn't help but be upset with him.

On my way out of the room, I sat down next to Humes, put my arm around his shoulders, and said, "You'll get it before the season's over." I knew these words rang hollow the second they left my mouth, but they were the best I could summon.

I stopped by Art and Helen's for a few beers, then dropped Joyce at her house. When I finally got home shortly after midnight, I found Dad in his recliner sipping a highball, a tape delay of our game playing on TV. Mom had already gone to bed. I could see he was feeling little pain.

"Want to watch this?"

"Nah, I've seen it."

"Great game, huh?"

I didn't say anything and slumped down into the love seat across from him, my coat still on.

"How was it after the game?" he asked.

"Rough. Larry was pretty upset."

"I bet. It's not often you get benched three points shy of the record."

Both of us sat silently for a minute. "You know what?" I said. "Beating up on LSU got lost in the Humes drama. But there were some really good moments out there."

"Yeah?"

"Yeah. I don't know if you could notice it from where you and Mom sat, but the guys started passing up their own shots to get the ball to Larry. We put our egos aside."

"You too?" Dad asked, grinning. We both knew he referred to the self-doubt he struggled to get me past, going all the way back to my Little League days.

Dad drained his glass and leaned forward to get up and go to bed. "What do you think will happen Monday?"

"I don't know," I said. "I hope this doesn't ruin everything. We've got a good thing going."

• • •

I SLEPT SOUNDLY THAT NIGHT, weary from playing two games in two nights. I awoke the next morning to the smell of bacon and the opening and closing of kitchen cabinets. The bright light shining through the window told me I had slept later than usual.

Mom greeted me with a cheery "Good morning, dearie" as I shuffled to the dining room in my slippers and flannel robe. A glass of orange juice awaited me.

"Here, boy," Dad said, sliding the Sunday sports page over to me. He had circled in red a quote Jerry Sloan had given the night before to sports editor Tony Chamblain: "You know why the players respect McCutchan? Because he sticks to his philosophy. He could please the crowd by giving into them when they boo, but he sticks to his guns. That's important."

"What do you think?" Dad asked.

I took a deep breath and let out a sigh. "I think we just dodged a bullet. Larry respects Jerry. If Jerry gives Coach the okay, Larry will too."

When I got to Carson Center on Monday, I heard the tearing of tape from the trainer's room, locker doors slamming, and the thumping of basketballs on the practice court. Dressed for practice, I walked onto the court and saw Sloan, Watkins, Williams, and Humes, each with a basketball, practicing their shots. Coach McCutchan, wearing his usual khaki shorts and gray T-shirt, watched it all.

*Thank God,* I thought, relieved to find things back to normal.

I grabbed a basketball from the ball rack, dribbled to Larry, and asked, "You okay?"

"Yeah."

"For sure?"

"Yeah."

"Well, you better put up a few more in the first half next time, don't you think?" I said and smiled.

"Yeah," he said, smiling back.

# 14

## THE BLACK HILLS AND THE BADLANDS

FIFTEEN HOURS AFTER BLASTING THE University of Massachusetts with a withering barrage of dynamite and thunder, the Aces sat aboard a chartered airplane on the tarmac of Evansville's Dress Memorial Airport. It was Sunday, December 27. We were bound for the Black Hills and The Badlands to play our first road game against the South Dakota State Jackrabbits Monday night in Brookings. The University of South Dakota would follow the night after in Vermillion.

The plane picked up speed as it roared down the runway. When its front wheels lifted off the ground, Jim Forman yelled, "Up, up, and away!"

Someone then chanted, "Go, go, go," and we all joined in, urging the plane skyward.

Sitting next to me, white-knuckling his armrests, Sam Watkins said, "I hate this." His wide eyes looked the same as both of ours had on our bumpy flight back to Evansville from South Bend after we'd played Notre Dame the season before.

The plane climbed steeply at first, its engine grinding hard against gravity, and then eased into a slow, steady ascent to its cruising altitude. I leaned my forehead against the cool window and watched the earth's landmarks diminish below. Roads became chalk lines, barns looked Monopoly size, houses clustered together into miniature hamlets.

Once the plane leveled off, I looked around. Coach McCutchan sat in the front row by the window next to Coach O'Brien. I could see blue sky and white clouds above the pilot's instrument panel. Jerry Sloan and Larry Humes sat in the row directly in front of Sam and me, Herb Williams and Ron Johnson across the aisle. Larry Denton, Gary McClary, and the others lounged throughout the cabin. A stewardess in a navy-blue skirt and white blouse walked past to the back of the plane, smiling reflexively as she went. Our eyes met and I returned her smile.

I settled back into my seat, feeling liberated and adventurous as the plane propelled us west. Just as I began to hatch an excuse to walk back to talk to the stewardess, the plane started bumping and lurching, throwing me sideways in my seat. I tried to grab my armrests, but Watkins beat me to it. He sat upright and stiff, his eyes fixed straight ahead.

"You okay?" I asked, trying to mask my own fear.

"Yeah," he said. "Are we there yet?"

I looked behind me to see if the stewardess had swung into some kind of emergency action. She walked slowly up the aisle, turning her head left and right. I hoped when she got to me she'd say something friendly. Instead, she said, "Make sure your seatbelt is fastened."

When the air smoothed out, I reached under my seat and grabbed the black gym bag I used to tote my schoolwork on road trips. I had slipped in the Sunday sports page that my dad had stuffed under my arm when he'd dropped me off at the airport. Studies could come later. I pulled out the newspaper, which was dominated by Aces basketball. I read down Don Bernhardt's column until a quote from Massachusetts coach Johnny Orr caught my eye.

"Hey, guys," I called out. "Listen to what Orr said about us after last night's game."

Sloan and Humes turned. Williams leaned across the aisle. I read: "I've never seen anything like this team. They're by far the best we've seen or played. There is no question about it. I think you have to go way back to someone like Ohio State when they won the national title to get a comparable team."

I glanced up and caught Sloan's eye. "Damn straight," he said. Coach McCutchan stopped in the aisle to listen on his way to the bathroom at the back of the plane.

"And here's what their assistant coach said: 'I've been looking at Eastern teams for seven years. And I haven't seen a team compared to Evansville. They're the best I've seen since UCLA a year ago.'"

"Wow!" Humes said.

We had just been favorably compared to the great Ohio State NCAA champions of 1960, led by NBA superstars Jerry Lucas and John Havlicek, as well as the UCLA Bruins who'd defeated Duke, 98–83, for the Division I championship the year before.

"Ain't we pretty?" said Williams.

"Now, hold on, boys," Coach said, pointing at the newspaper. "We've only played six games. I think it's a little early to jump on the greatness bandwagon, don't you? We haven't even played a road game yet."

I peered sideways at McCutchan. "By the way, Coach, you're also quoted." I paused to see if I'd get a negative reaction. Seeing none, I went on, "'I said it before and I'd have to say it now. I believe this is a better five-man team than last year's.'"

"Did I say that?" he asked.

"Don Bernhardt said you did." The guys chuckled and Humes patted Coach's arm, a sweet, understated smile on his face.

"Well, I must have gotten carried away. We'll see about that after this road trip." With that, he walked to the back of the plane.

Once Coach was out of earshot, Williams said, "I still think we're pretty."

We landed at the Brookings Regional Airport to twelve-degree temperatures. I peered out the window as we taxied to a stop. The ground was hidden under fresh snow. A flock of blackbirds swooped across the sky. Three snowplows lined the runway next to a fence. Next to them, a man wearing a red flannel jacket and a hat with flaps covering his ears warmed his hands over a fire blazing in a trashcan. We deplaned and pushed our way single file into a squat, square terminal as wind gusts slapped our faces.

"Cold enough for you?" Sloan asked an attendant inside the terminal, blowing into his hands.

"Not too bad," he said. "It was twenty-seven below two days ago."

We caravanned into Brookings on a two-lane highway that ran alongside fields dotted with bales of brown hay and grazing horses. Every third vehicle we passed was a pickup. Shivering in the backseat, I saw no buildings taller than two stories, no movie theaters, no cozy restaurants. The few people who walked the streets huddled inside three-quarter-length coats, the men in cowboy hats.

By the time we pulled up to our dreary motel, just east of the Jackrabbits' campus, it had begun snowing. I knew this trip would in no way resemble the one we'd taken west the year before. That trip had begun in Las Cruces to play

New Mexico State. It had continued the next day with a layover in El Paso, Texas, where we crossed the Rio Grande into Juarez, Mexico. It cost one penny to get into Mexico and two to re-enter the United States. The following day we jetted to Tucson to play the University of Arizona before returning to Evansville. There we found sunny skies, tanned coeds in shorts and sleeveless blouses, and grassy quadrangles on which students tossed Frisbees and lounged on blankets. As I waited in the shabby lobby for Coach McCutchan to check us in, I resigned myself to the fact that this trip would be about nothing but basketball.

After our team supper, Jim Forman poked his head into the room Jerry Sloan and I shared. We were lying back on our beds in our sweats. Herb Williams sat on a chair with his feet propped on my bed. Watkins and Humes were stretched out on the floor, leaning back against the wall, the door to their adjoining room wide open.

"What are you guys doing?" Forman asked.

"Building a canoe," Sloan said.

"Thanks, smart ass." A gust of wind rattled the window. Jim looked at me and added, "Looks like we're not going out tonight."

"Nope," I said, "too cold out there," I nodding toward the window.

"Guess I'll just hang out with you superstars then."

"That'll make you feel pretty special," Sloan said.

"Speaking of special," Humes said in his low-voiced way, "that was pretty cool what those coaches said about us in the paper."

"Yeah, but don't forget Coach's warning," Forman said. "This is our first road game. Lots of pressure."

"Pressure, hell, I love playing on the road," Sloan said, his voice pitched higher than usual. "I like nothing better than sticking it to them right in front of their own fans."

The wind rattled the windows again. Watkins chuckled and nodded his head. Williams said, "Yeah!"

"That's right, guys," Sloan went on. "The Redshirts already love us. Nothing to prove there. But we can show these people. They don't know who we are, but they sure as hell will afterwards."

No one said a word. I recognized the force of what Sloan had said. It was like he had lifted a veil and revealed a new source of inspiration. He obliterated the concept of the home-court advantage, turned it on its head. Rather than the other team's home court being threatening, it could become a source of motivation, even pleasure. We could drink in the enemy's venom as a stimulant, be better in hostile gymnasiums than at Roberts Stadium. Hell, I could even put aside my concerns about my personal performance. I sensed a hardening of the resolve among the guys in the room, a resolve fueled by a potent mix of testosterone, insolence, and pride.

*Damn!* I thought.

"Okay then," Sloan said, "time for this ol' farm boy to get some shut-eye. Let's do it tomorrow."

The next night we ran onto the South Dakota State Fieldhouse floor without rah-rahing, our jaws tight and eyes straight ahead. Built in 1918, the field house reminded me of all the aged and worn gyms I'd cut my teeth on in high school, especially Central Gym in downtown Evansville. The floor was dulled by the scuffs of countless gym shoes and the soft yellow glow of overhead lights. A few thousand people crowded onto bleachers pulled out to the very edge of the inbound lines. Cheerleaders stomped their feet and spun so that their dark-blue skirts swirled like matadors' capes. The sound of thumping basketballs punctuated the steady din of a thousand conversations. The smell of popcorn wafted across the arena, and the sense of anticipation reached a fever pitch.

We harassed the Jackrabbits all over the court, smothering the man with the ball and blocking every passing lane. This kept their guards from penetrating our perimeter and forced them into countless errors. Sloan started strong, hitting four of his first six shots from the field. I too started strong, hitting two long jumpers in the first few minutes of the game and a total of five in the first half. One from near the sidelines required such an arch that it seemed to take minutes to reach the basket. It dropped down as if from outer space, popping the net up inside the rim and evoking a low murmur from the crowd. Running up and down the court, one thousand miles from home, we were as one, in sync, fulfilling our mission, kicking ass. I felt as light on my feet as the snowflakes falling outside the field house.

We blasted ahead 26–11 only ten minutes into the game and coasted to a victory that was easier and more dominating than the final score of 73–63 portrayed. Larry Humes, magnificent as always, totaled a game high of twenty-six. Sloan and I each tallied thirteen, with Watkins contributing eleven. Williams drew a collective "ooh" when he grabbed an offensive rebound in the second half and leaped high to dunk the ball two-handed into the basket from a standing position.

Unlike Roberts Stadium, our postgame dressing room was empty of fans. Grateful for the privacy, I showered, dressed, and walked out to the playing court. Partially darkened, it stood empty except for a few fans scattered in the bleachers. The whisk of a janitor's broom and the occasional slamming of doors echoed from far away. I felt the same sense of reverence I did when I walked into St. Benedict Catholic Cathedral in Evansville.

One after another, my teammates exited the dressing room and wandered about as I sat alongside Sloan in the third row of bleachers. Both of us slouched on the bench, our feet outstretched. Two men walked slowly by, both buttoning their coats under their chins, then pulling stocking caps down over their ears, and finally wrestling into tight-fitting gloves. One said to the other, "I'd like to see how those guys would do against the Lakers."

Sloan elbowed me in the ribs and said, "That's what I'm talking about."

• • •

BACK IN THE HOTEL, HERB Williams poked his head into the room and said to Sloan and me, "Let's go get some beer." We collected Humes and Watkins and, bundled up as warm as we could, walked gingerly over ice-sheathed sidewalks to a corner pub.

Inside it was dimly lit with a bar along the wall left of the door and a jukebox playing Patsy Cline's "I Go Out Walking After Midnight" from across the room. Groups of young people about our age—students, I figured—crowded at tables, drinking beer and eating snacks.

We settled at a table at the back right corner, farthest from the bar. A waitress appeared, wearing cowgirl boots, jeans that hugged her hips, and a red plaid flannel shirt tucked in at her waist.

"Hey, fellas. What can I get you?"

"A pitcher of draft and some chips," Sloan said.

"You got it. But first I got to see that guy there's ID." She pointed at Williams. Herb was only nineteen at the time.

"Give us a break," I said. "He's older than most of the people in the room."

When the waitress looked at me, Sloan slipped his driver's license under the table to Williams, who held it up to her, his thumb over Jerry's picture.

"That'll work," she said and walked away. We looked at each other and burst out laughing.

"Guess we look almost like twins," the black Herb Williams said to the white Jerry Sloan.

"Yeah, like Amos and Andy," Sloan said, stimulating laughter that almost brought tears to our eyes.

We made quick work of the first pitcher and began on a second. The talk centered on the game that night, one after another of us recalling plays we admired from each other. In the midst of this, Watkins suddenly slumped in his chair and said, "Oh, shit!"

"What?" Humes asked.

"There's Coach O'Brien, over there, at the bar."

There he was, sitting with his back to the room, alone.

"Let's get out of here, quick," I said, grabbing my coat and throwing a ten-dollar bill down on the table.

We hugged the wall as close as we could and made a quick getaway. Once outside, we hustled back to the hotel, careful not to slip and break our necks.

"What a night," I said to Sloan, safe and sound back in our room.

"Yeah, but another one tomorrow night to look forward to," he replied.

◆ ◆ ◆

THE NEXT MORNING WE AWOKE to heavy snowfall and gusting winds that grounded our flight. We packed into five cars, and for close to five hours we slipped and slid the 125 miles south from Brookings to Vermillion.

I sat in the front seat of the lead car alongside Coach McCutchan. Herb Williams, Ron Johnson, and Ron Eberhard cramped together in the back. The heater rumbled steadily but barely kept us warm so that we had to keep our coats buttoned.

On edge because of a one-car spinout on a rain-slicked highway two summers before, I kept a tight grip on the dashboard and focused my attention on the feel of the tires on the road. I tensed with every sway of the back wheels, fearful of fishtailing, giving no thought to the University of South Dakota Coyotes lying in wait ahead.

Sixty miles into the trip, Coach McCutchan had had it with my gasps and grunts. He said, "Lordy, Grieger, if you don't settle down, I'm going to drop you off at the Sioux Falls airport and fly you back to Evansville."

"Sorry, Coach," I said as the guys in the back burst into laughter.

Despite treacherous roads, Coyote students and fans filled the gymnasium, more pumped up than last night's crowd. We trotted from our dressing room, past a trophy case that belonged more in a high school than a university gym, hearing a brass band and feet stomping on wooden bleachers. We ran onto the court to a chorus of boos and catcalls that continued off and on throughout our warm-ups.

Just before tip-off, Sloan gathered the five of us together near half-court and said, "Let's beat them down—every single person in this place."

And we did, playing as cruelly as the weather outside. Two and a half minutes into the game, Humes hit two free throws to put us ahead 5–4, following that with two short jumpers to extend the lead to 9–4. Watkins then hit three straight jumpers to run our lead to 20–8. By halftime, we led 52–31, with Humes hitting nine of his fourteen attempts, Watkins and me five of seven, and Sloan three of five.

During this first half, I sensed something happening that Sloan had touched on two nights before, something I had not had the time to think through or put into words. It was the sheer power of our team's developing personality. We were becoming a team that did not need fiery speeches or psychological tricks to jack up our emotions—tirades from our coaches, the fanaticism of our fans, the fear of loss or humiliation. What was beginning to drive us was a desire to play with such ruthless efficiency that we would obliterate anyone in our path. On one hand, we played with joy, on the other, to disassemble and destroy.

We walked off the court at halftime to a stunned and humbled crowd. "All right!" Sloan yelled when we got into the dressing room.

We showed no mercy in the second half. Though Williams never found his shooting touch, he snatched a game-leading twenty rebounds, leaping so high at times that his feet reached above our waists. "They ought to get that Williams a pilot's license," South Dakota coach Dwayne Clodfelter remarked after the game. "He goes so high I bet they pick him up on a radar screen."

Jerry Sloan flaunted his All-American skills on both ends of the court. With his knees and elbows sometimes flying in four different directions, he scored twenty points, pulled down ten rebounds, and limited the Coyotes' high scorer to a measly ten points. Humes proved magnificent, scoring thirty-six points (on fourteen baskets in only twenty-two attempts), and Watkins, relentless as always, dropped in eighteen points. I did my part with ten.

During the second half, the outcome no longer in doubt, the crowd gave us as many "oohs" and "ahhs" as they did cheers for their own team. Coach substituted for all five of us with the Aces leading 75–48. A few Coyote fans stood and applauded.

I sat on the bench, Humes and Sloan to my left, Williams and Watkins on my right. Leaning forward, I looked at Humes and Sloan and said, "Did you hear the applause?"

"Yeah," Humes said. "Sweet."

"I think these people know who we are now, don't you?" Sloan said.

"How could they not?" I settled back into my seat to watch our teammates mop up.

• • •

I SAT NEXT TO THE window on the flight back to Evansville the next day, enjoying the sunshine we hadn't seen for days. I wanted to be alone with my thoughts. The steady drone of the engines worked its hypnotic effect, and I watched the fields, towns, and rivers slip by below. I had the sense of floating above reality, as if in a dream.

My thoughts drifted to the Aces. I realized that our team had found its voice. We had started our season challenged by giants, the likes of Iowa, Northwestern, and Notre Dame, without knowing how truly good we were.

Now we knew we were good and relished the opportunity to show what we could do. We needed no pep talks or gimmicks to fire us up. We each put aside our individual egos and focused on doing what it took to achieve the one thing that mattered—winning the next game and then the next, one at a time. We had become a machine, fueled by pride and passion, determined to roll over any opponent without remorse.

Still gazing out the window, I spotted a small plane that had crossed paths with ours below us. It looked not much bigger than a bird. I looked around the cabin and located my teammates—Sloan and Williams, Watkins and Humes. Our future might be uncertain, but I didn't care. *There's no place I'd rather be right now than here with these guys,* I thought. With a strong tail wind, we touched down in Evansville an hour earlier than expected.

# 15

## LARRY, THEN THE HOLY GRAIL

IT WAS THE LAST DAY of 1964, and I felt that I was beginning to figure things out. I loved being introduced as an Aces starter. I relished the act of releasing a jump shot that dropped majestically through the basket. I thrilled at the pageantry and electricity of a jam-packed Roberts Stadium. Yet, I found myself letting go of basketball being only about me. A "we" was taking a foothold in my thinking, an "us" that was blowing aside my personal drama.

That evening, I took Joyce to F's Steakhouse in downtown Evansville to celebrate New Year's Eve. We sat at a corner table, me feeling overdressed in gray slacks, a dark-blue sports coat, and a white shirt and tie. She looked radiant in a soft white sweater that felt feathery to the touch. Couples packed the other tables, keeping up a steady din of conversation, interspersed with clinks of silverware and bursts of high-pitched laughter. I was about to tell Joyce how nice she looked when static interrupted the big band music piped into the room. A voice blared, "Call for Russ Grieger. Russ Grieger, please come to the lobby."

The room went quiet. When I stood to take the call, the diners erupted into applause.

I made my way through the room, acknowledging the clapping with small waves, trying to look unaffected and unflappable. On the phone, my buddy Gene said, "You and Joyce want to meet up later?"

"Absolutely. How about at the fraternity house in an hour or so?"

"Okay, see you then."

"Hey, wait a minute," I almost shouted. I told him what had happened, then added, "Give me five minutes to get back to the table and call again."

We both laughed. I walked back to my table, striving to look cool and detached, not wanting to betray the pleasure the recognition had given me. Waiting with a smile, Joyce looked more alluring than before. I smiled back at her but also at myself, appreciating that I had just poked fun at my ego-driven self, satisfied that, for the moment anyway, I had not taken myself so seriously.

What I didn't know, however, was that, within the week, I would be on that ego-driven roller-coaster ride once again.

◆  ◆  ◆

ON SATURDAY, JANUARY 2, THE Aces gathered at Carson Center to caravan to Muncie to play the Ball State Cardinals. We rode in five cars, three players per car. I sat in the front seat with assistant coach Tom O'Brien, Jerry Sloan and Larry Humes sprawling in the back.

We rode in silence, the three of us staring out our windows. It was bitter cold with sunlight illuminating the fields. I wished I'd brought my sunglasses. We passed country churches with knee-high tombstones standing in side yards, dingy row-house motels, dark and empty, and an occasional scruffy dog wandering along the highway. Trucks bustled by, buffeting us with blasts of wind. Roy Orbison, The Beatles, and Bobby Vale played on the radio.

Coach O'Brien finally broke the ice. "Hey, what's going on? It feels like a wake in here." Riding with Tom was the best. He had the crew cut and sturdy build of a marine drill sergeant. In his early thirties and unmarried, he liked to banter like one of the boys.

"Tell us what you really think, Coach," Jerry said.

"I'll tell you what I think," Tom said, pointing to a speed sign tilted off balance alongside the highway. "That sign's got more talent than Ball State."

"Hey, that's sacrilegious talk," I said. "You're supposed to convince us that they're as good as the Boston Celtics."

"I guess, but we've got two All-Americans right here in this car." Tom jabbed his thumb toward the backseat. "How can we lose?"

"What about Russ?" Larry asked, his voice low, his mouth curved in a barely discernable smile.

"That goes without saying," Tom said. "You two'd be nothing without him."

Although I knew what was said was in the spirit of playfulness, I still appreciated his comment. With a glance over my shoulder, I said, "Thanks, buddy."

We fell back into silence. I thought about how fortunate we were to have Larry on our team. After attending a segregated, all-black elementary school, he'd started four straight years for the Madison Cubs, losing only one regular-season game during all that time. In his senior year he was named Mr. Basketball, the best prep player in Indiana, and gathered offers from eighty schools to play basketball.

But it was more than that. I thought about how Larry's lighthearted comment in my defense captured his sweetness. Try as I might, I could not recall even one instance, in all the time I'd spent with him, on and off the court, when he had raised his voice in anger or made a cutting remark toward anyone. I remembered one day, when I brought Larry home for lunch, he'd stood awkwardly by the front door until my mom had coaxed him to the dining-room table. He "Yes, ma'amed" her repeatedly.

When we arrived at Muncie, I turned to Larry and said, "Wouldn't hurt if you went crazy tonight and broke that scoring record."

"Yeah, not a bad idea," Sloan agreed.

"So why don't you two see to it that he does just that," said O'Brien.

That night Ball State opened the game with the same collapsing zone as had our two previous opponents, tucking three and sometimes four players around Humes. This strategy worked for a while as the rest of us clanged easy jumpers off the rim with maddening regularity.

During a time-out, McCutchan said, "Keep taking your shots, boys. They'll start to fall. But keep looking to get the ball down to Larry so he can get to work."

We did, they did, and Larry did. Sloan and Watkins started finding the range, pulling defenders away from Humes. Then, bumping and grinding his way into position to receive our inlet passes, he became unstoppable. With bodies surrounding him, clutching and clawing for the ball, he managed to squirm through their defenses, scoring twenty-one first-half points, helping build our lead to four, then to twelve, and finally to fifteen by halftime.

I sat in the locker room waiting for Coach McCutchan to come in and dispense his second-half adjustments. Larry sat across the room from me, in a corner by himself, neither speaking to nor looking at anyone. I studied him and noted the faraway, ethereal look in his eyes. I remembered when I'd experienced the same transcendent state I imagined him to be in. He looked as if he had reached deep inside himself and touched base with some emotional truth that for him looked to be magnificent in its purity. Out of respect, I neither approached nor said anything to him, not wanting the break the spell.

In the second half, Larry continued to pile in baskets, topping thirty points within just minutes. Sensing that he could very well break the Aces' single-game scoring record, we started focusing more on getting Larry the ball than looking for our own shot or playing our usual in-your-face defense. This let Ball State close to within eight points on four occasions. Each time, we picked up the slack and again increased our lead. This worked to Larry's advantage as our lead was never so great as to warrant full-scale substitutions like during the LSU game, when Larry was removed only three points shy of the record.

Larry hit the forty-point mark with five minutes left in the game. Ball State called an immediate time-out. Coach McCutchan instructed us on what he wanted us to do to seal the victory. But not one of us did what he said. Instead, we poked and probed the perimeter until we discovered a passing lane to Humes. First he banked in a ten-foot jumper. Then he added two free throws after being fouled driving to the basket. Next he hit one of his sweeping hook shots that glided off the glass and slid through the net as if guided by radar. Larry's total rose to forty-six. Everyone on our bench, even Coach McCutchan, stood and cheered.

The record-breaking moment came with forty-eight seconds left on the clock. Sloan zinged a sharp-push pass over his defender's shoulder to Larry deep in the paint. He caught it with his back to the basket, faked upward with his whole body, twisted and jumped to shoot, only to be hacked so hard on both forearms he could not get the ball up to the basket. He stepped to the free-throw line, took a deep breath, and bounced the ball twice. He then dropped his thirteenth free throw of the night clean through the net to tie the Aces' single-game scoring record of forty-seven. After another deep breath and two bounces of the basketball, he swished his fourteenth free throw, breaking the record with his forty-eighth point of the night.

Larry turned and ran back to play defense. Sloan ran alongside, his arm around Larry's shoulders. Watkins gave him a sharp swat on the butt. Williams yelled, "You da man!" He looked sideways at Coach McCutchan, who smiled and nodded. Larry's return smile reassured me that they shared a bond not unlike that between a proud parent and a grateful son. I felt happy for Larry and proud of all of us.

In the dressing room after our 108–92 victory, Larry sat shirtless, accepting congratulations. Coach came in and called for attention. At the center of the room, he said to Larry, "I'm proud of you. You got that record when it counted."

Indeed, it was a win all around. Coach retained his honor after being maligned for yanking Larry only points shy of the record just weeks earlier. We won our ninth straight game, hitting 52 percent of our shots and totaling 108 points. And Larry not only broke the Aces' record but the Indiana Collegiate Conference and Ball State Fieldhouse single-game scoring records as well.

I walked across the dressing room, my coat in hand, to where Larry sat putting on his socks and shoes. Reaching down, I put my hand on his shoulder, looked him in the eye, and said, "It was an honor being a part of what you did tonight."

He held my look, nodded, and squeezed my hand. I felt whole and complete, happy for Larry, not noticing that I did not feel one whit of jealousy or envy.

• • •

IT WAS WEDNESDAY AFTERNOON, JANUARY 6, when I stood near center court in Butler Fieldhouse. The Aces had motored that morning to Indianapolis to play the Butler Bulldogs. We were here for a light workout, more to loosen our muscles than to practice.

Butler Fieldhouse was the Holy Grail for every Indiana basketball fan, the dream destination for every Hoosier schoolboy who'd ever picked up a basketball. It was here, on this very court, that the Indiana High School Basketball Championships had been played every year since 1928, when Muncie edged Martinsville 13–12.

I scanned the field house, trying to absorb as much of the atmosphere as I could. The place looked old and worn, like an ancient cathedral, cast in yellows and browns. The ceiling was convex from one end of the court to the other, so high in the middle you'd have to shoot a basketball from a cannon to reach its apex. Over ten thousand seats surrounded the playing floor, gradually ascending on both sides of the court to seven huge rectangular windows behind the top rows. Beyond them shone the bright blue sky, which looked endless. I had the impression of looking at a giant staircase that ascended into heaven.

My mind traveled back to 1954 when I'd watched my first state championship on my parents' seventeen-inch black-and-white Philco TV. Through a snowy, flickering screen, I'd seen tiny Milan, the team that inspired the movie *Hoosiers*, defeat Muncie Central on a last-second jump shot by the real-life Jimmy Chitwood, Bobby Plump. It would have been impossible to count the number of times on the concrete court behind my parents' house that I'd fantasized about holding the ball right here on the spot I now stood, letting the clock wind down to just a few seconds, dribbling hard to the right of the free-throw arc, stopping short, and launching a rainbow over the helpless hands of my befuddled defender, the ball touching nothing but net.

That memory transported me forward to March 1956, when I was an eighth-grader. It was a Saturday night, and I'd gone to a party thrown by one of my friends, a year older than me and a freshman in high school. Under dim lights, a few couples slow-danced in the middle of the room to the haunting melodies of The Platters' "The Great Pretender," Morris Stoloff's "Moonglow," and Gogi Grant's "The Wayward Wind." Others sat on three beanbag chairs or on a white vinyl couch pushed against the wall. Still others munched potato chips and pretzels while standing at a white-clothed refreshment table.

I had just turned fifteen and felt I had reached the big time as I stood talking with these older guys and girls. And yet my thoughts were preoccupied by the Indiana State High School Basketball Championship game that night between Lafayette Jefferson and Indianapolis Crispus Attucks. Attucks, an all-black school led by superstar Oscar Robertson, had won all of their thirty games that season, an encore after winning the state championship the year before. I had to watch this game.

At eight o'clock, I made my way to the tiny TV in the corner of the room and turned it on. I pulled a chair up close, bent forward, and cupped my hands around my ears. From the opening tip, I recognized that Oscar Robertson was different from everyone else. His teammates got him the ball on each possession, and he controlled the game. His moves were precise, with no frills, no wasted motion or effort. He found a way to get open for a jumper anytime he wanted. He seemed to cut through the Jefferson defense on his drives to the basket, like Moses parting the seas. His dominion over the court both electrified my nerves and numbed my brain. I forgot I was at a teen party in Evansville and felt somehow connected to Robertson on the court in Indianapolis. It was as if I scored each of his thirty-nine points that night.

"Hey, Russ!" Hearing my name, I snapped back to Butler Fieldhouse in 1965. "You do want to get in a few shots before we close practice down, don't you?" Coach O'Brien said.

"Yeah, thanks." I dribbled to the basket. I felt a bit intimidated being on this court, as if on holy ground. This thought was not conscious in my mind, but the tightness in my gut gave proof that it was there and palpable.

We ran onto the court at seven thirty to be greeted by ten thousand crazed fans who meant us no good. The students stood as one and thrust their index fingers at us like weapons, shouting, "You! You! You!" I didn't know what that meant, but I knew it communicated ill will.

Butler opened with a hot hand, hitting everything they threw up. They led 10–5 and 14–7 before we finally caught them at 20–20, nine minutes into the game. The Bulldogs played sound, fundamental basketball, blocking out on the boards, playing hard-nosed, man-to-man defense, running their offense with precision. They bumped and hipped and elbowed under the basket, hand checking and clawing on the perimeter, exactly the kind of game this court deserved. I realized we would have to fight to win this one. We traded baskets back and forth. But, on the wave of Humes's dazzling and unscripted twenty points, we forged a 44–40 halftime lead.

In the second half, neither team conceded an inch. I worked hard on both ends of the court, but I felt frustrated and uncoordinated, unable to contribute much of anything. I couldn't get open for a shot and grabbed few rebounds. I felt irrelevant, wanting to do so much more than just take up space on this court.

The score was tied at fifty-seven, then fifty-nine, and again at sixty-one before Watkins swished a free throw to put us ahead by one with under ten minutes left to play. Humes then stuffed one in from under the basket, and Sloan hit two free throws to push our lead to 66–61.

This was the moment Jerry Sloan took over the game, reminding us amid all the splendor of Larry Humes's artistry why he was the All-American backbone of the team. On his own initiative, he moved out to the perimeter with Sam and me and took over the ball-handling duties. He dribbled circles around his six-foot-seven defender, taking time off the clock and doling out precise passes to Watkins and Humes for easy baskets. We led 77–69 with twenty seconds remaining when Sloan canned two free throws. A meaningless tip-in by Butler at the buzzer made the final score 79–71.

We rode back to Evansville through a lamp-black Indiana night. No stars twinkled, no lights glimmered in the farmhouses we passed, only a rare car met us going the other way. Sloan and Humes dozed in the backseat while Tom O'Brien drove, sipping coffee from a paper cup to stay awake.

I leaned my head against my window. If someone had asked me my mood, I would have said, "Confused." I felt happy for and confident in my team but disappointed that I hadn't made more of a contribution. Humes had scored thirty-three, Sloan twenty, and Watkins seventeen, while Williams had grabbed fifteen rebounds. My two for three from the floor and three rebounds felt puny. Even worse, I felt shame for letting Sloan carry the ball-handling duties near the end of the game.

Just then Tom said, "Penny for your thoughts."

"Dunno," I said, not wanting to share my negative thinking. "What about you?"

"Well, I'd say we've got something pretty special going. I don't see anybody we can't beat the rest of the year."

"Yup," I said, finding it hard to get into the flow of the conversation.

We rode without talking, Tom sipping at his coffee. After a few miles, he said, "Let me ask you a question: Why do you think you guys are so good?"

"You mean in addition to those two guys in the backseat?"

"Yeah," he said, throwing a quick look my way.

"I don't know, what do you think?"

"I agree with Mac. I think you starters are better than last year's, and, don't forget, last year we won it all. I think you five match any five in the country. Together, you're smooth as glass."

I didn't say anything, gratified by what he'd said but amazed that he wasn't critical of my play that night. Thankfully, we drove on without going there, only the hum of the wheels interrupting the silence. In my mind, I continued to berate myself. In the past, I had been at center stage. I'd played the game with originality and daring. Tonight, I felt more an extra rather than a leading man, and not a very good one at that.

The car heater whirred, but I rolled down my window halfway and let the wind blast my face. I hoped it would blow away my sour mood. *Get over yourself,* I thought. I knew I needed to get back to where basketball was basketball and I was me.

# 16

## FANS INTO REDSHIRTS

WE RETURNED TO ROBERTS STADIUM on Saturday, January 9 to do battle with the DePauw Tigers. Outside, the wind blew and snow swirled. Swarms of Redshirts—some in parkas and scarves, others in overcoats and hats—pushed forward, heads down, shoulders hunched, to get to the turnstiles. Here and there stood a man, hands gloved and shivering, holding a sign that read, "Need A Ticket!"

None of that mattered inside the stadium. Our purple-clad cheerleaders led us onto the court, shaking white pom-poms above their heads. The 12,416 fans stood, hooted, and stomped until I thought my eardrums would burst. Our last home game had only been two weeks before, but they still seemed to be starved for us, as if we and they were lovers reunited after being separated by great time and distance.

First in the layup line, I dribbled to the basket and laid the ball off the glass and in and then ran to the back of the rebound line. The cheering continued. "Unbelievable," I said to Sloan when he trotted in line behind me.

When we broke into our shooting warm-ups, I walked to midcourt and looked around. Three rows behind the scorer's table sat Evansville mayor Frank McDonald and Evansville College president Melvin Hyde, both clapping in rhythm and wearing red sport coats. I located my sociology teacher, Ludwig Petkosic; my psychology advisor, Delbert Sampson; and the drama department chair, Sam Smiley, all outfitted in red V-neck sweaters. Paul Grabill slouched in his seat at the end of the court, his rust-red goatee and ruddy complexion matching his red tartan vest and crimson blazer. I saw lawyers and doctors, merchants, pharmacists, and barbers, salesmen and teachers, men I had met at one Aces reception or another. Each wore some piece of red clothing.

Though it had been a staple in my life during these last two years, I still felt intoxicated by such adulation and hoopla, particularly after my lackluster performance against Butler the game before. It was as if all had been forgiven and they still loved me. And yet I didn't understand it. I wondered, *What would drive all this craziness about a bunch of boys playing a child's game?*

Herb Williams ran by to retrieve a basketball as it rolled over the centerline. On his way back, he tugged at my shirtsleeve. "Hey," he said, "you going to play basketball or what?"

"Here I come," I replied, but the question stuck in my mind. It seemed important, though I didn't know why. *Focus on the game,* I told myself.

If all this fury and turbulence was meant to intimidate, nobody bothered to tell the DePauw Tigers. They surprised us with a full-court press and a collapsing two-three zone defense. Diminutive guards, five-foot-eight Jack Hogan and five-foot-nine Dan Schermer, pestered Watkins and me like mosquitoes. They double-teamed whichever of us controlled the ball, hacking and slapping us on every possession.

These strategies worked for much of the first half. We couldn't find our rhythm. We missed shots we normally dropped, made our cuts and passes a half-second too late, and reacted a step or two slow on defense. The ear-crushing noise from the sea of red died to a worried murmur.

With four minutes left in the half, Coach McCutchan called a time-out. Our substitutes offered words of encouragement, our team managers passed out water and towels. Without raising his voice, Coach simply said, "Boys, how about we knuckle down and play Aces basketball?"

Then he instructed us to make two adjustments that turned the game into the fastest rout in Evansville College basketball history. He switched defensive assignments, interchanging Watkins and me with the six-foot-four Humes and the six-foot-six Sloan, putting them on DePauw's pint-sized guards. Humes and Sloan engulfed Hogan and Schermer, forcing them into numerous ball-handling errors, ones we immediately turned into easy baskets.

Coach also reminded us that DePauw played a two-three zone defense and instructed us to focus on attacking them with our one-three-one zone offense. The goal was to get the ball to the Aces positioned near the foul line, which would create a four-on-three advantage for us. If one of the three defenders moved to guard him, he could pop the ball to the open man for an easy shot; if the three defenders stayed put on the man in their zone, he could drop an easy jumper.

On our first possession back on the court, I stood at the point and lobbed the ball over the guards' heads to Humes at the free-throw line. He quickly pivoted toward the basket, with Sloan on the wing to his right, Watkins on his left wing, and Williams under the basket down low. The defenders in the middle backed off Humes to cover Williams. Humes immediately took a fifteen-foot jumper that plopped through the basket as if settling into an easy chair.

From then on, we played precise and seamless basketball, running our offense to perfection. I hit a couple of jumpers, as did Humes, Watkins, and Sloan. In the four minutes between Coach's time-out and halftime, we outscored DePauw 23–7 and opened up a 58–43 lead. All told, Humes accounted for twenty-one and Sloan ten of our first-half points.

The rumble that started with Humes's basket at the four-minute mark escalated to the roar of a jet about to take off when we walked off the court on our way back to the locker room. The Redshirts thundered their hallmark cheer: "Aces, Aces," *clap clap, clap clap clap* . . . "Aces, Aces," *clap clap, clap clap clap* . . . Just before disappearing under the stands, I spotted Dr. Grabill standing with everyone else, stomping his cane in rhythm to the chant. I couldn't help but think, *Him too.*

Back on the court, we picked up where we'd left off before halftime, outscoring DePauw 14–2 in the first four minutes. With 14:38 left in the game, Coach subbed for all five of us, our lead a whopping 78–47. The noise before was only a prelude to what rained down now. The Redshirts applauded for a full minute before settling back into their seats. They kept up their clamor as our second-stringers continued the onslaught. At the 4:38 mark, our substitutes gave way to the third team, who brought home the 117–88 victory.

Just before I left the court on the way to the locker room, I waved my arms over my head, trying to catch Dr. Grabill's eye, and then mouthed to him, "I need to talk to you." He nodded and mouthed back, "Monday." I figured he'd put me on the right track to understanding all this insanity surrounding the Aces.

In the crowded locker room, everyone wore bloodred except for the Aces in white uniforms. McCutchan had to practically shout to be heard over all the celebrating. "That's about the greatest eight minutes of basketball anyone has ever played for me," he said to reporters. I sat and unlaced my shoes, my jersey practically dry from watching most of the second half from the bench. I took in the backslapping and congratulations, observing the total joy spread across the faces of our well-wishers. I had the thought that we held the key to their happiness in our hands. *God forbid we should lose a game,* I thought.

After the game, I met up with my girlfriend, Joyce, outside the locker room. We drove to Art and Helen's, the neighborhood bar my fraternity had adopted as our official watering hole. Set in a seedy neighborhood away from campus, it had a tough, blue-collar atmosphere and tolerated underage drinking and good-ol-boy hijinks. Art always wore a short-sleeved white shirt that looked a size too small and emphasized his barrel chest. He slicked his hair back into a 1950s ducktail and called everybody "sport." Helen had a full body and a glob of dyed-black hair bobby-pinned to the top of her head. Her salty language captivated the fraters as much as her cleavage.

When I walked in behind Joyce, a few patrons at the bar spotted me and offered "Good game." Joyce pulled me by the hand through the low-hanging smoke, the smell of stale beer, and the sound of clicking billiard balls into the large back room situated behind the bar. There, fraternity brother Jerry Gray's band, The Fourmosts, played honky-tonk on a small makeshift stage. Couples danced on a cramped dance floor carved out between them and the tightly packed tables that filled the rest of the room. The lights were dim, so we had to peer hard to spot Jerry Linzy and his girlfriend, Mary, along with Eddie Paxton and his steady, Suzanne. We settled into chairs, Joyce and I, with our backs to the dance floor.

With pretzels in front of me, I leaned back, my left arm around Joyce's shoulders, my right hand gripping a Budweiser. I felt a hand on my shoulder, looked up, and saw a man I didn't recognize. He wore a red cardigan over a white golf shirt and also held a Budweiser in his hand. "Great game," he said. "Can I buy you a beer?"

"No thanks, you never know when Coach McCutchan might pop in," I said, raising my longneck in a salute. Everyone guffawed.

"He's insufferable," Eddie said to the man, rolling his eyes at Joyce as if wondering how she put up with me. I grinned and nodded a thanks to the fan as he smiled and walked away.

Two couples sat down at a table to the right of me. They ordered a pitcher of beer and lit cigarettes. One of the guys tilted his head back to exhale a cloud of smoke, spotted me, and said to his companions, just loud enough for me to hear, "Hey, there's Grieger."

"That's me," I said, turning my head toward him.

"Hey," he said. "You guys were great tonight."

"Thanks," I said and turned back to my friends. Then, in a low voice, I added, "Redshirts everywhere," putting a hint of derision into my voice to hide how puffed it made me feel.

"You love it," Linzy said. "Much more of this and you'll get a swelled head."

"Much more?" Paxton said. "His hat size is already bigger than his waist."

"Not much chance of getting cocky around you guys, is there?" I said. "But, I gotta say, these people are nuts."

Later, after I dropped Joyce off at her house, I lay back on my bed and thought about how this Redshirt mania had grown to such enormous proportions. It was over the top last year but even more so this year. I admitted to myself that I lapped up the experiences that came with being an Ace, experiences only a very few people are lucky enough to have. I felt humbled that so many people opened their hearts and gave so fully of themselves so that I could run the court and express what artistry I had.

At the same time, I couldn't wrap my mind around it all, why they cared so much. I sensed that there was some connection between what fueled their passion and what drove me to such heights of exhilaration and despair. But what? *Dr. Grabill will help me figure this out,* I thought, then I turned onto my side and went to sleep.

• • •

I SHOWED UP EARLY FOR class on Monday so I could take a seat at the back of the room. I wanted to gather my thoughts before talking with Dr. Grabill. Students shuffled in, shed their coats, and settled in around me.

I opened my three-ring binder to jot down notes. Evansville had always been a sports-crazy town. I figured there must be some connection between that and the Redshirt phenomenon.

I remembered, as a kid, playing Little League, Pony League, and then Colt League baseball during summer days on ball fields complete with dugouts, outfield fences, and pitcher's mounds. We wore uniforms like those the big leaguers wore. On warm summer evenings, Mom and Dad would often take

Gary and me to watch the Evansville Braves Three I League baseball games at Bosse Field. There, nestled among five thousand other fans, we stuffed ourselves with hotdogs and peanuts still in their salty shells. At home, on other summer nights, we listened to Harry Caray, the voice of the St. Louis Cardinals, on the radio. My mom would sit at the dining-room table and keep a box score of what happened each inning. All of this didn't include the nighttime softball leagues for adults all over the city.

I recorded all these points, one after the other, in my binder. Then I listed all the other sports I could think of. There was high school football in the fall on Friday nights, dominated by the Reitz High Panthers, who beat up the other Evansville schools and regularly contended for state championships. Sometimes it got so cold at those games that the thermos of hot chocolate Mom brought barely kept our insides warm. Across the Ohio River in Kentucky, Evansvillians swarmed to thoroughbred racing at Dade Park on summer afternoons and harness racing at Audubon Park on spring evenings. Next I noted the public golf courses, Fendrick and Helfrich, crowded with thousands of Arnold Palmer wannabes, the summer playgrounds for kids run by the Evansville Recreation Department, the gambling on every conceivable sporting event through local bookies.

This took me to high school basketball, the epicenter of Evansville sports, the heart that had pumped excitement into every neighborhood throughout the city before the birth of the Aces mania. I wrote the words "Bosse—state champions in 1944 and 1945," then below that "The Central High Golden Bears," the team in the 1950s led by Jerry Clayton, which the whole community either supported or hated. It occurred to me that the Evansville College Purple Aces were merely one source of entertainment back then, hardly the most important or glamorous star in the Evansville sporting firmament.

While I wrote down these items, feigning taking notes by glancing up now and then, Dr. Grabill sat at his desk at the front of the room and read various scenes from *Macbeth* in dramatic fashion. He paid no attention to me, so I went back to my notebook.

Thinking of the Aces took me to Evansville College basketball. It was with the opening of Roberts Stadium on December 1, 1956, at the start of the 1956–1957 basketball season, that the Aces began their ascendancy. I remembered sitting high above the court on a bench seat, one of 10,500 fans watching the Aces battle the Purdue Boilermakers. That was the biggest crowd I had ever been in, and I was thrilled by the noise and color and passion in the stands.

That was the season that gave birth to the Redshirts. Coach McCutchan's wife, Virginia, gave him a pair of bright red socks as an early Christmas present to brighten his wardrobe. He wore the socks to a Holiday Tournament game. When the Aces won, he decided to keep wearing them. Fans across the court noticed the socks and decided to wear red as well. As the number of red socks in Coach's dresser multiplied, so did the number of people who wore red to the game. By season's end, the whole stadium looked as if a giant balloon filled with red paint had burst upon all those in attendance.

The opening of Roberts Stadium meant that the Aces were able to lure high-profile teams to Evansville with the promise of a huge payday and the expectation of an easy win. Instead of a paltry $250, Evansville College could now offer visiting teams a choice of $5000 or half the gate, whichever they chose. As the increased revenue attracted a higher caliber of competition, the competition brought better players to Evansville, which translated into increased victories. This in turn led to ever-growing enthusiasm and support for the Aces.

When the Aces captured back-to-back NCAA titles in 1959 and 1960, my junior and senior year in high school, the city's love affair with the Aces took off. Socialites scheduled events so as not to conflict with home games. Restaurants, movie houses, and bars sat three-quarters empty on game nights. Players took on a celebrity status. The stadium became the place to be and be seen. It seemed at this point that the city merged its identity with the Aces.

That was as far as I got by the time class ended. I understood that Evansville was a sports-obsessed town, one that took their games and teams seriously. But I knew that there had to be something else to it, something that would congeal all these thousands of people together as Redshirts and lift the Aces to the equivalent of a manic obsession. But what?

I walked with Dr. Grabill to his office after class. I knew he'd want to talk about the DePauw game, but he didn't know that I wanted to discuss the Redshirt insanity. He made his way down the hallway, bracing himself with his cane as he shuffled. He stepped into his office, careful not to trip on the books and papers that littered the floor, then dropped his textbook onto his desk with a thump before easing himself into his chair. He took a deep breath and let it out in a long sigh, as if to gather himself.

I jumped in before he could speak. "You Redshirts sure are crazy."

Dr. Grabill smiled. "You're just figuring that out, are you, Mr. Grieger?"

"Yep. I watched all that insanity at the stadium Saturday night and wondered why in the world all you people would carry on like that about a bunch of boys running around in their underwear."

"Well, I can see you've been using your brain for more than just jump shots and girls."

"I'm trying," I said, pursing my lips and nodding. Dr. Grabill was the first person to treat me as a person of intellect, well before I ever imagined that I might be. I enjoyed these conversations, but I also felt out of my element. He was the only professor who pushed me to think critically.

"Well then," he said, "so you want to understand the Redshirt phenomenon, do you?" He leaned back in his chair and clasped his hands in his lap. "Okay, let's see if we can get to the nut of it. You start. Why do you think we do it?" He waited.

"I don't know," I said, put back on my heels by his Socratic approach. "I suppose some are true basketball fans. They understand what's happening on the court and appreciate good basketball when they see it."

"Not bad," he said, nodding. "But you know as well as I that most of those people at the stadium don't know a whole lot about the ins and outs of basketball. Go a little deeper. What else could drive them?"

"Well, how about the entertainment factor? It's exciting; Hoosier Hysteria and all that. It beats going to the movies on a Saturday night."

"Okay?" Dr. Grabill fastened his eyes to mine, waiting for more.

I thought for a moment, feeling inept. "How about hero worship?" I finally said. "The Redshirts put us on a pedestal, like we're some kind of special beings. They stare at us when we're out in public, want to be in our presence, go out of their way to get us to pay attention to them."

"Now you're on the right track." Dr. Grabill leaned forward, his forearms on his knees, his hands clasped together. "But let's go one layer down. Put on your psychology hat. Why would a whole community worship a bunch of boys playing what's just a game, as you said?"

I thought for a minute and shifted in my chair. Nothing came to mind. "I don't know."

"Well, okay then, let me try to help. Besides life itself, what's the most precious thing that each of us owns?"

"Beer," I said and grinned. Dr. Grabill just sat there, unsmiling, waiting. I sat still, my mind a blank. Then I got it. "It's self-worth, isn't it?" I blurted with a titled head and wide eyes, recognizing the truth of what I'd just said the moment I said it.

"That's it!" Dr. Grabill sat up, his eyes intense, staring into mine. I knew something significant was coming.

"Look," he went on, "all people want to feel important, to be somebody, to think they and their lives have meaning. That is the deepest longing of the human spirit. You want to understand that Evansville's stuck down here at the toe of Indiana, the state's redheaded stepchild. What once made it important, the riverboat transportation of goods on the Ohio River, is long gone. Industry has dried up, the economy suffers. There's the big schools to the north—IU, Purdue, Notre Dame—and puny little Evansville College down here. Except for Bosse in 1962, high schools from Indianapolis on up have dominated basketball. So, guess where this community gets its self-esteem from?"

Dr. Grabill looked at me for a moment, letting all this sink in. Then he said, "They've become melded with the Aces, Russ, don't you see? As you do well, so do they. As you win, they do too."

"So it is all about self-esteem, isn't it!" I said, astounded by the thought.

"Exactly. It's intoxicating to be transported to that special place of being somebody."

"Don't tell me that applies to you as well?"

"You don't think I'm like them, do you?" He chuckled.

I sat there, nodding, awed.

"Okay then, there's something for you to think about." He turned to his desk to signal the end of the tutorial. "We'll talk soon, okay? I've got to prepare my next class."

I left Dr. Grabill's office and headed to Carson Center. I threaded between the limestone buildings, past others students, beneath barren trees. My eyes were open, but I didn't notice where I walked. All I could think about was what Dr. Grabill had explained to me.

Suddenly, with no warning, a truth hit me like a slap to my face. *Just as me and basketball are separate, so too are we Aces and the Redshirts. Though we may have defined each other as one before, it doesn't have to be that way any longer.*

I stood there, at Walnut Street, across from Carson Center, as if in a stupor. It was like one of those moments in a movie when the hero looks off into the distance, ethereal music comes up, and the scene dissolves from the present into the past. Only now, time seemed to stop dead, and I understood something faster than I ever had before.

I understood that we Aces did depend on the Redshirts. Without them, there would be no Roberts Stadium, no Aces basketball as we knew it, no richness and texture beyond the actual playing of the game. They made it possible for us to have all that, and we would forever be in their debt. But, in another way, we didn't need them. Once the game began, they receded from our focus, even our consciousness. They were separate from us. They provided a giant, writhing backdrop of color, motion, and sound, but we played the game for ourselves—indulging our competitive drives, frolicking in our boyish pleasures, rejoicing in our moment-to-moment creativity. We were the conductor and the orchestra, and we let the Redshirts sit in and listen to our music.

I don't know how long I stood there. A horn woke me from my reverie, and I picked my way across Walnut Street and into Carson Center. My mind raced with all these new realizations. But I had no idea how to make use of them. That would have to come later. Right now, I had to get into my practice togs and prepare for the next game.

# 17

## SOUTHERN ILLINOIS SURPRISE

I WALKED INTO CARSON CENTER the Monday before the Southern Illinois game to find Humes, Sloan, and Williams playing a game of H-O-R-S-E. Humes lofted a high-arching hook shot from near the sideline that skimmed the glass and slid into the basket.

"Are you kidding me?" said Sloan, who then missed his hook.

"H on you, big fella," said Williams.

Williams then dribbled to the basket, jumped up from a standstill, and slammed the ball two-handed through the basket.

Settling back to the court, he grinned at Humes and said, "Your turn."

I laughed along with Sloan, then picked up a basketball and dribbled the length of the court to the far basket. There Watkins worked his way around the perimeter, practicing his jumpers, one after another. I watched the smooth flip of his wrists as he released the ball from above his head, holding his shooter's pose till the ball made the net sing.

"The man!" I said to Watkins, who nodded and smiled.

Coach McCutchan walked to midcourt at precisely three o'clock. He blew his whistle and shouted, "Gather up, boys!"

We surrounded him, our shirts not yet damp, some holding a basketball on their hip, others cradling one against their belly with two arms. I noticed Sloan scuffing the centerline with the toe of his sneaker and could sense his urge to swing into action.

"Listen up," McCutchan said, rubbing his hand from his forehead back over his hair to his neck. "Southern Illinois is good. They have a six-foot-four forward named Walt Frazier who may be the best player we'll face all year. And their guards, George McNeil and David Lee, are both feisty and good shooters. We'll have our hands full."

"Yeah, that Wormy is good," said Sloan.

We all looked at him. "Wormy?" I said.

"That's what I nicknamed Lee when we played together in high school. Somehow he could worm through the smallest spaces on the way to the basket."

*Great*, I thought.

"Okay," said McCutchan. "We'll get all over them. But we're going to focus on ourselves, being the best we can be. If we play our game the way we can, we'll be okay."

*That's the closest he's come to an out-and-out pep talk*, I thought.

Coach then glanced around the circle and said, "Let's get to work, first defense to offense."

The scout team positioned themselves to simulate the SIU offense as we, the starters, got into our defensive positions. McCutchan blew his whistle and the subs angled and cut, eventually getting off a shot that bounced high off the back of the rim. Sloan leaped high, grabbed the ball with one of his massive hands, brought it down cradled between his palm and wrist, and slammed it to the court to dribble up the middle. Williams and Watkins filled the lanes while Humes and I trailed for an outlet pass should the initial thrust fail to produce a basket. The gym erupted in whoops and shouts when Williams took a pass from Sloan and laid the ball into the basket without breaking stride.

The subs restarted SIU's offense. Watkins deflected a pass into my hands near the sidelines, and I hustled the ball up court. Humes sprinted ahead and hipped and elbowed to establish position six feet in front of the basket, trying to position his defensive man behind him. The rest of us spread ourselves around the perimeter to open up passing lanes. I bounced a pass to Sloan on the right wing, and, in one motion, he caught it and flung it two-handed into Humes. Yellow shirts immediately surrounded him, and he tossed the ball out to an open Watkins on the left wing. Watkins floated a feathery jumper that hit nothing but net.

On our next possession, Watkins stood with the ball at his favorite spot on the left wing, facing the basket, his right foot anchored to the floor. He faked forward with his left foot, shoulder, and head, holding the ball behind him and to his right, deciding whether to take his jump shot or power to the basket. We all recognized the move and slid away from him to give him room to maneuver, each of us ready for a pass if he could not create his shot. When he dribbled to his right, my defender shaded toward him to block his path to the basket. Seeing this, he flipped the ball to me ten feet away. I caught the pass and, in one motion, sprung up and swished a jumper. It felt so good I wanted to call time-out and savor the feeling.

We repeated this process over and over, each possession smooth and crisp. At some point, while I ran the court, an image flashed through my mind that almost brought me to a standstill. It was a fleeting impression of the five of us, in our practice gear, dancing around a blazing fire, embers breaking free and spiriting upward toward a coal-black sky. Each of us high-stepped and gyrated, doing his own moves, though we still moved in perfect rhythm. It was as if our individual consciousness had disappeared and our nervous systems melded, down to our DNA.

*Holy Christ,* I thought, *where did that come from?*

I glanced at the other guys, wondering if they'd seen what I had. But they looked the same as always. Williams yipped and hooted like a kid on a playground. Humes glided as he ran, panther-like. Sloan thrust his body one way, then another, never letting up for an instant. Watkins, his body taut and eyes intent, ran up and down the court as if nothing mattered but winning the next possession.

Coach McCutchan must have also sensed something special happening between us. Beaming an uncharacteristic full smile, he blew his whistle and said, "That's enough for today, boys. We don't want to leave it here on the practice court. Go home. See you tomorrow."

As the Aces walked back to the locker room, I grabbed a basketball and dribbled toward the far basket.

"Don't you think you're good enough yet?" Sloan shouted over his shoulder as he walked from the court.

"Almost, but not yet," I yelled back.

Once the gym emptied, I sat down on the floor beneath the basket and leaned back against the concrete wall. From this level, the two side-by-side basketball courts looked enormous, the size of a football field. I stared at the waxy shine on the floor that gleamed all the more brightly without the distracting sounds of thumping basketballs, screeching rubber, and players yelling. I wondered if my voice would echo if I yelled.

I knew I had experienced something unusual, perhaps significant, and I wanted to truly grasp it before it got lost in my memory. I conjured up the starless night, the fire, the five of us dancing in a circle. Then I understood. What I realized was that the five of us—Sloan, Humes, Watkins, Williams, me—were each expressing something from deep within, but something that could only be realized alongside and with each other. I wasn't alone. I danced with others who heard the same music and felt the same beat as I did.

*Wow!* I thought. A sense of wonder spread through me. I smiled and thought, as if I had just found the Holy Grail, *I don't dance alone.*

Just as I was pushing myself up from the floor, Jerry Sloan walked back in the gym. "You still here?"

"Not for long."

I dribbled toward the locker room, the *thump, thump, thump* of the ball lost in the cavernous space. At the free-throw line, I flipped the ball toward the basket, not bothering to watch whether it went through the net or not.

"Just dance!" I said as I walked off the court.

•  •  •

WEDNESDAY NIGHT, JANUARY 20. THE massive black scoreboard hung high above the stadium's empty basketball court. Below, and all around, 12,123 red-shirted fans shimmered like a fiery sunset over the Ohio River.

At exactly eight o'clock, a grating sound called both teams to action. I walked with my teammates to center court and exchanged "good lucks" with the Southern Illinois Salukis, communicating with my expression and gestures that they were to be just another one of our victims. The surrounding throng stood and blasted their familiar cheer, "Aces, Aces," the power of its volume emphasizing my message.

Then the roof fell in.

The Salukis started hurricane strong, hitting eleven of their first twenty attempts while we clanged one shot after another off the rim. The peals of anticipation at the launch of each shot at the game's beginning morphed into a chorus of groans when the misfires continued to hit metal as the game progressed. It took more than eight minutes before Sam Watkins scored our first basket, making the score 22–7 in their favor.

I felt ham-handed. A few plays after Watkins's basket, Sloan sped past his defender and flipped the ball to me on the wing. I promptly missed my third straight jump shot. But I had little time to berate myself, since Southern Illinois's six-foot-one guard, David Lee, grabbed the rebound and dribbled the ball up court. Thin and wiry, he was quicksilver fast, just as Sloan had warned, both on his feet and with his hands. As he closed in on me, I watched his dark eyes survey the court, deciding which direction to attack. I crouched low, legs spread. When he switched the ball from his right hand to his left, I reached to swat it away, only to swish air. He quickly crossed the ball back to his right hand and drove toward the basket. Stride for stride we ran together, so close I could hear him breathe, until he jumped, my hand in his face, and sank an incredible twenty-footer, his third of the game.

*Dammit,* I thought, my jaw tight and my face expressionless so as not to give him the satisfaction of seeing my frustration.

Had I been less self-critical, I would have noticed that not one of my teammates had slacked off. Sloan kept on the balls of his feet, playing defense, contending for rebounds, and slashing at the ball as if civilization depended on it. Williams jumped and bumped for every rebound, conceding nothing to our maroon-shirted tormentors without a fight. Humes positioned himself deep under the basket to get his defender behind him, doing his best to get open for an inlet pass. Watkins, steely-eyed as always, crowded his man on defense and continued to take his shots as if he knew the law of averages would soon turn in his favor.

I stole a quick look at the scoreboard. *Southern Illinois 26–Aces 11,* the clock blinking from 8:01 to 8:00. That's when it all came together, as if the basketball gods had decided to take the lid off our basket. In the final few minutes of the half, Humes and Sloan each scored after a steal. Humes then added two free throws and, in our next possession, rebounded a missed shot into the basket. Watkins followed by grabbing an offensive rebound and converting his short jumper. To end the half, I laid the ball in on a fast break just before the buzzer, my one and only score.

The applause that escorted us off the court was as much out of relief as appreciation. I glanced over my shoulder at the scoreboard: 39–36, Salukis. We had outscored them 25–13 since the eight-minute mark, Humes alone accounting for thirteen.

Not one of us said a word when we walked into our locker room, sweat-drenched and spent. Team managers distributed Cokes and towels. With our legs outstretched and our arms dangling at our sides, we knew we had fought back from being stone dead, that it would be a struggle the rest of the way.

This sobering thought hung over the room when Coach McCutchan walked in and made his way to the blackboard. He slashed a few lines in white chalk to illustrate adjustments he wanted us to make. Then he took off his black horn-rimmed glasses and swiped his forehead with the back of his hand. "Boys, I'm proud of the way you fought back out there," gesturing toward the door with a sweep of his hand. "But this game won't be won with x's and o's. It's about what's inside of you. I know what you're made of, so go get it."

To start the second half, Sam Watkins hit two quick baskets that pushed us ahead for the first time, 40–39. Then the lead switched hands thirteen times in the next fifteen minutes. While Watkins, Humes, and Williams carried the scoring load, my shots continued to miss the mark, and my defense failed to stop their guards.

We trailed 70–69 when the game clock blinked from 5:01 to 5:00. *Crunch time!* I thought. The Redshirts must have agreed, for they stood and cheered as I dribbled the ball over the centerline. It sounded like a plea as much as encouragement.

At the top of the key, I spied an opening and sliced toward the basket. The man guarding Watkins stepped over to head me off, and I dropped a bounce pass to Sam, who popped in his twenty-footer. Evansville, 71–70. In quick succession, Humes then cashed in a follow-up, Watkins drilled another twenty-footer, and Humes knocked in a pair of free throws to make it 77–70 with 3:35 left in the game. The roar that had started at the five-minute mark escalated with each successive point to the level where it felt like the stadium would explode.

We had experienced moments like this many times before, moments when teams had given us their best shot, only to be broken in the end by our superior talent and relentless pressure. We would see it in their darting eyes and their slumped shoulders. Sometimes these moments came early, other times later. But I saw no surrender in the eyes of these Salukis from Southern Illinois. As my teammates ran by on their way back to play defense, I shook my fist at one and then another, sending the message, *Don't let up. It's not over.*

David Lee promptly dribbled up the court and drilled another twenty-foot rainbow. *Shit!* The next time down the court, he sank two free throws after I fouled him. *Dammit.* He then stripped the ball from Sloan at midcourt, dribbled hard to the basket, and drew Jerry's fifth foul. His two free throws narrowed our lead to 77–76 with 2:26 showing on the clock. The silence in the stadium felt oppressive as Sloan took his seat on the bench, replaced by Ron Johnson.

Each point Lee had scored stung me like a slap to the face. He and I had now tussled against each other, possession after possession, for almost forty minutes.

I had my shots but couldn't connect. I couldn't help but feel embarrassed at my paltry output—two measly points and two puny rebounds. I not only felt inept and inconsequential, but, worse, humiliated. I knew nothing else to do but tell myself, *Keep your head in the game; you can kick yourself later,* knowing full well that I would. I forgot all about dancing.

I brought the ball up court. Lee crowded me as I zipped the ball to Watkins. Trying desperately to steal the ball, Saluki Joe Ramsey committed his fifth foul, and Watkins dropped the first of his two free throws. Aces, 78–76. Watkins then pulled down a missed Saluki shot, was again fouled, and made one of his two free throws to extend our lead to 79–76. Thirty-nine seconds glared on the clock.

As we retreated back down the court, I screamed, "Don't foul! Don't foul!"

David Lee hustled the ball across the centerline. I played him tight, figuring that, if he was going to score, he'd have to do it with me in his face. He passed the ball to a teammate who probed for an opening before tossing it back to Lee. He then launched a desperate jumper from way beyond the free-throw arc that somehow found the net to close our lead to 79–78. Only twelve seconds remained.

Before I had time to slump my shoulders and curse at myself, Southern Illinois's Randy Goins picked off our inbound pass and banked in a layup to shove Southern Illinois ahead 80–79.

Coach McCutchan jumped off the bench and called time-out, the clock frozen with nine seconds remaining. The ebullience coming from the Redshirts only minutes before dimmed to a low murmur of disbelief, the dream of an undefeated season seemingly dead before their eyes.

We gathered around McCutchan in front of our bench, Jerry Sloan slouching helplessly at the outside of the huddle. I felt emotionless, whether composed or in shock I didn't know. In his strong voice, Coach told each of us exactly what to do, pointing dynamically over our shoulders at the court, as if we were alone in Carson Center.

"Got it?" he asked. We nodded. "Okay, go do it."

The referee blew his whistle and handed the ball to me under the basket. I took a deep breath and threw it over the head of a Saluki to Watkins, just short of midcourt near the scorer's table. He dribbled twice, leaped into the air just past the centerline, and slung the ball two-handed from above his head to Humes near the foul line. Larry pivoted and cut to the basket, half stumbled as he dribbled, recovered, and, twisting between two Saluki defenders, lofted a short running shot from off his fingertips in front of the basket. His momentum carried him under the backboard, as Watkins, Williams, and I crowded in front, ready to tip the ball in should Larry's shot roll off the rim.

The ball hit the back of the rim just where the flange attaches to the backboard. It bounced four times, for three whole seconds, tantalizing everyone in the building. Along with almost thirteen thousand other people, I stood and watched, waiting to see if it would break our hearts or theirs. With two ticks left on the clock, the ball dropped passively through the net.

The Redshirts erupted with a thunderclap that sustained itself for minutes.

The Aces' bench stormed the court and lofted Humes onto their shoulders, everyone jumping and shouting like teenage girls at a Beatles concert. Larry covered his eyes to hide his tears. We ran together off the court through a thicket of euphoric fans who had flooded to the tunnel to yell their hurrahs, pound our backs, and tousle our hair.

"We did it, dammit, we did it!" I said to no one in particular.

•  •  •

WE BARELY GOT SETTLED BEFORE the locker room filled with exultant fans. Humes stood in the back corner surrounded by a three-deep circle of well-wishers. With the widest smile I had ever seen on him, he said, "That was the best shot I ever made. I just stood there and watched it and prayed it would drop."

Opposite him, across the room, stood Coach McCutchan, still dapper in his checkered sport coat and black tie, looking at the stat sheet and talking before a tight semicircle of reporters, each jotting notes on a scratchpad. Across the room, I spotted Watkins and Williams sitting next to each other, looking up and accepting plaudits from the fans.

I sat next to Sloan, my uniform soaked and clinging to my body. People passed by, saying, "Great game." I felt drained, my mood a strange mixture of exhilaration and dejection. The relative lack of attention paid to Sloan and me reflected our contribution.

I leaned over to Jerry and said, "I sucked."

"You're not the only one," he replied.

Just then, sportswriter Al Dunning stuck his head between Sloan and myself and asked me, "Was David Lee the best guard you've played against this year?" All told, he had scored twenty points, along with Frazier's nineteen.

Anger flashed through me, and I looked in his eyes to see if he was taunting me. I wanted to say, "Screw you, and screw him," but I knew better.

"Yeah, he was, right up there with Larry Sheffield from Notre Dame," I said.

I turned to Sloan and said, "I gotta get out of here."

"Race you out."

I quickly dressed and made my way from the stadium to Rotherwood Avenue, a quiet neighborhood street where I used to make out with young ladies in high school. I didn't want to deal with my parents, my fraternity brothers, or even Joyce. I figured it was as good a place as any to brood. I pulled under a giant oak in front of a darkened house and, letting the car idle for warmth, settled back in my seat. Without warning, the image of my high school sweetheart, Jeanne, flashed through my mind, along with the smell of Shalimar, the feel of cashmere, the taste of lipstick. I floated along with these memories, my melancholy giving way to feelings of comfort and warmth.

Just then, I caught the reflection of car lights in the rearview mirror. Instinctively, I hunched down in my seat. Back in the day, I lived in fear of a police car pulling alongside and shining a spotlight into the car.

This startled me back to the moment. I thought about the game, replaying in my mind all my missed shots and failed defensive efforts. I pummeled myself with recriminations fit for a serial killer: *You should have made that bucket! How pitiful was that! Lee made you look inept!* My mood soured once again.

My mind then flashed to the final play of the game. I pictured the five of us executing McCutchan's strategy to perfection, first my pass to Watkins, then his to Humes, and finally Humes laying the ball into the basket, all of this in one flowing motion.

This reminded me of the vision I'd had at practice just two days before, my Aces teammates and I dancing around a huge roaring fire. I smiled, thinking that's exactly what we had done at the end of the game. "We danced," I whispered out loud.

I sat there for a moment, then sat up, put the car in gear, and picked up speed. As I pulled alongside Art and Helen's, I heard the heavy rock beat vibrating through the wall. I snuck a look in the rearview mirror to tidy my hair and caught the reflection of my eyes. I held my gaze, nodded at myself, and then said, "Just dance, dammit!"

# 18

## DEPAUW AND MORE

SUNDAY MORNING, THE LAST DAY of January, 1965. I laid in bed, clutching the covers tight under my chin. A sliver of sunshine snuck under the blinds and sliced across my face. My clothes on the floor were saturated with the acrid smell of smoke. My mouth felt dry, my eyes burned, and I had a headache, no doubt the result of staying so late at Art and Helen's the night before.

After our scare against Southern Illinois, the Aces had dispatched two more opponents, both at Roberts Stadium. On Saturday, January 23, we'd trounced the Ball State Cardinals, 117–81, with all five starters scoring in double figures. Last night, we'd beat Valparaiso University, the final margin of 83–78 not a true indication of our superiority. Sports editor Tony Chamblain wrote that our domination in these two games was so complete that Coach McCutchan's "sole duties consisted of talking to reporters and making sure the subs got in the game." Our record climbed to 16–0.

I'd just rolled onto my side, burrowed my head into my pillow, and pulled the covers over my eyes when I heard the telephone ring in the dining room. *Oh, no*, I thought. A moment later, Mom scratched her fingernails on my door and stuck her head in. "Gene's on the phone. Want to take it?"

"I guess," I said, throwing back the covers. I shuffled past Dad at the dining-room table. He smiled, holding his coffee cup up as a salute, and I raised my hand as I picked up the telephone. The smell of toast and bacon spiked my hunger.

"Have you seen the newspaper?" Gene asked.

"No," I answered, the thought racing through my mind that either something had happened to one of our fraternity brothers or maybe there was an article criticizing my performance last night.

"Cook's Barbecue is having an all-you-can-eat chicken special tonight. Want to catch it?"

"You bet," I said, relaxing, grateful for the opportunity to focus on life outside basketball for the day.

Before Evansville had assumed its identity as "The Home of the Aces," it had flirted with "The Barbecue Capital of the World." Mac's Barbecue on the west side reigned as king, but Cook's, along with numerous neighborhood bars dotting the city, competed for supremacy.

Sitting with Dad at the dining-room table, a glass of orange juice in my hand, I could taste the tang of Evansville barbeque. It had a robust, husky flavor that gripped the palette like a firm handshake. My favorite meal consisted of a slab of ribs sided by Mom's German potato salad. Nobody talked much during these meals. We gnawed on the ribs as we would an ear of corn, slurped sauce from our fingers without regard for civility, and dropped stripped bones into brown grocery bags Mom sat next to each of our chairs. We always ended these meals with a huge triangle of banana cream pie, its graham-cracker crust moist and gooey from sitting all day on the kitchen counter.

Gene pulled up in front of the house at five o'clock and beeped his horn. We made our way west on Washington Avenue, a short trip to Cook's that served as a mini-tour of my early life. We first passed Ross Center, a block-long strip mall with a hardware store, a dry cleaners, and a men's clothing store. On one end was Ross Theater, the neighborhood movie house where I'd taken in Saturday-afternoon double features as a kid. On the other end was H. A. Woods Drugstore, the sponsor of my Little League team.

A half-mile down the road, we came to Washington Elementary School, a huge, two-story, redbrick building. At its entrance, four Georgian-style columns rose from the ground to the roof, giving it a majestic aura. Behind it sprawled the massive playground where I'd spent my high school summers supervising a peewee baseball league. Blistered by the merciless sun, I'd umpired interminable games. The pitchers couldn't throw strikes, outfielders couldn't catch flies, and infielders couldn't field grounders. Sometimes I'd call strike three on a batter even though the ball sailed a foot over his head just to end an inning.

Farther down Washington we came to Bosse High. As we drove by, I pictured the nicked and scuffed floors, the dented lockers, and the tiny practice gym on the second floor where I'd cut my basketball teeth. I wished I could go back and do it all over again.

Just past Bosse, we turned left onto Highway 41, a major thoroughfare that divided Evansville east from west and led south over the Ohio River into Kentucky. Cook's Barbecue sat two blocks down, a square, white-plaster building distinguished by its wide rectangular front window which contained a large neon sign that blinked *Cook's Barbecue* in bold red script.

Gene and I entered to find ourselves the only customers. Square tables sat throughout the dining room, each table with a red-checkered tablecloth and four armless chairs with red vinyl seats and backs. Music crackled from speakers mounted ceiling level in opposite corners of the room, but not loud enough to drown out the eighteen-wheelers that accelerated past the window. The aroma of barbecue saturated the air.

No one greeted us, so we sat at a table close to the metal swinging doors that led to the kitchen. "Anybody home?" I called out.

Within seconds, a short, squat woman walked through the doorway. She wore a white dress, white shoes, and a red-checked apron that covered half her bulk. Without her apron, she could have passed for a nurse.

"Let me get you a menu," she said, smiling.

"Don't bother," Gene said. "We want the barbeque chicken special."

Minutes later, the waitress placed a plate in front of each of us, both containing two pieces of chicken, a leg and a thigh, coleslaw, and a pickle spear. She turned to walk away.

"Stay handy," Gene said, chuckling.

We gobbled our two pieces of chicken, shoveled down our coleslaw, and munched on our pickles.

I caught the waitress's eye as she leaned against the wall by the kitchen door, waved, and pointed at my plate. She nodded and brought a plate with four more pieces of chicken, two legs and two thighs.

"You boys sure are hungry," she said, smiling before walking away.

Then the drama began.

"More chicken, please."

She brought a plate with four more pieces, this time two legs and two wings, but no words or smiles.

"More chicken, please."

This time she brought only two legs.

"More chicken."

She delivered two lonely wings.

"I think she's pissed," I said to Gene.

"I care," he said.

Gene started to signal for more chicken when the door opened and in walked Dad. I thought that maybe Mr. Cook had called him to complain.

Dad sat down and looked at the plate of bones piled high at the center of the table. "Good Lord," he said.

"Your son did the damage," Gene said. "I only had a couple pieces."

"What are you doing here?" I asked.

"Joe Celania just called. He said he wants to tape an interview to be aired on his Saturday-morning TV program. He sounded pretty anxious to nail this down."

"No kidding."

"Yeah, he wants you to call to schedule a time," Dad said and motioned for the waitress to come over.

"Can he use the telephone?" he asked her, pointing to me.

"Only if he stops eating," she said.

I followed the waitress behind the counter to the phone a few feet from the table. As I dialed, Gene said, "Ask if you can bring chicken to the interview."

Joe and I arranged to meet next Friday morning, two days after our Wednesday night DePauw game and the day before the Aces were to play Indiana State in Terre Haute.

"What's the focus of the interview?" I asked.

"The angle I had in mind was your psychology training, you know, you being the psychologist on the team, stuff like that."

When I returned to the table, Dad sat with a bottle of Budweiser in front of him.

"Want to join us?" I asked.

"I think he does," Gene said as the waitress brought Dad a plate loaded with two pieces of chicken, a leg and a thigh, coleslaw, and a pickle spear.

• • •

THREE DAYS LATER, WEDNESDAY, FEBRUARY 3, the Aces caravanned to Greencastle, Indiana, to play the DePauw Tigers. We hummed north on Highway 41 under a cloudless blue sky, past naked trees, and through tiny hamlets with beguiling names like Haubstadt, Patoka, and Brazil. Neither I nor my teammates had any idea of what awaited us that night.

Dressed in our traveling uniforms, we left our locker room and walked down a narrow hallway toward the court. The *boom, boom, boom* of a huge drum pounded our eardrums on the way but did not soften the boos and catcalls that bombarded us when we stepped onto the court.

Bowman Gym was crammed to the rafters, mostly with boisterous students still angry from the 117–88 pasting we had given their Tigers three weeks earlier. The first row of seats crowded so close to the floor that hostile students could trip, grab, or claw at us if they wanted. I couldn't spot one inch of spare space, either in the stands or at the four exits, where people stood five across and three deep. It felt like we were trapped inside a box of Crackerjacks.

Ten minutes before game time, Coach motioned us to our locker room for final instructions. A chorus of catcalls ushered us off the court. As we wormed through a gaggle of people, one fan, wearing a gray DePauw sweatshirt and sporting peachy stubble on his chin, stuck his face in front of mine and hissed, "You shitheads gonna show us something tonight?"

And, by God, we did. We walked out of the locker room, eyes steely, no one clapping, jumping, or backslapping, in fact happy for the extra motivation this hostility stimulated. I could feel the power of our collective wills pushing us toward the court like a machine that would crush anything and everything in its path.

Herb Williams stepped to the centerline, coiled and wide-eyed. The referee tossed the ball up, and Williams tipped it forward to Jerry Sloan, who leaped and batted it sideways to Larry Humes on his run to the basket. Humes caught the ball, took two dribbles, and gracefully laid it off the glass and into the basket. Aces, 2–0.

Following four straight baskets, two by Sloan and two by Humes, the Aces opened up a 15–7 lead six minutes into the game, then expanded it to ten midway through the first half. Williams and Sloan grabbed every rebound in sight, pivoting without hesitation to find one of us to start a blistering fast break. Each of us popped jumper after jumper with the regularity of a metronome.

With six minutes left in the half, Humes banked in a long hook from so near the sideline that he stumbled into the bleachers on his follow-through. Fans pushed him back onto the court. A little later, Watkins drilled a twenty-foot jumper from the left side that popped up the net. I did the same from the right side off the dribble. A sprinkling of applause followed a fast-break basket by Williams on a perfect bounce pass from Sloan.

"You hear that?" I said to Watkins as we stood behind the free-throw arc waiting for Williams to shoot his free throw.

"Hear what?" he said.

"They're starting to cheer us. Can you believe it?"

Before Watkins could respond, Williams hit his free throw and play resumed.

We hit ten of our first fourteen shots to start the second half and extended our first-half lead of 56–35 first to 72–49, then to 92–67. With 5:30 left in the game, Coach McCutchan motioned down the bench. The second-teamers threw off their warm-up robes and reported together to the scorer's table, the first time he'd substituted all game.

Walking off the court with my teammates, I saw something that made my jaw drop. First a few, then more, and then all those formally hostile DePauw fans stood, faced our bench, and gave us an ovation that lasted well over a minute. Action did not resume until they settled down.

Watkins and I raised our eyebrows at each other.

Sloan elbowed me in the ribs. "Unbelievable."

Williams leaned forward and looked down the bench at the four of us. "Ain't we something?"

Once the crowd quieted, we settled back and watched our teammates finish the game. I knew that something extraordinary had just happened. I had never heard of a team being given a standing ovation by the fans of the team they had just beaten to a pulp.

Near the end of the game, I looked to my left at Sloan and McCutchan, then to my right at Humes, Watkins, and Williams. They all sat silently, watching the action on the court. I felt a wave of pride flow through me. I felt bonded with them for life.

• • •

TWO DAYS LATER, ON FRIDAY morning, I met Joe Celania at the local CBS studio to record his Saturday-morning TV show. Joe stood five foot ten, had the rugged body of a football linebacker, and wore his wavy, jet-black hair cropped short over a handsome, square face. Off the air, he had the reputation of being one of the better softball pitchers in Evansville, flinging a mean fastball and a wicked dropper. He oozed athleticism from every pore.

He led me from the claustrophobic reception area, with its miniature desk and blond receptionist, down a dingy, windowless hallway lined with file cabinets. We finally reached a large recording studio, which was still dark and chilly from not being used that day.

Joe flicked on the lights, and I scanned the room to get my bearings.

It looked like a large, unfinished basement. To the left was a desk and two swivel chairs on a raised platform that I recognized as the evening news set. Two cameras, each mounted on rollers, stood alone and motionless on the concrete floor, pointing toward the desk. On the right side of the room was a man's den. A brown leather chair sat at a right angle to a matching leather couch. A giant swordfish that looked as if it had been ordered from Field & Stream hung on the wall behind the couch. Before the couch sat a coffee table littered with a handful of magazines. The leather made a scrunching sound as I sat down, and I wondered if I'd have to sit stone still when the filming began.

Once we settled, overhead klieg lights clicked on so bright I could feel their heat. I had done these interviews several times before, but I still felt the same nervousness I did before a game.

Joe arranged his papers on his lap. "Ready?" When I nodded, he looked into the camera and introduced me. Several other people now stood behind the camera, one holding a clipboard and a pencil.

Joe started: "Basketball wisdom tells us that a team can only go as far as its guards take it. With the Aces sporting a perfect seventeen-and-oh record going into tonight's Indiana State game, you and Sam have certainly proven that to be true."

"Well, it doesn't hurt to have All-American Jerry Sloan and about-to-be All-American Larry Humes on the first team," I said.

"I think you're being a little too modest." Looking at his notes, he cited Watkins's and my statistics, Sam's more impressive than mine.

Back and forth we went, Joe making pithy statements or asking open-ended questions, me responding as if I held some store of wisdom the world needed. As we continued, I relaxed and started to enjoy myself.

Some thirty minutes in, Joe turned to the camera and said, "As you Aces fans know, Russ is studying psychology at Evansville College, and I thought we should tap a little into his training."

*Here it comes*, I thought.

He then turned to me and said, "Okay, Dr. Russ, put on your psychologist hat. The Aces are undefeated, unanimously ranked number one in the nation, and favorites to win the NCAA Championship. Not to get too far ahead of ourselves, but what is it that makes you guys so great?"

Joe couldn't have known, but this is exactly what I had pondered for a while, starting with our road trip to South Dakota and ending with the standing ovation at DePauw two nights before. Yet I feared I would sound heretical if I shared my thoughts publicly.

"Well, lots of things," I said, starting off on safe ground. "It begins first with our coach, Arad McCutchan."

"That's for sure."

"Then we have two great players in Sloan and Humes, and a couple of pretty darn good ones in Watkins and Williams."

"Don't forget Grieger," he threw in.

"Kinda set that up, didn't I?" I said, shifting on the couch and making a loud scrunching noise.

We both laughed.

I went on to lay out the rest of it, all true, but lifted from the official basketball cliché manual—we had a great offensive and defensive system; we accepted our roles and performed them to the best of our abilities without rancor or jealousy; we looked out for each other so that, when one guy was off, the others did what they could to pick up the slack; we cared about and respected each other.

"I think you've just given us a team-building clinic," Joe said, taking a sip of coffee from the cup sitting at his side.

I knew I had. But I also knew that I wasn't being forthcoming, that this was the moment to take a risk. I took in a deep breath and, before I had a chance to hold back, asked, "Can I add something?"

"You betcha."

I glanced at the people behind the camera, all of whom seemed to be staring at me with soulless eyes. The room took on the silence of a tomb.

"Well," I said, "what I think really makes this team great is that we play basketball for ourselves, selfishly."

Joe scooted to the front of his chair and leaned forward. With a quizzical look on his face, he said, "Selfish? That's about the last word I'd ever use to describe you Aces."

"Maybe that's not the right word," I said, "but what I mean is that we all love playing the game so much that there's no other place we'd rather be than on the court. It's like, when we're playing, especially when we're grooving, like at DePauw the other night, it's like we're totally alone on the court and nothing else matters for us except the playing."

"You get into a zone," Joe said, pulling out a sports cliché.

"I guess," I said, feeling emboldened, "but it's more than that." I too scooted to the front of the couch and leaned forward toward Joe, my elbows on my knees. "On the count, it's like we're in our own little world, playing for ourselves. It's very personal. It's like we're all alone, playing to win, but also for the pure joy of doing it. We do it, and we welcome you all along on the ride."

I shot a glance at the people behind the camera. They just looked at me, no one laughing or rolling their eyes. Joe sat back, either waiting for me to go on or not knowing what to say.

"I guess that sounded kind of crazy," I said, leaning back myself, feeling a little uneasy, wondering if I'd gone too far.

"Well, that's certainly not your run-of-the-mill jock talk. I asked for psychology and I sure got it."

"You sure did."

"Well then, let me ask you this. You said you let us go along for the ride. I presume you meant the Redshirts?"

"Yes, the Redshirts, and everybody else. Maybe it's like a giant bull's-eye. We're at the center, playing on the court, in the game; that's ours alone, doing our thing. Then the Redshirts are in the next ring out. Then in the outer ring comes all the rest—the media, the pollsters, and all that. It's all one bull's-eye, for sure, but it's that center circle, where we play for ourselves, that makes us great, I think."

One of the people behind the camera held up two fingers. Joe glanced at her and, without missing a beat, asked, "Have you talked to any of your teammates about this?"

"No," I said. "They'd laugh me out of the gym." I threw him a sheepish look. "Can we keep this between just the two of us?"

He laughed as I slouched back into the leather couch, having nothing more to say.

At the end of the hour, Joe thanked me and said his goodbyes to the camera. The klieg lights clicked off. I felt keyed up but drained, much as I did after a game.

"That sure was interesting," Joe said as he leaned forward to shake my hand.

"Well," I said, pursing my lips, "I hope I didn't offend anybody with my last comments. Maybe I went too far."

"No, you did good. It was just what I was after. And good luck tomorrow at Indiana State."

"Thanks." As I walked out of the studio, I wondered if I'd be a target of ridicule come Saturday.

•  •  •

THE INTERVIEW WITH JOE CELANIA aired the Saturday morning of February 6, my twenty-third birthday. That night we trounced Indiana State on their home court in Terre Haute, 97–76. With hot shooting and a sticky full-court press, we jumped into an early 12–3 advantage and led comfortably at halftime,

52–34. All five starters scored at least a dozen points, led by Humes's thirty and followed by Watkins's twenty-one and Sloan's nineteen. Williams and I each tallied thirteen. It was our eighteenth game without a loss.

The next evening, Gene drove me and three of our fraternity brothers to Cook's to again feast on their all-you-can-eat barbeque chicken special. This Sunday, though, half the tables already held patrons. A different waitress than before greeted us.

She placed menus in front of us and said, "Let me get you some water and then I'll take your orders."

"No need for that," Gene said. "We all want the barbeque chicken special."

"Sorry, guys," she said. "We took that off the menu."

"No way!" I said. "It was great. What happened?"

"Yeah, well," she said, "a couple of guys came in last Sunday and ate so much chicken Mr. Cook realized he couldn't make money on the deal."

"No shit," Gene said.

"No shit," she echoed and walked away.

# 19

## FIVE GAMES, FIVE SNAPSHOTS

O N WEDNESDAY, FEBRUARY 10, THE day of the St. Joseph's game, I settled in the back corner of the room for my psychopathology class. I expected to be bored by yet another in a series of useless lectures. My professor had a balding head, drooping jowls, and a rounded stomach that protruded from the front of his rumpled suit. He spoke without life or drama and had yet to offer even one morsel of information not drawn from the textbook. I glanced out the window and spied two of my fraternity brothers tossing a football on the grassy lawn below and wished I could join them.

Right then, in walked a man who perfectly fit the stereotype of a practicing shrink. He wore khakis, a dark-brown corduroy jacket, and a neatly trimmed goatee like that of Sigmund Freud.

Introduced as an expert on the treatment of addiction, this visitor mesmerized me with case studies that revealed how compelling is the alcoholic's desperation for drink. He paced slowly across the front of the room, telling the stories of an insurance agent unable to stop drinking despite his doctor's warning that he'd die within a year from liver disease, a mother of two who lost her parental rights because of alcoholism, an engineer who embezzled money to support his habit. He spoke of broken families, lost careers, and incarcerations, all the result of people so alcohol dependent that the horrific consequences of their actions mattered not one whit to them.

I listened, rapt, too captivated with what this man was saying to take notes. He spoke with enthusiasm, as if he loved his job. I saw in front of me the living, breathing embodiment of what I wanted to do with my life.

I couldn't help but connect what this man said to my immersion in basketball. He talked about the alcoholic being powerless to resist the bottle, and I thought about how compelled I was to run the court and shoot a basketball. When he talked about the alcoholic's damaged sense of self, I recognized how I had lost myself in basketball, so much so that Russ and the basketball player had become one and the same. He talked about the euphoric effect the alcoholic found in the booze, and, in the same way, I realized how I had come to depend on the elation that basketball gave me.

He took a breath, then clapped his hands together and said, "Okay, let's take a look at how to get these people sober."

He jabbed the air with his hand and laid out the strategies for addiction treatment. He introduced the tools for defeating denial, embracing sobriety, and slaying the inner demons that drive it all. He emphasized that the addict would never be free of the craving but could learn to manage it with a "one day at a time" philosophy.

*One day at a time*, I repeated to myself. I knew I had come a long way in rehabbing my dependency to basketball. Maybe I could never completely rid myself of this monster, but perhaps I should think about fighting it one day at a time.

Class ended. I walked to the front of the room, right up to the speaker. "Hey, thanks," I said. "That was great."

"You're welcome." When I turned to leave, I felt his hand on my elbow. "Go get 'em tonight," he added.

"I will," I said, neither of us realizing that at that moment he fanned the embers of my addiction.

I walked out of the building and snapped my purple letter jacket close at my collar. I felt invigorated and free of the game-day jitters I had carried into class. It crossed my mind that the Aces lived the principle of recovery; we actually did take each game, even each practice, one at a time. The thought added bounce to my step.

That night the Aces assembled in the locker room minutes before tip-off. No one spoke. We starters stripped off our warm-ups. The subs slipped on their floor-length satin robes, each in a lustrous color, either blue, red, green, yellow, or silver.

Coach McCutchan, natty in a brown tweed sport coat, called us to order and reviewed what he wanted us to do that night. Once finished, he tossed his chalk to the student manager standing in the corner. "Okay, boys, let's go do it."

"Yeah, one game at a time," I blurted.

"One game at a time, hell," said Sloan. "Let's kick ass."

We set a frantic pace from the opening tip, pouncing on the Pumas like wolves devouring a defenseless rabbit. St. Joseph's rarely got more than one shot at the basket. We ran our offense fluid and relentless. When we weren't cashing in on a fast break, we got the ball down low to Humes, who twisted and contorted for layups or short jumpers that left me asking myself, *How'd he do that?*

We led 38–22 thirteen minutes into the game and then 51–34 at halftime. We built the lead to 61–35 only three minutes deep in the second half and then to 98–69. The final score read a whopping 103–73. Humes's thirty-eight points dwarfed my fourteen and Watkins's ten. I felt smooth and graceful all game as I swished seven out of twelve field-goal attempts, all from long range. Sloan played defense as if he were high on amphetamines and attacked the boards as if every rebound belonged to him. Before game's end, he had grabbed twenty-nine rebounds to complement his twenty-six points.

Afterward, the locker room filled to bursting. Fans wedged past each other to backslap, high-five, and recall memorable plays. A behemoth of a man wearing a red V-neck sweater, which did nothing to hide his world-class beer belly, yelled, "Nineteen down, five to go!"

Sitting to my right, Herb Williams bellowed, "No way! One game at a time!" and shot me a grin.

On my left, Sloan elbowed me in the ribs and said, "Happy now?"

·  ·  ·

I WALKED ONTO THE CARSON Center court the Thursday before the Butler game. There stood a tall, lanky man, looking to be in his late twenties. He had black hair that hung long in back and bushy over his ears, hippie-like, but wore a blue double-breasted blazer, a white dress shirt starched and open at the collar, and tan slacks with a sharp crease. His left hand rested casually in his pants pocket, giving him the air of a young Cary Grant. *This guy's not from Evansville*, I thought.

Coach tooted his whistle to gather us around him. "Boys," he said, "this here is Frank Deford. He's from *Sports Illustrated*, and he's going to write a story about us."

By this time, the Aces were used to national recognition, having already been featured in *Time, Newsweek, The Sporting News,* and *Ebony.* But *Sports Illustrated* was the premier sports magazine of the day, the magazine I devoured each week, reading about my heroes: Mickey Mantle, Arnold Palmer, and Bob Pettit. I had even saved the magazine's first issue, published in 1954, with Milwaukee slugger Eddie Matthews on the cover.

Turning to Deford, Coach said, "Say hello to the Aces, Frank."

"Hi, guys," he said in a confident tone. "I've heard a lot about you, and I'm looking forward to seeing you in action." Looking toward McCutchan, he said, "And don't worry, Coach, I won't get in anybody's way. I sure don't want to run those Armory steps."

Along with Frank Deford, a raucous crowd of 12,500 red-clad fanatics greeted the Aces the night of Saturday, February 13. It was Family Night, when we were to escort our parents to midcourt for the Redshirts to show their appreciation.

After warm-ups, we congregated with our parents off court. When it was my turn, the public address announcer said, "With their son, Russ, I present Mr. and Mrs. Russ Grieger." I walked onto the court between Mom and Dad, each lacing an arm through one of mine. I could feel Mom's grip tighten, and I wondered if she felt nervous like me or was just making sure she didn't trip in her high heels.

Once we got to half-court, a cheerleader handed Mom a dozen roses. She smiled that sweet smile of hers, the one she had greeted me with thousands of times before. I wanted to pull the three of us together for a group hug but thought better of it and settled for giving her a kiss on the cheek.

As we stood there, I watched Mom look up at the people, all dressed in red, extending from the court to the ceiling. I followed her gaze and noted for the first time all season the perfect geometry of the fan-filled stadium—the concentric rows, the sections divided neatly by concrete staircases, the order and symmetry that would disappear once the game began.

"Oh my," she said to me, "look at all those people. Aren't you scared out here?"

I smiled and gave her a hug. *If only she knew,* I thought.

Frank Deford sat somewhere within the billow of red and witnessed the Aces play sloppily but still dominate the Butler Bulldogs. Sloan and Williams controlled the boards, and Humes kept up a steady stream of baskets that helped him maintain his thirty-points-per-game scoring average.

But stats don't tell the whole story. We played great defense that night. Halfway through the first half, Butler tried to inbound the ball under their own basket. Each of us played chest to chest with our man, bumping him from his route as he tried to get open, so close to him we could intercept an attempted pass. They were unable to do so within the required five seconds and relinquished possession to us out of bounds without even getting off a play.

Deeper in the half, I crowded my man into the corner at midcourt, close to the scorer's table, forcing him to pick up his dribble. Seeing this, my teammates crowded their man to close off all passing lanes. When my man couldn't get rid of the ball within the allotted time limit, the referee tweeted his whistle for a jump ball, which we won, and we then preceded to take it to the basket for a score.

Our halftime lead of 44–34 was solid and irrefutable. The Bulldogs opened the second half by jamming the middle against Humes, a ploy that gave the rest of us easy pops from medium range. Sloan hit two, I hit three, and Watkins hit three. When Humes dropped a sweeping hook shot from the right side of the basket with 13:18 left in the game, we had outscored Butler 17–6 to take an insurmountable 61–40 lead. We coasted from there for an 84–73 victory.

A week later, I motored home after practice and parked the car underneath the basketball hoop behind the house. Its chain net hung silently from the rim. I walked into my bedroom, threw my coat on my bed, and headed into the kitchen where I immediately inhaled the hearty smell of Mom's goulash. She stood, ladle in hand, wearing a matching yellow skirt and blouse. Her smile communicated nothing but love.

"I'm starved. How soon do we eat?" I asked.

"Soon," she said. "Dad's in the living room. He's got a surprise for you."

In the living room, Dad held up the February 26, 1965 issue of *Sports Illustrated*. "Here. Page twenty-four," he said.

I sat down and read the headline, "Aces Are High In Evansville," with the byline, "Best small-college basketball team in the nation, the Evansville Purple Aces are the inspiration for a tidal wave of civic pride that has engulfed a three-state area in the great bend of the Ohio River."

"Pretty cool, huh?" Dad said.

I read the story twice. Frank Deford served up a glowing picture of Evansville that was both warmhearted and lifelike. He described in luminous detail the obsessive love affair between the community and the Aces, the color and pageantry inside Roberts Stadium, and the rightful credit Arad McCutchan deserved in making it all happen. He emphasized the powerful simplicity of our strategies and the depth of our talent. He concluded: "Despite their small-college status, the Aces could compete favorably with any team in the country—they are among the best by any definition."

I found my name mentioned once, near the bottom of page twenty-six. I felt proud of my team, but I couldn't ignore the twinge of disappointment in that I had occupied such a minor part of the story. I still harbored the desire to be Mickey Mantle and Arnold Palmer and Bob Pettit, all rolled into one.

• • •

THE LARGEST CROWD TO EVER witness a game in Valparaiso, Indiana, turned out for our February 17 game against the Crusaders. When we took the floor, a loud, screeching gathering of lunatics stood and chanted staccato-like, "Beat Evansville."

In the layup line, Herb Williams snapped his fingers and danced in time to the crowd's incantations. I smiled, once again appreciating his bubbly spirit. Looking over his shoulder, he said, "I love this. Don't you?"

"Uh, no!" I said.

"Hey, lighten up," he said, then sprinted to the basket for his layup.

The Valparaiso students kept up their chanting until the player introductions. When the announcer intoned, "Let's give a big Crusader welcome to the Evansville College Purple Aces," the students fell totally silent and stood stock-still. This felt eerie and surreal. Then, he introduced me: "At one guard, Russ Grieger." As I loped to the free-throw line, they blasted me with a clipped, synchronized, "Hi, Russ!" Once again, total silence.

Standing there, I scanned the bleachers, only to spot my fraternity brother, Gene, some thirty rows up, waving his arms frantically over his head in a crisscrossing motion. Next to him stood a dark-haired lady, the top of her head barely reaching his chin.

While Watkins received the same treatment I had, I spread my hands to my sides, palms forward, as if to ask Gene, "What the hell are you doing here?" A month ago, he had been stationed in Elkhart, Indiana, some sixty miles northwest of Valparaiso, to undergo management training for Gulf Oil.

Between the greetings for Humes and Williams, and again between those for Williams and Sloan, Gene shouted a solitary, "Hi, Russ!" Both times I practically broke up, feeling a mixture of appreciation for him being here and relief from the tension.

At exactly eight o'clock, the referee tossed the ball skyward at center court and Williams out-jumped his opponent to tip it forward to Jerry Sloan. But then an alert Valparaiso player leaped in front of Sloan to take possession, causing an earsplitting roar. Before it reached its crescendo, Sloan stole the ball away, dribbled the length of the court, and laid it in for our first basket. The decibel level immediately dropped by half. Thirty seconds later, Sloan zipped the ball between two defenders to Humes under the basket for an easy layup, deflating the crowd's volume again by half. Then Sloan drilled a jumper from the corner to put us ahead 6–0. The crowd fell nearly silent.

Valpo immediately called time-out. In the huddle, Herbie flashed that wide smile of his and said, "Can we slow the scoring down so we can have a little fun? We don't want to blow them out too early."

Sloan reached across the huddle to ruffle his hair. I grinned.

Coach said, "Now, boys, let's not get too far ahead of ourselves."

We hit fourteen out of our first seventeen shots, jumped ahead 28–14 eleven minutes into the game, and led Valparaiso 55–38 at halftime. We increased our lead to 63–40 four minutes into the second half, making the game all but over except for the mop-up. That night, we sunk forty-eight of our ninety-one shots, and out-rebounded Valpo 57–33. The final score: 109–88. When McCutchan took the first team off the floor in the final minutes, the Valpo fans gave us a respectful round of applause, not quite as dramatic as that at DePaul, but still noteworthy.

We showered and dressed in the relative peace of our Valparaiso locker room. Carrying my winter coat over my shoulder, my hair still wet, I hustled back into the gym to find Gene and his girlfriend. The floor lights had been dimmed, and it was whisper-quiet. At the opposite corner of the court, I saw Valpo players leaving their locker room and walking to the exit doors without speaking.

Just as I started to walk to center court to look around, I heard a shout from behind me: "Frater!"

Gene came walking toward me, holding the hand of an attractive young woman—about five foot four, dark-brown hair, bangs hanging over her forehead, sparkling eyes, a generous smile.

"What are you doing here?" I asked Gene.

"Came to see my buddy. Elkhart's only an hour away."

"So, who is this?" I asked, turning to his date.

"I'm Jan," she said, extending her hand. Then, before I could speak, she added, "You're a lot taller than you look from way up there in the bleachers."

"Well, you could have sat closer to the floor if Gene wasn't so cheap."

"Wanna get out of here and go to Art and Helen's?" Gene said.

"You have no idea how much I'd like that."

We chatted and joked for a few minutes until Coach called me to catch our ride back to the hotel.

"Gotta go," I said. They walked me out of the gymnasium to our vehicles. Just before getting into the car, he leaned forward and mumbled low under his breath, "She might be the one, frater."

I shot him a glance and said, "Yeah? Well, she does look like a keeper."

•  •  •

I SAT SOME TWENTY ROWS above the court in the vast emptiness of Roberts Stadium, fully dressed in my practice gear—white shorts, red shirt, and Converse All-Stars. The dim lights and gentle silence on this Friday afternoon was soothing, so unlike the frenzied chaos that the thirteen thousand screaming Redshirts would create the next night.

Two seats to my left sat *Evansville Press* sports columnist Bill Fluty. Looking nothing like an athlete, he was in his late thirties with close-cropped hair that receded at the temples, carried a slight paunch, and wore glasses whose dark frames circled his eyes. He had a spiral notebook on his lap, flipped open at the top, and a yellow pencil shoved behind his ear.

"Tools of the trade?" I asked, pointing at his notebook.

He smiled, but kept his eyes down, no doubt reviewing the scribbled questions he had prepared for me.

We were about to begin a dance whose steps both of us would follow but neither would voice out loud. We were there to use each other: he would use me for spiffy quotes, insider anecdotes, and team insights for his next day's column; I would use him for the ego rush of seeing my picture and words in print. We both knew this, yet neither of us would acknowledge that it was true.

"Ready?" Bill said. Before I could answer, a door slammed from deep beneath the stands and echoed throughout the stadium.

"Da, da, da, dumm," I said, mimicking the opening of Beethoven's Fifth.

Bill ignored me. "First question: The Aces are twenty-one and oh and go for number twenty-two tomorrow night against Kentucky Wesleyan. An undefeated season, the Aces' first ever, is a possibility. How does the team handle the pressure?"

"To tell you the truth, we never talk about it. I don't think we feel any pressure."

"What?" he said, ignoring his notebook and looking at me. "You've got to be kidding."

"Nope. We only think about it when somebody like you brings it up."

"Well, how do you explain that?"

"I don't know," I said, shrugging my shoulders. "I guess it's one game at a time and all that. We just go out and play, do our best, and let the chips fall where they may."

I watched Fluty scribbling notes on his pad, pacing what I said so he could keep up with me. I knew what I'd said to be true. But what I didn't say, also true, was that, unlike in high school, I wasn't the star of the team. My role carried fewer expectations and responsibilities, less pressure. This realization had been a blow to my ego at first, but a fact I had learned to accept, though wistfully.

Fluty asked more questions, some about basketball, others about me. About basketball, he quizzed me regarding the role of our conditioning to our success, memorable moments from the season so far, our strategy for Kentucky Wesleyan the next night. He asked me about my transfer three seasons before from St. Louis University, my psychology major, and even the Bachelor of the Year contest I'd won last season. I knew he was searching for an angle to wrap his story around.

At about two thirty, Sloan and Watkins walked onto the court and started warming up. The thump of the balls banging against the hardwood floated throughout the stadium as if in a giant echo chamber.

"I gotta get down there in a couple of minutes," I said. "Don't want Coach mad at me."

"Okay, almost done." He cocked his head and squinted at me, pencil at the ready. "You played right here in this very stadium as a high-schooler at Bosse, and now, a hometown boy, you're a member of the undefeated number-one team in the nation. What has all that come to mean to you?"

I paused to gather my thoughts. "Well, I remember my first game here in the stadium, in my high school freshman year. There were maybe two thousand people in the stands. You might have been one of them. It was against Madison, and I scored fourteen points in the first quarter before they put their all-stater on me. He shut me down pretty good after that."

"I was there," he said.

"Yeah? Well, now look at it," I said, sweeping my hand around. "Those bleachers added above the chair backs, the whole place packed to the rafters every game, me playing alongside Sloan, Humes, and all the other guys. Who'd a thought?"

I paused to let him finish scribbling his notes. I watched more Aces walk onto the court. When he looked up, I said, "How was that?"

"Not bad," he said, "but can we go a little deeper? It's been eight years since you played your first game on that very court down there. What have you learned from all of that?"

"What have I learned?" I repeated, more to myself than to Bill. I stared off into the bleachers and scratched my head. *Be careful*, I told myself, not wanting to lay my self-doubts and insecurities out for the whole community to see. He waited, pencil poised.

"Well, there are lots of things," I said, "but one thing I think I've learned, I guess, is humility."

"Humility?"

"Yeah, humility. I think that's the right word."

"Can you expand on that?"

"Sure. There are lots of good basketball players, many better than me." I paused. "I learned I don't have to score tons of points like in high school to contribute to the team. I can play defense and make assists and rebound here and there. It's not all about me."

"There's no 'I' in team. Is that what you're saying?"

"That's right," I said, inwardly chuckling, thinking, *I just dodged a bullet.*

I glanced toward the court and saw Coach McCutchan.

"Uh oh, I better get going," I said, getting up. "That deep enough for you?"

"You bet."

"Okay then." I gave him a friendly jab him in the arm and double-stepped it down to the court to warm up.

The next night, Saturday, February 20, more than twelve thousand blood-thirsty Redshirts refused to quiet down, from pregame warm-ups until the final buzzer as we battled our cross-river rival, the Kentucky Wesleyan Wildcats. We dominated every phase of the game and dispatched them with relative ease, 99–70.

Our strategy was simple—pressure them into the ground. On offense, we fast broke every chance we could and, when we couldn't, we pushed the ball down low to Humes to do his magic.

On defense, we planned to hound the Wildcats all over the court and sic Jerry Sloan on their six-foot-four scoring phenom, Dallas Thornton. Sloan started out defending him, but, early in the game, when the man I guarded set a screen on Jerry, I yelled "Switch!" and picked up Thornton while Jerry crowded my man.

Thornton stood two inches taller than me and must have felt like a shark smelling blood in the water. He immediately put the ball on the floor to drive to the basket. Something in me anticipated his move. I slid in his path, causing him to run full force into my chest. The referee blew his whistle and called him for a charging foul, giving us possession of the ball.

A blast of applause rewarded my effort. Sloan reached down, grabbed my hand, and yanked me to my feet. I felt my testosterone spike.

When play stopped for a free throw a few seconds later, I impulsively said to Jerry, "Hey, let me take Thornton, okay?"

From that point on, whenever Wesleyan had the ball, the first thing I did was locate Dallas Thornton so I could stay so close to him we could have whispered into each other's ears. To deny him the ball, I always kept half my body between him and the Wildcat with the ball. When he did get the ball, I crowded close in front of him, keeping my hands forward, ready to snatch the ball should he get careless. My reflexes felt trigger quick, and I reacted sometimes the split second he moved. I knew he couldn't lose me that night, no matter how hard he tried.

By halftime the Aces held a 42–28 lead, and Thornton managed to get off only four shots, just one finding the basket. When Coach took the starters out with two minutes left in the game, I had held him to just three field goals. After the game, I felt particularly pleased when Coach McCutchan, facing the press in our dressing room, pulled me to him and said, "I was particularly pleased with the job Grieger here did on Dallas Thornton."

I held no delusions that I was the star that night. Humes led the way with twenty-nine points, Sloan chipped in with twenty-four, and Watkins and I contributed thirteen and eleven, respectively. Yet I felt proud of my performance. Let veteran sports reporter Bill Robertson tell it as he did in his Monday-evening column:

> Grieger's workmanlike performance Saturday night was another in frequent critical deliveries which the former Bosse star has made generally unnoticed— in the Aces remarkable saga this year.
>
> With the experience of 29 games last year and the advantage of an added year's maturity due to his transfer from St. Louis University, he has functioned as defender, feeder, rebounder, and long shot this season.
>
> Saturday night he hit five of eight shots, grabbed five rebounds, passed off for five baskets and made only one error in one of his typical performances.

Reading what Robertson had written, I beamed with pride. *So much for humility*, I thought.

◆  ◆  ◆

FIFTEEN MINUTES INTO OUR TWENTY-THIRD game of the season against Indiana State at Roberts Stadium, Sam Watkins lofted a high-arching jumper that seemed to take forever to reach its apex and descend toward the basket. As soon as the ball left Sam's hands, Larry Humes elbowed his way around his defender and crouched under the basket, his knees ready to spring for a rebound. The ball bounded high off the rim. Humes leaped and snatched it, faked up with his arms to get the Sycamore defenders to leave his feet, and laid the ball softly into the basket.

The near-capacity crowd sprung to its feet and let out a booming ovation that was way out of proportion for the seventeen-point lead Humes's basket gave us. They knew that Larry's eleventh and twelfth points had broken the Evansville College single-season scoring record of 730 points recorded five seasons before by Aces great Ed Smallwood.

Though Larry had his record, Sloan didn't see it that way. "Come on, guys!" he yelled as we ran back to play defense. "We've got more work to do."

What he meant was that Humes was still vying with Indiana State's Butch Wade for the conference scoring championship. Going into the game, Wade trailed Humes by only seven points. Sloan wanted us to do all we could to help Larry win the title.

Each time down the court, we probed to worm the ball down low to Humes, passing up all but the most open shots for ourselves. Larry struggled to establish position, sometimes bouncing off his defender, other times thrusting them sideways out of his way. Once one of us got the ball into his hands—a sharp push pass over a defender's shoulder, a soft floater over a defender's head, a bullet bounce pass—two or three defenders converged on Humes to force him to give up the ball.

Sometimes he did just that, flipping the ball to one of the four of us for an easy basket. More often, with his eyes wide, computing in a fraction of a second the position of the basket and the Indiana State defenders, he slithered to the basket for a twisting layup, an abrupt jumper, or a soft hook.

I watched all this unfold. The player in me felt proud, not only of Larry, but of all of us who had wanted him to break the record almost as much as he did. My spectator side made it difficult to stay focused on my job. I watched Larry make split-second decisions that created one masterpiece after another. Often during that game I wanted to stand and clap.

That night, Tuesday, February 23, records fell left and right. The Aces set an all-time home attendance record of 149,616. The 112 points we scored put us over the century mark for the eighth time that season. We went undefeated in the Indiana Collegiate Conference for the second year in a row. As for Humes, he scored thirty-nine points to run his season total to 748, breaking the old record of 730, set a school field-goal record of 290, established a record point-per-game average of 33.6 for conference play, and won the ICC scoring title to boot. Most important, we won our twenty-third game in a row without a defeat.

Coach McCutchan sent in substitutes for the starters with just over two minutes left in the game. The bench, along with everyone else in the building, gave us a standing ovation. Before we could settle in and enjoy the rest of the game, the Redshirts in this slap-happy Tuesday night crowd began to chant: "We want Southern. We want Southern."

I draped my arm around Larry's neck and said, "I think they mean the Southern Illinois Salukis," our opponent in our twenty-fourth and last regular-season game, the team we'd beaten with a miracle basket by Larry as time expired nine games ago.

He rolled his eyes and said, "No rest for the weary."

The next morning, I sat at my desk, bleary-eyed, waiting for my modern drama class to begin, not quite ready to tackle the plays of Lillian Hellmann, Eugene O'Neill, or Tennessee Williams. Only excitement from last night's game kept me from dropping my head on my desk and dozing off.

I sat along the wall next to the window, near the back of the room. Theater and drama students drifted in—Duane Campbell, Ron Glass, Curt Ball—people I had seen perform in various Evansville productions over the last three years. I felt a kinship with these students, though I knew them only slightly. They, like me, felt love for what they did and dared to stand up in front of people who could judge them without mercy. I knew I could take any of them on the basketball court, but here I felt out of my element.

At exactly ten o'clock, Professor Sam Smiley strolled into the classroom and dropped his thick textbook on the desk with a thud. He cut a striking figure, dressed all in black—black loafers, black slacks, black turtleneck sweater—with the lean, taut body of a long-distance runner. His bald head would have glistened had it not been slightly tanned.

He settled astride the corner of the desk and flipped open his book.

"Okay, boys and girls," he said in the sonorous voice of a radio announcer, "let's do a reading from *Death of a Salesman* and then discuss what's there. Duane, you read Willy. Sandra, you're Linda. David, you play Happy. Russ, how about you do Biff."

My eyes snapped to him and then to the class. I had not planned on acting—not that day. Not any day, for that matter. I didn't like the idea of standing in front of an audience who could see through my cultivated self-assurance into a heart petrified with self-doubt.

I disengaged myself from my chair, walked to the front of the room, and stood next to Sandra, the four of us facing the class and holding our textbooks open like hymnals. This young woman, now playing my mom, had featured many times in my lascivious imaginings. I hoped my hands wouldn't shake.

Professor Smiley read the author notes that set the stage for Act One. When he finished, he nodded to Sandra for the play's opening word: "Willie!"

My mouth felt dry. My heart pounded. I looked at the students sitting in the front row and saw nothing but critics, ready to mock me.

Then it hit me: *That damn ego thing again!* I stood in front of twenty people, not twelve thousand, and realized I had given them the power to denigrate me. Recognizing this gave me some comfort, yet not the ability to calm my anxiety. I wondered, had I made any progress in slaying this dragon called ego?

After what seemed like hours of shifting my feet, I came to the word "Biff" on the page, followed by a colon. I uttered my first line: "What's the matter?" I got it out without hurling.

Happy/David held his textbook in his left hand. He raised and lowered the volume of his voice to inflect his lines with the meaning and emotion the author had intended. He paused his delivery at times, slowing down and speeding up his words, mimicking a real conversation. He gestured with his free hand and even put his hand on my shoulder at one point to convey brotherly affection. My delivery sounded flat, emotionless, like a stenographer proofreading a legal document. I neither smiled nor gestured. I could not forget the audience in front of me and only occasionally looked up from my book, more to see if they were snickering than anything else.

Smiley finally said, "Good, that's enough."

I released a giant sigh.

"You did just fine," he said, nodding at me. "You all did." Then, turning to the audience, "How about giving The Mighty Smiley Players a nice ovation."

Discussion followed the reading that I only partially followed. When twelve thirty rolled around, I felt drained. I couldn't wait to get out of that room and hook up with my fraternity brothers at The Indian.

"All right, that's it for the day," Smiley said as he grabbed his textbook and headed toward the door.

We shuffled to collect our books.

"Oh, one more thing," he said, pausing at the door. "Don't forget that the Aces go to Carbondale Saturday to play Southern Illinois. Our undefeated season is on the line."

He looked at me with his laser eyes.

"Russ, from all your fellow thespians, break a leg."

Then, turning to the class, he raised his fist and shouted "Go Aces" to applause from everyone in the room.

# 20

## SOUTHERN ILLINOIS REDUX

WE LEFT CARSON CENTER ON Saturday, February 27 to play our last regular-season game against Southern Illinois University in Carbondale. We had beaten the Salukis earlier in the season on a last-second miracle shot by Larry Humes. Since then, SIU had trampled nine straight opponents and climbed to number three in the nation, two slots behind us. With three minutes left in their last game, a forty-foot banner had unfurled from the rafters, declaring in large black letters, "Beat Evansville." This prompted ten thousand supporters to chant "We want Evansville" over and over until game's end. SIU's opportunity for revenge had arrived.

No one spoke as Coach O'Brien eased his Ford Fairlane west. Sam Watkins and Herb Williams stared out their windows in the backseat, while I sat in the front. As we drove, I watched Evansville pass by—the snow-spotted lawns of the east side, Memorial High, downtown, Johnson & Johnson Laboratories, Lamasco Field. As neighborhoods and filling stations gave way to open fields, I had the sensation of being pulled away from the safe and the familiar.

I felt tight, on edge, as I always did on game day. But this was more than typical game-day jitters. I knew that all we had accomplished so far this season—our twenty-three straight wins, our season-long ranking as the nation's number-one team, our accolades and approbations—would mean nothing if we lost tonight.

Coach O'Brien accelerated as we hit open highway. Herb said, "That's it, Coach, put the pedal to the metal."

No one responded.

A moment later Herb tried again. "Hey, guys, don't you just love this, going to battle together?"

Sam glanced at Herb, then looked back out his window.

"Hey, Herbie," I said, "save your energy for tonight."

"Thank you, Lord, for putting me in this car," he said. "I know you put me here to save these lost souls from the gloom and doom of themselves."

No one took the bait. He muttered, "Well, I tried," and settled into gazing out the window, his forehead pressed against the glass.

We rolled along the two-lane highway, past billboards touting Burma Shave and Camels, through cornfields fallow from winter and still splattered with patches of snow that refused to melt. We rode in silence for what seemed an eternity before we passed through New Harmony and across the state line into Illinois.

"Back home again . . . in Illinois," Herb sang and then added, "Hey, guys, how about we slip by Centralia and pick up my dad?"

I bit. "Okay, Herbie, why do you want to pick up your dad?"

"Because," he said, "if we're going to have a funeral in this car, we might as well have a preacher."

Everybody laughed.

"That's more like it," Herb said. "Now how about turning on some music so we can boogie?"

I dialed the radio until I found a rock station. For the rest of the trip, through the hamlets of Eldorado, Harrisburg, and Marion, we bounced along to Sam the Sham and the Pharaohs, the Righteous Brothers, and the Supremes.

We knew we'd hit Carbondale when we passed a Holiday Inn whose marquee read, "Beat Evansville." The farther we drove into town, the more such signs we spotted. After a while, it seemed that "Beat Evansville" occupied the window of every restaurant, bar, and shop we passed. "Beat Evansville" even played alongside *Mondo Cane* at the local movie palace.

Then we saw the SIU arena. From a distance it resembled a giant flying saucer, with its circular top and square, florescent-lit underside. Surrounding it was an unbroken cavalcade of cars filled with students wearing green bowler hats and blaring long Alpine horns extending out of the windows. The noise drowned out the radio. I imagined what it would sound like once those maniacs let loose inside the arena.

Coach O'Brien inched the car through this circular parade and into the parking lot. I pictured us in the middle of the mob, pulled out onto the street and pummeled.

"We made it," O'Brien said, parking the car. "Let's check out where we get our twenty-fourth win."

Inside the arena, the court was brightly lit. The ceiling resembled the interior of a giant scallop shell with rib-like beams extending from its center down to the outer walls. There hung that forty-foot banner from the ceiling proclaiming, "Beat Evansville," bigger and more menacing than I'd imagined.

By six thirty, we had stowed our gear in the locker room and settled onto seats above the court to watch the freshman game. Just after halftime, the festivities in the street began spilling into the arena. The buzz of voices steadily grew, eventually 10,300 strong, dwarfed by the students tuning up their horns with hundreds of deafening blasts.

With every step we had taken closer to the start of the game—driving into town, getting to the arena, checking out the court, seeing the hostile crowd arrive—my stomach clinched tighter, my heart beat faster. I only half followed the action on the court.

Just then, I felt a hand on my shoulder. Sitting behind me, Sloan yelled, loud enough for me to hear over the din, "Hey, this guy here has something for you."

Next to Sloan stood a man in black slacks, a maroon blazer, and one of those caps cabbies wear. "You Russ Grieger?"

"Yes."

"This telegram's for you."

I tore it open. Inside, under my name and the words "Evansville Team Player," it read:

Be cock!
Gene.

I snorted, read it again, and then snickered with a tight-lipped smile on my face and a bob of my head. A calm spread through me.

I looked around at the people already seated in the arena. There were the students crammed under the basket and around the corner to half-court—boys in jeans and sweatshirts and girls in sweaters and skirts, many wearing those ridiculous bowler hats. Everywhere else there were adult men and women, wearing sweaters and coats, hooded sweatshirts, and hats, looking in no way special or exceptional. *Just people,* I thought, *no different than those at Roberts Stadium or Art and Helen's.*

I looked around for the usher who'd delivered Gene's message. I spotted him as he disappeared behind the bleachers courtside, too late for me to flag. I wanted him to send a two-word reply: "I will!"

• • •

WE RAN ONTO THE COURT at exactly seven thirty. Two thousand Redshirt diehards let it rip from the upper corner of the arena behind our bench. Moments later the Salukis trotted onto the court, David Lee and Walt Frazier leading the charge. Their loyalists drowned out the Aces fans with a cacophony of throaty screams and bleating horns. A hyperactive pep band played "Hold That Tiger." The clamor continued throughout the warm-ups so that talking became impossible. In that instant, I realized as clearly as I ever had that these were the moments I lived for, yet also the ones I most dreaded.

The ball went up and the Salukis surprised us with a modified one-three-one half-court zone press. Guard David Lee manned the point at midcourt. Doing jumping jacks, he tried to guide Sam or me, whoever brought the ball up court, sideways to trap us with one of his wingmen, Frazier or George McNeil. Their goal was to force us out, far from the basket, so we could do no harm from the perimeter nor get the ball to Humes near the basket. Teammates behind Lee readied themselves to attack should Watkins or I penetrate the perimeter.

The zone forced us out of our usual patterns and into areas of the court we rarely visited. We struggled to make snappy passes and had a hard time getting the ball to Humes. When we did, the Salukis swarmed him. Every pass took effort, every point was hard-earned—a jumper by Sloan, Watkins, or myself; a put-back by Williams; a twisting hook by Humes. It felt like a dream in which you run but are barely able to move your legs.

I settled into a grudging acceptance that this was the way the game would play out—trench warfare, hand-to-hand combat, each possession a begrudging battle of wills. But I took comfort from the fact that not one of us backed down, not even for one second. I watched Williams soar for rebounds, Humes squirm to get open, Watkins battle even harder than usual on defense. And then there was Sloan, all elbows and knees, scrapping and clawing from one play to the next.

I, too, did everything I could to help us win. Ten minutes into the game, Saluki Boyd O'Neal ripped a rebound off the boards and looked like he would fling the ball to forward a teammate at midcourt. I anticipated his outlet pass and hustled myself just behind the Saluki so that, when he leaped, caught the ball, and turned to dribble, he would find me planted in his path. As predicted, when he caught the ball, he turned straight into me, stumbled, and was called for traveling.

Back and forth we went for twenty minutes, two bands of gladiators, neither willing to grant superiority to the other. The Aces and Salukis tied seven times. We led once by two points, they by five on one occasion. When the half-time buzzer sounded, the Salukis had a 42–40 advantage.

I walked off the court toward our dressing room, sweat dripping from my chin. I glanced up at the packed stands and saw the 10,300 people slumped in their seats. What I heard was a low murmur, the kind of muted sound a group of exhausted people make after a full-out effort. I had lost awareness of this hoard for the entire first hour.

In the locker room, some of us sat on chairs, leaning forward, elbows on our knees. A few paced and fidgeted. Others stood, passively leaning against the wall. Nobody said a word. I didn't sense fear or defeat, just acceptance that we were in a dogfight with a job to do.

McCutchan walked in, looking as sharp as if he had just dressed after a shower. He stood at the center of the room, the first-half stats gripped in his left hand, focused and businesslike. He opened by complimenting us on our poise, considering this madhouse impersonating a gymnasium. Then he started his tutorial, precise and without emotion or drama.

"Sam, put a little more pressure on McNeil once he crosses the centerline. He's getting them into their offense a little too close to the basket. Russ, you need to overplay Lee on his right hand. Force him to go left where he's less effective." He looked down at the stat sheet. "Herb, you want to tighten up on O'Neal. He's killing us with those short jumpers. Larry, keep fighting to get open. The points may not come easy tonight, but every one counts." He swept his hand around in a semicircle. "Now, all of you, you need to be fierce on the boards. This is one of those grind-it-out games. Rebound baskets, one way or another, will make the difference." He glanced at his stat sheet one more time. "Okay, boys, that's all I've got." Looking at Coach O'Brien, he asked, "Anything you want to add?"

"That about covers it, Coach," O'Brien said.

"All right then. All we need to do is score three more points than they do in the second half and we'll take number twenty-four back to Evansville."

Herb Williams won the second-half tip, which went to Jerry Sloan. He pounded the ball on the dribble to the basket for a quick two points. That tied the score at 42–42.

*All we need now is one more point than them,* I thought.

In the next four minutes, the Salukis took seven shots, all jumpers, and hit five. They kept up their half-court zone, cutting off passing lanes and continuing to make it difficult for us to get the ball to Humes. With each of their baskets, the crowd exploded. In this flurry, they stretched their lead to 53–46.

This was one of those moments that I later came to understand defined the character of our team. When challenged, we became icy cold, more determined, kicking our focus into a higher gear. We had a reptilian calm on the outside but a quiet rage inside.

Down seven points, I inbounded the ball to Watkins and trotted parallel with him as he dribbled up the court. We poked and probed the SIU defense, struggling to find an inlet lane. I drifted down the left side of the court and found an open space some twenty feet from the basket. Watkins got the ball to me on the bounce with a two-handed sideways sling. I took the ball waist high, jumped, and lofted my shot. It didn't feel smooth as it left my hand, but it nonetheless curled inside the rim and dropped through the net. This cut their lead to 53–48.

The Redshirts sent out a cheer, but not one of us on the court said a word. We ramped up our defensive intensity. Whoever was guarding the man with the ball got right into his breadbasket. The rest of us did our best to cut off the passing lanes. On the right wing, Sloan slapped the ball from Walt Frazier's grasp as he started his dribble. It bounced off David Lee's leg out of bounds. Aces' ball.

This trip up the court, we got the ball into Humes close to the basket. Three Salukis immediately crowded around him. Unable to get off a shot, he flipped the ball out to me in the exact spot where I'd made my prior basket. Wide open, I leaped and, with a smooth flick of my wrist, swished this one through clean and pure: 53–50.

This last basket spurred us on to even more in-your-face defensive playing. We forced two consecutive Saluki turnovers—one on a cross-court steal by Watkins and another when Humes tipped the ball out to me after an attempted inlet pass. The score reached to 55–52, and then to 58–56. When Williams banked in a ten-foot jump shot just left of the free-throw lane, we tied the score at 58–58.

With just under seven minutes left, we took our first lead of the second half, 63–61, and then, at the 4:30 mark, increased it to 65–61. By the time the clock ticked to 3:00, we clung to a slim 67–65 margin, despite missing three straight crib shots under the basket.

Anybody in the arena suffering from heart disease would have had an attack by now. The noise was constant and deafening, so loud in fact that the only thing I could hear anymore was my own heart beating. SIU fans roared when the Salukis scored and pleaded when the Aces had the ball. The Redshirts responded in kind. The Saluki students became so caught up in the game they even forgot to blast their horns.

Sloan brought the ball up court and bounced it to me at midcourt. I stood there, the ball in both hands, protecting it by holding it off my right hip. I saw my teammates spread out across the court, as far away from me as they could get. I understood in an instant the plan was to run out the clock without giving away possession.

The Salukis abandoned their zones and closed in on me. I dribbled around and between two and sometimes three Salukis. Out of instinct, I paused and juked in mid-dribble and pounded the basketball from one hand to the other as a Saluki reached to snatch it. All semblance of organized basketball disappeared. At times I lost my orientation to the basket, but that didn't matter; my sole purpose was to keep possession of the ball. Seconds ticked away at a glacial pace: 2:30 . . . 2:15 . . . 2:00. As I dribbled, I heard an incoherent guttural sound, half a whimper, and realized it was me. I was making the feral sound of an animal trying to survive.

With a minute and a half left, three SIU players boxed me in at the corner between the centerline and the side of the court, forcing me to pick up my dribble. In desperation, I lofted a cross-court pass to Watkins near the centerline, a move I knew was a mistake the moment the ball left my hand. Saluki forward Walt Frazier catapulted out of nowhere and snatched the ball in midair and streaked down the court to tie the score at sixty-seven.

The SIU fans bellowed in ecstasy. I felt a mixture of rage and shame, but I had no time to indulge myself in expressions of self-hatred or self-pity.

I retrieved the ball as it fell through the basket and immediately inbounded it to Watkins. He forwarded a pass to Sloan who, in turn, dribbled across the centerline and got it to Humes just right of the free-throw line. Larry didn't hesitate. He wheeled toward the basket, drove down the right lane to the glass, and drew a foul on the way up for his shot. The clock stopped at 1:07.

With the sound of horns blaring in the background, Humes bounced his first free throw off the back of the rim. A groan went up from the Redshirts, a mighty roar from everybody else. Larry toed the free-throw line a second time, took a deep breath, and spun the ball toward the basket in a perfect arc. It plopped through the net without touching the rim. Aces, 68–67.

"No fouls," yelled McCutchan from the bench as we scurried back to play defense.

Putting every ounce of concentration and energy we could muster into our defense, we forced SIU's Joe Ramsey to take an off-balance shot from the corner. Herb Williams snatched the ball off the rim and tossed it into Sloan's hands. Forty seconds showed on the clock, the Aces leading by one.

Sloan brought the ball up court and bounced it to Watkins at thirty seconds. A Saluki bumped him in a desperate attempt to steal the ball. Unable to spot an open teammate and afraid he was going to travel, Sam lofted an off-balance shot that careened off the backboard and into a Saluki's hands. They called a quick time-out with eighteen seconds left on the clock.

We crowded around Arad McCutchan, who simply said, "Make them shoot from the perimeter. Keep a hand in their face. No fouls. Go do it."

SIU inbounded the ball to David Lee, who rushed up court. I guarded him tightly but carefully. He looked to pass it under the basket but found no one open. With time ticking away, he flung the ball to his running mate, George McNeil, on the perimeter, just left of the key. McNeil took one dribble to his right and, with Watkins's hand in his face, let fly a twenty-footer from the top of the free-throw arc.

A hush fell over the arena. Ten thousand hearts pounded. All eyes fixed on the ball as it arced toward the basket.

The ball bounced high off the rim, hovered over the basket as if it might fall through, and then ricocheted off. Joe Ramsey tried to knock the rebound back up and in, but Herb Williams once again leaped into the air, seized the ball with both hands, and flung it to me as I was knocked out of bounds.

The final buzzer sounded. We had won our twenty-fourth straight game.

$\bullet \quad \bullet \quad \bullet$

OUR BENCH RUSHED ONTO THE court, as did our coaches and cheerleaders. We embraced, whooped, and hollered. High up in the balcony, three thousand fans, all outfitted in red, stood and cheered. The Salukis pep band dutifully played on, but the SIU faithful weren't listening, their zeal lay on the floor along with their green horns. Without speaking, they shuffled toward the exits.

I sat on a stool in the corner of the locker room, still in my sweat-soaked game uniform. I munched ice from a soft-drink cup, my face chalky, the game tension still in my eyes. My teammates also sat still, quiet and drawn, an unintended compliment to the team we had just beaten.

Coach McCutchan stood in the corner to my left, his back to the wall, semicircled by reporters. One of them asked, "What about the pressure of going into the NCAA tournament with a perfect record?"

Coach paused, then said, "These guys don't feel any pressure." He rubbed his forehead, then his neck, squinting, an expression I had come to recognize as exasperation. "Do you think they showed any pressure tonight?"

I half-smiled, half-smirked. *If only he knew how I felt those last few minutes.*

Motoring out of Carbondale, we passed the same Holiday Inn we had coming in. This time the signs read: "Good People, Good Ballplayers, Evansville."

We cruised toward home, a bright moon casting a silver sheen over the landscape, illuminating farmhouses and barns, billboards and signs, tractors and livestock. I switched on the radio, hoping to find some peppy music to pass the time. A velvet-smooth voice said: "This is KMOX Radio, 1120 on your AM dial, the voice of St. Louis. Stay tuned to the second half of our delayed broadcast of the Southern Illinois–Evansville clash in Carbondale. We'll be right back after these messages."

"I hope the Aces win," I said.

I listened with rapt attention to the play-by-play of the second half, lost in what the announcer described, seeing the scenes as if I were still on the court. I saw Williams leap and elbow for rebounds, Watkins dog his man, Sloan fly across the court wreaking havoc, Humes driving toward the basket.

When the broadcast got to the point at which we fell behind by seven and I made my two key jump shots (my only two of the second half), the announcer declared, "This Grieger is sure underrated."

Tom glanced at me and nodded. I looked toward the backseat, but Watkins and Williams both slept. I appreciated Tom's affirmation, but I realized how much my teammates' approval meant to me.

Later, when I dribbled to try to run out the clock, the announcer exclaimed, "A wizard with the basketball, this Grieger is." Near the end of the game, he described my cross-court blunder that was intercepted and converted into the tying score.

"Don't say it, Coach, I know, a really stupid move."

"I'm not saying a word," Tom said.

After the final buzzer, the announcer extolled the virtues of the Purple Aces—talented, gritty, courageous, a perfect blend of talent.

He concluded, "Stay tuned, folks. Evansville and SIU are seeded in opposite brackets of the NCAA tournament and could meet once again for all the marbles."

To that, his color man said, "And remember, it's hard to beat any team three times in one season."

Tom and I looked at each other and rolled our eyes.

# Part Four

## The Aces Triumph

It is not in the stars to hold our destiny, but in ourselves.
—William Shakespeare

# 21

## THE NCAA REGIONAL

I WALKED ACROSS CAMPUS THE Monday after the Southern Illinois game and surveyed the two- and three-story limestone buildings that made up Evansville College. Stately and eternal, they seemed capable of absorbing the mood of whatever Mother Nature bestowed—the brilliance of summer, the somber gray of winter. On this overcast day, they looked dark and menacing, the way things look after a loved one's death.

I knew why. The Aces had reached the NCAA tournament. Thirty-two teams, the best in the country, all faced the same awesome truth: our season records, our national rankings, our tributes and accolades, all meant nothing. We had to start from scratch and play head to head for survival. Win and advance or lose and go home.

As I broke free of the buildings and crossed Walnut Street to Carson Center, I realized that this truth applied to the Evansville College Purple Aces more than to any other team in the tournament. For nothing would be so brutal than for us, the team ranked number one the whole year, the team with the spotless 24–0 record, the team already voted national champions by United Press

International's Board of Coaches, to lose. Coach McCutchan had said that his Aces felt no pressure. *Yeah, right!* I thought.

Dressed in white gym shorts and faded red practice jersey, I sat in the far back corner of our Carson Center meeting room and worried about what the team's mood would be. Nobody said a word as Coach McCutchan scratched x's, o's, and slashing lines onto the blackboard. Whooshing sounds from cars and trucks speeding past Walnut Street penetrated the window. From across the hall, I could hear the thump of basketballs pounding the floor of the intramural court.

I tapped my right foot to the floor in rapid succession and looked around at my teammates, hoping to find reassurance from them. Jerry Sloan sat impassively in the front row by the door, his arms lying across the backrests of the chairs on each side of him. Larry Humes and Sam Watkins, sitting two rows in front of me, watched McCutchan diagraming plays at the board, saying nothing. In the middle of the room, Herb Williams whispered into Ron Johnson's ear, like he might at church. Johnson simply nodded while looking straight ahead.

Just then, Larry Denton hustled into the room, eyeing the board to his left. Sloan shot his left leg forward, tripping Denton, and then gave him a "Who, me?" look. Everybody burst out laughing, followed by Williams standing up and doing a little boogie in front of his chair. The tension that hovered over the room lifted like the morning fog.

*We're okay*, I thought. I knew right then that Bethune-Cookman, our first-round opponent, would have to take it away from us.

Coach McCutchan finished his diagramming. He rapped his knuckles on the blackboard, turned, and said, "Okay, boys, let's get to work. I've got good and bad news." The room went silent. "First the bad. Bethune-Cookman has the top rebounder in the country, six-foot-nine Carl Fuller."

"Does that mean I guard him?" quipped Jim Forman, our diminutive last man off the bench, who topped out at five foot seven on a good day.

With a grin, McCutchan said, "Did I mention he scored sixty points Saturday night?"

"Then you better have Sloan take him," Forman said.

Laughter rippled through the room. Coach went on, "That's why we have Forman on this team, boys—to help me coach. Jerry'll take Fuller, but the rest of you had better be ready to help out."

"Are we getting to the good news, Coach?" Williams asked.

"Not quite. Our second challenge is their speed. They're fast, they run every chance they can, and their guards shoot from anywhere on the court. Got that, Grieger? Watkins?"

"Hell, we can run with anybody," Sloan said.

"That's right," Coach said, nodding at Sloan. "That's the good news. Cookman's running is our meat. We'll run them into the ground."

Clapping filled the room. I sat in the back, nodding. I itched to get onto the court.

All that week we practiced hard, repeating the same drill over and over when not scrimmaging. It started with playing defense against the scout team that ran Bethune-Cookman's offense. Every time we grabbed a rebound or forced an error, we pushed the ball up court as fast as we could to either score on a fast break or hustle into our offense. Once the play ended, we repeated it in the opposite direction. Coach paced along the sidelines with the flow of the action and urged us on: "Push it!" "Keep up the pressure!" "Run!"

Monday's practice blended into Tuesday's, Tuesday's into Wednesday's. Each day, I saw the fire in the guys' eyes and the set of their jaws. No one fooled around and no one hesitated. My confidence grew.

At four o'clock Thursday afternoon, an hour before our normal quitting time, Coach McCutchan blew his whistle and gathered us at midcourt. We settled around him, shirts drenched, sweat splattering the hardwood. I braced myself for the pep talk that would remind us of all the hard work it had taken to get to this point and the supreme effort it would take to finish our job.

Cradling a basketball against his hip, Coach said, "Boys, you're ready. You don't need any more work. Get a good night's sleep. I'll see you here tomorrow at noon to caravan to Louisville."

• • •

BETHUNE-COOKMAN'S CARL FULLER CONTROLLED the opening tip backward to one of his guards. Watkins immediately picked him up tight in the backcourt, forcing him to struggle to cross the centerline. He darted a pass cross-court toward my man, who I had already crowded shoulder to shoulder. I wrestled the ball away from him and took a foul as I drove to the basket. Making one of my two free throws, we inched to an early 1–0 lead after only seconds.

The 1,500 Evansvillians who'd made the 120-mile trip to Bellarmine College's gym let out a roar. The rout was on. The Aces dominated the game with such speed and ruthlessness that the court looked like a cross between a stampede and a mugging. Everything worked to perfection, a seamless continuation from where we'd left off Thursday afternoon at Carson Center. Williams and Sloan battled the boards all night, the rest of us grabbing a missed shot here and there. One of them would snare a rebound, then whip the ball to Watkins or me on the wing. The rest of us would fill the lanes, and off we'd streak to our basket on a thundering fast break.

After ten minutes we led 36–14, then extended that to 62–32 at halftime. Back on the court, we opened up a thirty-five-point lead, 83–48, with twelve minutes left in the game. At that point, McCutchan not only pulled all five of us from the court, but he sent us to the showers to get a head start on resting for the next night's regional championship.

We headed to our locker room single file, receiving a standing ovation till we disappeared from sight. We looked neither right nor left, nor did we smile, nod, or wave. To do so, we felt, would make us circus performers, not athletes.

Showered and dressed in our street clothes, the five of us walked back into the gym, again arousing an ovation from the Evansville faithful. Sitting in the first row of bleachers behind the bench, Humes and Williams on my left, Sloan and Watkins on my right, I felt full of myself, proud to be one of these Aces.

With a few minutes left in the game, sub Ron Eberhard drilled a jumper to put the Aces over the century mark. Just then I felt a tap on my shoulder. I turned and saw a young woman smiling at me in a confident, beguiling way that shot electricity through my body. She had Elvis-black hair that spilled to her shoulders, ebony eyes, ivory skin, and high cheekbones. She wore a short-sleeved white sweater and a dark-blue skirt that stopped at her knees. She was breathtaking.

Before I could react, she said, "You're number twenty-four, aren't you?"

"Yes," I said. "How'd you know?"

"I've been watching you run around in those cute little shorts all night."

I wanted to say something clever, but nothing came to mind, so I just smiled. She extended her hand and said, "I'm Amy."

"Russ," I said, taking her hand, noticing the softness of her skin.

Just as I was about to slide up to sit beside her, I heard Sloan's voice in my right ear. "Hey, you'd better keep your mind in the game. Coach sees you fooling around and you're in deep shit."

"Yeah, okay," I said. I turned back to Amy and asked, "Can you stay for a little while after the game?"

"Yes," she said, the sweetest sound I'd heard all night.

While the reserves finished the game, the capacity crowd dwindled, leaving mostly Evansville fans cheering till the game's end. The final score: 118–77. Humes scored thirty points in his twenty-eight minutes of action. Williams contributed sixteen, Sloan fifteen, Watkins eleven, and me nine. Though Carl Fuller did collect sixteen boards, we out-rebounded the Wildcats 70–56, chalked up eighteen assists—five by Sloan, four by me—and forced too many errors to count. Best of all, Sloan held the six-foot-nine Fuller to an inconsequential ten points.

After the final horn sounded, I gestured to Amy that I'd return in a minute, then joined the Aces on the court for congratulations. As they left to shower, I hustled back to the bleachers and settled into the seat next to her.

"Welcome back," she said.

I sat and listened to the outline of her life. She attended Bellermine College, our next night's foe, majored in theater and drama, and was unsure of what to do after graduation. She lived off campus in an apartment with her roommate, belonged to no sorority, and did not have a boyfriend. Her voice rang clear and confident, the voice of a woman who knew her allure. I felt myself drawn to her and lamented that this encounter was taking place in Louisville rather than Evansville.

I saw the Aces drift back one by one onto the court in their street clothes. "I'm sorry," I said, nodding toward the team. "I gotta go in a minute."

"Can we meet up and go somewhere?" she asked.

"No, as much as I'd like to."

We both sat silently for a few seconds, the first pause in our conversation since I'd sat down. I wondered if she felt as wistful as I did.

"Hey," I said, "how about tomorrow night after the game? You bring your car, and I'll figure out how to get away. Okay?" I hoped my enthusiasm wasn't over the top.

"It's a date."

"Okay then. You know where I'll be." I gestured toward the court. "Stand up and give me a wave before the game."

"I will," she said. "Look for me."

As I got up to join my teammates, Amy grabbed my hand from behind and gave it a squeeze. She looked me in the eye and said, "I'm going to think about you tonight."

I stepped off the bleachers and made my way across the court toward the guys. I imagined her watching me as I walked away and liked the feel of her gaze.

Jerry Sloan and I barricaded ourselves in our stodgy downtown hotel room after the game. It had a lived-in look—reddish carpeting worn dull by thousands of feet, white bedspreads curdled to a hint of yellow, a register painted white that emitted a rattling sound and, along with heat, gave off a musty odor. At the foot of our beds sat a TV that took a full minute to light up and whose picture periodically rolled up as if it were blinking.

I switched to channel three to catch the late-night sports news. In a dark-blue blazer that buttoned off to the side in ship-captain fashion, the sportscaster told us he had just come back from the Bellermine gym and seen the best team in the country. He breathlessly reported the stats of our victory over Bethune-Cookman and called us "wizards of the hardwood," "ballerinas in basketball shoes," and "in a class all their own." He compared our speed with that of a thoroughbred and likened our artistry to Nureyev's.

"Sounds like he likes us," I said to Sloan, trying to sound cool, careful not to betray how much I relished the praise.

Like an attorney presenting evidence, he showed video replays—us fast breaking, Humes out-finessing two and sometimes three defenders, Sloan firing a bullet to an open man for a score. He punctuated each play with "See that?" or "What a move!"

Once the sportscaster turned to other stories, Sloan said, "We better not let that go to our heads or we'll take a fall."

"For sure," I said.

"Turn that thing off so we can get some sleep. We've got more work to do tomorrow."

The lights of downtown Louisville snuck through the window shade and sliced across the six-foot-six form of Jerry Sloan, asleep in his too-short bed. I felt too pumped up to go to sleep. As I lay there, I replayed the events of the evening—the game, for sure, but also my encounter with Amy. I knew I was taken with her, captivated by her interest in me, bewitched by her seductive way, excited by her beauty. I pushed thoughts of my girlfriend, Joyce, out of my mind, not wanting to think of the loyalty, affection, and support she had given me over the past year. What I did not understand was that my heart was a hungry little muscle, underused too long, and starved for romance that I had sacrificed for comfort.

◆ ◆ ◆

BELLERMINE'S FANS MUST NOT HAVE watched TV. When we took the court the next evening, they chanted: "They were Aces, now they're Jokers." The Redshirts countered with "We're number one, we're number one" but were out-shouted with a massive "Not for long, not for long." Locating Amy sitting in this hostile crowd did nothing to comfort me, nor did her demure wave and smile.

*We're in for a dogfight,* I thought.

Bellermine's coach, Alex Groza, a former University of Kentucky All-American, based his game plan on the belief that his team could not beat us by way of talent and finesse. Instead, he decided to challenge us with a bare-knuckle game resembling a brawl between two caged animals.

The Knights pounded the boards, sending three and sometimes four men to the glass after every shot, elbows flying and hips bumping. They packed their defense tight to the basket to prevent Humes from getting the ball, hipping and elbowing him every time he made a move. When we succeeded, three defenders swarmed him, so that he couldn't move without running into someone. They dove to the floor and flew headfirst out of bounds to retrieve every loose ball.

The Aces fell behind 7–2. Everyone in the gym, except those dressed in red, howled so loud that I thought the walls would collapse. Standing behind the free-throw arc, I noticed Coach McCutchan motion to Sloan to speak to him on the sidelines. He stood, half turned toward the court, and spoke close into Jerry's ear. Sloan nodded, trotted back onto the court, and yelled loud enough for us to hear, "Okay, dammit, let's pick it up!"

As he had all season, Sloan showed his fighting spirit. He hit a line-drive jumper from the corner to tie the score at 7–7. Minutes later, he hit another jumper from outer space to give us the lead for the first time, 20–18. At 23–22, Aces, he dropped a screamer from the top of the key to make the score 25–22, then another from the wing, 27–22. Putting an exclamation point on his one-man assault, he threaded the needle between two defenders to Humes for an easy layup, 29–22, and then rocketed the ball to me for another basket, 31–22.

Bellermine called a time-out. The Redshirts cheered and howled, our purple-skirted, white-sweatered cheerleaders leading the chorus: "Aces, Aces," *clap, clap . . . clap, clap, clap*; "Aces, Aces," *clap, clap . . . clap, clap, clap*. The rest of those surrounding the court sat in silence.

We circled Coach McCutchan in front of our bench. I snuck a look at Amy talking to the girl at her side, but did not make eye contact.

We kept up our pressure and extended our lead to eleven, 37–26. With minutes left in the half, Sloan ripped a one-handed rebound off the defensive glass and slowly dribbled the ball across the centerline. He fired a bullet to Humes on the right side of the free-throw lane. With his back to the basket, Humes spied me open as my man went to double-team him. He looked left, then dropped a no-look bounce pass off his right hip to me. I banked in a ten-foot jumper and was fouled after the shot. My two free throws increased our lead to 41–26.

We took a 49–38 lead to the locker room. As usual, Humes led the scoring with twenty, collecting almost as many bruises as he did points. Sloan totaled twelve, his last basket a sensational leaping tip-in over the hands of two Bellermine grapplers. I tallied ten. Though the Knights outscored us twelve to eight down the stretch to cut our lead to eleven, this game felt to me like many others we had played: we struggled for a while but assumed command by halftime and then blew it wide open in the second half. I felt relaxed and confident, glad to have my teammates around me.

We trotted back onto the court to find a rejuvenated Bellermine crowd. "There they are, there they are" morphed into "You'll get yours, you'll get yours" from the student section.

While warming up, Sloan said, "They're not done."

The tone of his voice sent a shiver through me.

The Bellermine Knights started the second half with pinpoint accuracy on offense to complement their roughhouse tactics on defense. They hit seven of their first ten shots without a floor error, cutting our lead to 55–52. The crowd howled, thunder-clapping with each basket that brought them closer to us.

Tightness gripped my chest, but Sloan remained unstoppable. Eyes darting, nostrils flaring, he fired a precision pass to Humes, who made the layup, 57–52. Then another for 59–52. After Bellermine converted a three-point play, Sloan hit Humes once again under the basket to make our lead six, 61–55.

Back and forth we went. We stretched our lead, they closed the gap, we again separated ourselves, they reeled us back. My emotions followed this seesawing, feeling relief one minute, tension the next.

The clamor surrounding us never let up. A small group of Bellermine students started a cheer that the rest of the crowd quickly picked up: "Beat their Aces! Beat their Aces!"

I wiped sweat off my forehead and glanced at the student section. I locked eyes with a young man wearing a scarlet Bellermine sweatshirt.

He had curly red hair and a matching goatee. His mouth was fixed in a sneer. He extended his arm, pointing at me, and nodded, as if to say, "Yeah, you, you're going down."

I felt like giving him the finger.

Leading by six with five minutes left to play, I dribbled up the side of the court to hear Coach McCutchan yell, "Grieger! Grieger!" I stole a quick glance and saw him pushing downward with both his palms. "Slow it down!" he yelled and continued to make the gesture to the other guys so they also got the message.

"Smart move," Coach Groza said after the game to reporters. "We were forced into a zone because of foul trouble and that brought us out of it."

I didn't like it. For the first time all season, I questioned one of Coach's decisions. Playing defensive basketball went against the grain of our team's personality. I thought it made us look weak and scared.

With one and a half minutes to go, leading by five, a Knight guard swiped the ball from my grasp and passed it to his running mate, who sped toward the basket unmolested. The crowd erupted with an avalanche of noise until they realized the official had called traveling on the ball thief and had given the ball back to us.

After that, I took special care to protect the basketball when it was in my possession. With us in full keep-away mode, Bellermine desperately fouled Watkins, who dropped both his two free throws. Seconds later they fouled me. My two gave us a nine-point cushion, so a Bellermine basket that cut our lead to seven was inconsequential.

The horn sounded. We'd won the regional championship: 81–74. I felt more relief than anything else.

When I left the court, I glanced into the stands at Amy. She looked radiant in a lavender sweater and black skirt, an outfit I took as a statement of allegiance to me.

I waved and then pointed down to the court to signal for her to wait for me while I dressed.

She smiled, nodded, and put her hand over her heart.

◆   ◆   ◆

WELL-WISHERS AND REPORTERS JAMMED INTO our locker room. They circulated from one of us to another, like in a wedding receiving line, and offered "Good game" and "Atta boy." Coach stood in one corner, surrounded by media, Sloan in another, trapped by his own gaggle of reporters.

I showered, dressed, and hustled out to the gym. There Amy sat, by herself, in the same seat she'd occupied these last two games. Her black hair glistened under the fluorescent lights, every strand in place, and her lavender sweater contrasted with the maroon bleachers behind her. She saw me as I crossed the court and smiled. I wondered how I looked to her, whether she felt the same excitement I did.

We said hi as I settled next to her. I had not touched her except to briefly hold her hand, but I wanted to.

"Listen," I said, "I have to ride to the hotel with the team. Give me about half an hour and meet me out front. Keep your motor running for a fast getaway. Okay?"

"Okay." She smiled. "Any place special you want to go?"

"Anywhere."

"How about my apartment? It's quiet and comfy."

"Great," I said, hoping she'd thought to get rid of her roommate for the night.

At the appointed time, Amy sat in her red Chevrolet Chevelle across the street from the hotel, the motor running. I glanced both left and right to make sure the coast was clear. Seeing nothing but the glare of streetlights and cars stopped at the intersection, I double-stepped down the marble steps to the passenger side to find she had already scooted to the middle of the seat. "You drive," she said.

I slid behind the wheel. "Which way?" I asked, trying to sound lighthearted.

Amy's apartment was more modest than I'd anticipated—a living room with a kitchenette off to the side, a hallway with a bathroom at the end, and two doors on either side with a bedroom behind each. I flopped down next to the armrest on a couch that sat with its back to a window, its blinds twisted shut but not totally keeping the lights from an occasional car from sweeping in around its edges. A green lava lamp sat on the coffee table and gave the room a soft glow. Amy sat Indian style, her skirt over her knees, facing me. "I'm glad you're here," she said, reaching out to hold both my hands in hers.

"Me too."

Talk came fast and easy, as if we both wanted to cram a whole semester's worth of getting to know each other into this one night. We discussed school and majors, families, friends, hopes, and dreams. I relished the details from her life and shared mine with her.

"When do you need to get back to the hotel?" she asked sometime after midnight.

"By six," I said. "I think I can sneak into my room without getting caught if I get back early."

"That's good." Then she stood up and, taking my hand, pulled me down the hallway.

We stayed up all night, me engulfed by a feeling of enthrallment that I had not felt off the basketball court in a long time. Later we drove in silence back to the hotel as soft morning light filled the car. She sat close to me as we pulled up across the street from the hotel.

I glanced out my window and saw Coach McCutchan and Doc Whetstone, one of our drivers, walk down the steps of the hotel. They both wore overcoats, hats, and gloves.

"Holy shit," I said, sliding down as fast as I could.

Amy also slid down and laughed. "I knew there was some desperado inside you," she said.

With a satisfied grin, I peeked out the window and spied Coach disappearing around the corner. "I gotta go."

"I know." She gave me a quick kiss. "Think about me."

"I will, I promise," I said as I opened the door and ran into the hotel, desperado style.

A few hours later, the Aces assembled outside the hotel to caravan back to Evansville. I sat in the front seat next to Doc Whetstone, exhausted. Jim Forman and Jerry Sloan sat talking in the back. We drove past downtown Louisville on our left and the Ohio River on our right, then over a four-lane silver bridge back into Indiana toward Evansville.

The car moved silently as we passed restaurants with glaring red letters on their roofs announcing *Truck Stop* and run-down motels that looked like they would only appeal to the most desperate travelers. Flocks of black birds swirled across plowed dirt fields and around leafless trees. I leaned my forehead against the window, too spent to talk.

I thought of Amy. I could still smell her—her perfume, her hair, her passion. I could picture her eyes, sweet and inviting. I could feel the softness of her skin and the curve of her body from her shoulders to her waist and down along her hips. With a mixture of longing and sadness, I wondered if I would ever see her again.

I woke from this reverie and saw a white rectangular church, two stories high, with a huge stained-glass window above its front door and a steeple that reached to the sky. Sunshine washed over a man wearing a white shirt and black suit and holding a Bible as he stood passively atop the concrete steps of the church's entrance. He met my eyes and held his Bible up toward me, half a greeting, half an admonishment. Joyce came to my mind and guilt spread through me like a prairie fire.

I looked over at Doc Whetstone, as much to see if he saw the man as to check out if he could sense my guilt. He peered over the steering wheel with a faraway look in his eyes. "What are you thinking?" I asked, leery of his answer.

"Funny you should ask," he said. "I was thinking about the start of the Bethune-Cookman game when you stole that pass and took it to the basket. Kind of set the tone for the whole weekend."

"I guess," I said, thankful for the turn toward basketball.

My mind drifted to last night's game against Bellermine. I had scored thirteen points, ten in the first half, three in the second, all on free throws. *Why only thirteen?* The truth was, from the beginning of the season through this game, I did not look for my shot, did not aggressively work to score. *What if I had last night? What if I had all season? Could I have averaged more than my ten per game? Maybe twelve, or fourteen, or even sixteen?*

The wheels hummed over the pavement, an occasional thump over a crack. I realized these were the wrong questions. The real one was *why* had I not been more conscious of scoring, more aggressive with the ball, more insistent on being upfront and center stage? My first answer was that it had to do with fear—fear of failure. I remembered the apprehension I'd felt during the tenuous moments of last night's second half.

Then a second answer popped into my mind. Maybe it wasn't fear at all. Maybe I had accepted my role, not that of a high scorer or a star, but of a solid player, willing to do what he could to help the team. Maybe it was indeed about self, not a doubting self, but more an accepting self.

Doc Whetstone left me off in front of my parents' house. No sooner had I gotten in than the phone rang.

"I'm glad I got you," Joyce said. "My dad had a heart attack yesterday afternoon."

"Oh, my God. Is he okay?"

"Yes, he's resting comfortably. Looks like he'll be okay."

"I'm so sorry," I said, meaning much more than just about her dad.

"Can you come over?"

"Sure. Let me settle in. Then I'll be over."

The minute I hung up, a mixture of both guilt and apprehension consumed me. I felt very much like the drunk who'd sobered up to discover the next day how badly he'd behaved. *Okay, now what?* I realized that, above all else, I had to support Joyce through her crisis. Also I'd have to give all my attention to the NCAA finals next week.

After that, who knew.

# 22

## THE NCAA FINALS

I PLOPPED DOWN AT THE breakfast table in my red plaid robe the Monday before the NCAA finals. I took a deep breath, slowly expelled it, and then massaged my eyes.

Dad sat to my right, dressed in a starched white shirt and blue tie, ready for work. Early-morning daylight eased through the window behind him, as did the voices of Dexter grade-school children on the playground across the street, enjoying their last minutes of freedom before the bell called them indoors. Mom stood at the stove in the kitchen to my left, still in her blue wraparound, preparing breakfast, the smells of sizzling eggs and bacon drifting my way.

"Read this," Dad said, sliding the *Evansville Courier* sports page in front of me. The headline read: "Toughest Field After Aces Title."

*Christ!* I thought, feeling Dad's eyes on me, not yet ready to deal with the next challenge after the drama of the last few days.

In the article, Dave Powers extolled the virtues of each of the other seven teams in the field, but especially those of Southern Illinois University. He wrote: "Southern Illinois, anxious to tangle with the Aces again, rate a real threat after dropping a home-and-home series by one point both times (81–80 and 68–67)."

"Okay," I said, tossing the paper aside. I didn't say the *so what?* that completed the sentence in my mind.

"Well, what do you think?" Dad asked, raising his eyebrows. Mom sat my breakfast in front of me and leaned against the doorjamb that separated the kitchen from the dining room.

"I don't know," I said. I grabbed a piece of bacon and tore off a bite. "I guess anyone can win it."

Dad gave me a quizzical look. "Don't you think you'll win?"

"Of course I do, but I'm just being realistic here."

"I hope you're not as nervous as I am," Mom said. "I can't stand it. It would be horrible to lose."

I sat there, a piece of toast in my left hand and a fork full of egg in my right. I glanced at both of them and realized that they were looking to me for reassurance, the kind Dad had given when I stepped up to the plate as a Little Leaguer, the kind Mom had given when she'd rubbed Vicks salve on my congested chest when I was a boy.

I dropped my fork back on my plate and said, "Look, win or lose, it's just a game, not really that important. Okay?"

No one moved for a moment. With a tilt of his head, Dad pursed his lips and nodded, as if I had just delivered the Eleventh Commandment.

Mom smiled her sweet smile and patted me on the shoulder.

I munched on my toast, secretly affected by what I had just said. I knew in part that I was expressing the image I had cultivated as an Evansville College Purple Ace, the kind of bravado I reserved for the public. I also knew my words contained some irritation. I was frustrated by the pressure my parents had thrown at me first thing on a Monday morning. But there was more. I was startled by the fact that what I had said contained a ring of truth to me.

*Wow, just a game, not life and death.* My mind flashed back to September and October, to the Armory, to preseason practices at Carson Center, to when I thought my existence depended on being an Aces first-teamer. I marveled at the distance I had traveled in these few short months.

"What are you thinking?" Dad asked.

I blinked back to the table. "Nothing, just about the tourney," I said, wanting to shut the conversation down.

"Well, you better eat up. You don't want to be late for school."

"Yeah," I said, hoping I could hang onto this perspective until game time Wednesday night.

•   •   •

DRESSED IN OUR HOME WHITES, ankles taped and shoelaces tied, we sat in our locker room a few minutes past nine, Wednesday night, March 10. No one spoke. I stared at the floor, lost in my pregame jitters, wanting to get onto the court and settle down.

Scout Dave Fulkerson stuck his head in the door and said, "Time."

"Okay, let's do it," Sloan said.

We walked single file through the concrete bowels of Roberts Stadium, dim and concrete gray, toward the bright lights and hubbub of the court. We passed the Southern Illinois Salukis heading in the opposite direction, having just completed their quarterfinal victory over Washington University, 76–67. Their shirts clung to their bodies; their faces dripped sweat. We did not look at or speak to them. We wanted to show indifference, a hint of disdain, because acknowledgment communicated respect, and respect might be seen as weakness.

Once on the court, routine took over. Layups, stretching, jump shots. Everything felt familiar—the color red surrounding us, the faint smell of cigarette smoke from the concession areas above, the drone of thousands of conversations.

Yet I felt the atmosphere was different. The conversations sounded concerned, as if the spectators were waiting for a jury's verdict. I located Dad, standing, his arms folded across his chest, bending down to say something to Mom, her hands clasped over her red-skirted lap, prayer style. I found Dr. Grabill studying the Philadelphia Textile Rams, a serious look in his eyes, pointing toward them and barking into the ear of the gentleman next to him. Sportswriters Bill Fluty, Tim Tuley, Al Dunning, Tony Chamblain, and Bill Robertson sat silently at the press table, forgoing their usual banter.

Textile had the second-best record in the tournament—twenty-four wins, three losses. They stayed close to us for two-thirds of the first half by packing in their zone defense and dropping bombs from long range. Tied at 27–27, Herb Williams leaped between two Rams and tipped in Watkins's missed jumper. This move ignited some invisible spark in both Sloan and Humes, who began popping fifteen-foot jumpers from each side of the basket until we opened up a 49–37 lead at the break. Forced out of their zone, we broke Textile's back in the opening minutes of the second half and coasted home for a 92–76 triumph.

I walked off the court and gave no thought to the next night's game, enjoying the feeling of dominance.

While I untied my shoelaces, Watkins, sitting next to me, shoved a stat sheet in my face. "Look at this," he said.

Humes had scored thirty, Watkins fourteen, and me eleven. Underneath my name came Sloan's: twenty-seven points, twenty-six rebounds. We looked at each other and shook our heads.

The next night, Thursday, March 11, again wearing our freshly laundered home whites, I stood with the Aces in the tunnel, waiting to take the court for our national semifinal game against St. Michael's. We watched Southern Illinois finish their thrashing of the North Dakota University Sioux. The squint in their eyes and the set of their jaws let us know they had a mission that did not end with this game. We did not need to look at the scoreboard to know that they were making a statement.

I thought of none of this as we raced onto the court, though it stirred my blood. We started the game against St. Michael's as intense as Southern Illinois finished. We raced ahead 27–15 six minutes into the game, made it 35–20 after ten, and expanded that lead to 51–33 at halftime with Sloan's tip-in at the buzzer. After Humes made a basket with nine minutes left on the clock, his thirty-seventh and thirty-eighth points, Coach McCutchan flooded the court with substitutes, who brought home our 93–70 victory.

We walked together into the locker room, the last time, I realized, we'd gather there with a game still in front of us. I carried a mixture of feelings I hadn't the ability to straighten out: a sense of pride in what we'd accomplished; an awe in that we were about to battle for the NCAA title; and a nagging dread that, should we lose, our undefeated season, our number-one ranking, and our reputation would be lost in an instant.

I woke the next morning to find that sportswriter Bill Robertson had captured the situation simply and best in his *Evansville Courier* headline. In bold, black letters, spread across the top of the sports page, he declared:

Aces, SIU To Go At It Again, And This Time It's For Keeps.

•　•　•

SO WE CAME TO THE NCAA Championship game, the game that would decide our destiny. It seemed fated, as if the basketball gods would not allow any other teams but the Southern Illinois Salukis and the Evansville College Purple Aces to contend for the prize. The Aces ranked number one in the nation, the Salukis number two. Only two points separated our team from theirs after eighty minutes of feverish play this season—an Aces victory in Evansville on a last-second, miracle basket; another Aces victory when the potential winning basket by the Salukis clanged off the rim as the buzzer sounded.

The day began gray and drab. Low, heavy clouds seemed to stifle what was possible, hanging so thick and motionless it seemed to slow time to a crawl. I could barely stand the tension gnawing at my stomach.

I felt grateful that Coach McCutchan had scheduled a noon team meal at Evansville College's student union. I drove my parents' blue Ford Galaxie to campus. It was eerily vacant, since President Melvin Hyde had declared a school holiday for the game. I saw only a stray dog sniffing the grass and a flurry of birds pecking the ground for nourishment.

We sat at a long table at the center of a banquet room directly above The Indian. Light from high rectangular windows, bordered by thick crimson curtains, illuminated a white tablecloth and the polished wood floor. Before us lay porcelain plates and silverware with EC engraved on the handles. I imagined that President Hyde used this room for official functions.

Waiters dressed in black slacks, white shirts, and bow ties served us steak, baked potato, and hot tea loaded with honey. Everyone spoke quietly. Now and then only the clanging of silverware could be heard. Herb Williams said something to Sam Watkins, which I couldn't quite catch, and Sam responded with one of his wry smiles. Then I heard Sloan say from across the table, "They ain't beat us yet, and I'll be damned if they're going to do it tonight."

I felt comforted being with the guys. Yet I knew I would have to endure this dread till game time.

The clock in the Administration Building chimed one o'clock. Coach McCutchan stood up at the head of the table and said, "Okay, boys, listen up. Finish your meal and get yourself over to Carson Center. I'll see you on the court in half an hour, in street clothes, for a walk-through."

I saw no need for such a rehearsal. Both Southern Illinois and the Aces would start the same lineup they had our first two games. We knew their plays as well as they knew ours. Each coach could predict the other's maneuvers. Yet I felt grateful for something to do to occupy my mind.

Sloan and I walked across campus, each wearing our dark-purple letter jackets snapped tight to our necks. The clouds had started breaking, and slivers of sunlight pierced our pathway. Neither of us said a word, both of us lost in thought. We turned left between the Olmstead Administration Building and the McCurdy Library and made our way beneath a smattering of trees. Approaching Carson Center, Sloan broke the silence. "This is it."

"Yeah," I said, my hands deep in my pockets, knowing he meant both the NCAA Championship and our last game as Aces.

We walked a few more strides, the only noise the crunching beneath our feet.

"I say we take it to them from the opening tip," I said.

"Yeah," he said, "let's kick ass."

"Yeah, let's," I echoed.

I got to the stadium that night midway through the consolation game to find that the 12,797 seats had already filled. The fans, almost all wearing red, bellowed, "We want Southern! We want Southern!" the game in front of them an afterthought.

We dressed without a word, the only sounds the tearing of tape, shouts from the faraway court, and an occasional locker closing. Evansville College had played big games before, but there had never been one with so much at stake. I felt the tightness in my chest, a strange mixture of hotness and trembling.

Pushing nine o'clock, Coach McCutchan walked to the center of the room. He wore a black-checked sport coat with a red flower in his lapel, a red vest over a white shirt and red tie, and his lucky red socks under black slacks. The room became deathly quiet.

Finally, he spoke. "Boys, I've only got two things to say to you before you take the court. One, I want to let you know that I've never been so proud of any team of mine in my life. You're the greatest in my book, bar none. Okay?" A pause. "But I also want you to hear something else. Win or lose, we're going to get up tomorrow morning and have breakfast. So go out there tonight and have fun."

I considered him as I had never done before, my respect now mixed with love.

He then slowly looked around at us, as if acknowledging each of us in turn, and said a simple, "Okay, let's go."

We rose as one and trooped toward the court, wedging through more people in the tunnel than I'd ever seen. Nearing the playing floor, Sam Watkins grabbed my arm, pulled me to the front of the pack, and said, "You're our senior, Russ. Lead us out."

I did, bursting through a huge paper oval held up by my TKE fraternity brothers, my teammates close behind. The Redshirts roared, "Aces! Aces!" *clap clap . . . clap clap clap*; "Aces! Aces!" *clap clap . . . clap clap clap*. They continued this chant, like a needle stuck in a record groove, for minutes.

At nine thirty, the buzzer blasted to signal game time.

The announcer at the scoring table introduced the Salukis first: David Lee and George McNeil at guard, Boyd O'Neal at center, and Walt Frazier and Joe Ramsey at forward. After eighty minutes of furious action already this year, these were opponents whose games I'd come to know as well as the neighborhood boys I had played against behind my house on Chandler Avenue.

"And now, for the Aces . . ." the announcer blared.

The Evansville College cheerleaders, wearing purple skirts and matching purple sweaters, immediately hustled from the sidelines to form a semicircle under the basket. They kicked their legs high and shook their white feathery pom-poms over their heads as they ran.

". . . Number Twenty-Four, Russ Grieger."

I trotted loose-limbed to the free-throw line, turned to the bench, and clapped, waiting for my teammates to join me. It didn't register then, but this would be the last such introduction I'd ever get in my lifetime. Next came Humes, followed by Williams and Watkins, and then Sloan, the screaming growing louder as each Ace ran onto the court.

We gathered around Coach for last instructions. "Everybody ready?" he asked.

"Yeah!"

"Okay then, you're forty minutes away from NCAA immortality. Go get it!"

We walked out to start the game and exchanged "Good lucks" and "Play wells" with the Salukis. I always approached the opening tip-off with respect, but the gravity of all that was at stake filled me with a sense of solemnity I hadn't expected.

David Lee controlled the ball for Southern Illinois in the backcourt. He had the look of a warrior, scanning the court as if it were a battlefield. He dribbled toward me, and I met him at center court, crowding him close, shuffling my feet to keep his movement lateral, holding my hands low and forward to snatch the ball if given the opportunity. I could feel the adrenaline coursing through my body, but knew I'd soon settle into the rhythm of the game.

Lee bounced the ball to Walt Frazier on his left and cut right to the basket. Frazier then winged a pass to Joe Ramsey in the left corner, who, in turn, bounced the first shot of the game high off the rim. After a scramble, the ball went out of bounds to the Aces on the sidelines.

The Redshirts howled, all thirteen thousand of them, as if smelling first blood.

The referee handed me the ball, and I gripped it hard with both hands, absorbing the feel of it. I tossed it to Watkins, who hustled up court and shoveled it to Humes on the right side of the lane. Humes dribbled to his left, cautiously at first while scanning the court, got a pick from me at the top of the key, then another from Sloan, and gathered speed to the left baseline to take a ten-foot jumper. Swish. Aces, 2–0.

The Redshirts howled again.

I knew we were on our game as I whomped Humes on the fanny, an expression of relief as much as praise.

I took my turn flipping the ball to Humes the next time down the court. With his back to the basket, he faked left, dribbled to his right, and lofted a running right-hander over his shoulder that kissed off the glass and dropped through the net. Minutes later Watkins drilled a twenty-footer from the left side. The Aces led 9–3 four minutes into the game.

The Salukis quickly called time-out. The crowd, already erupting after every shot, every pass, every official's decision, drowned the court with thunderous jubilation. It felt like a nuclear wave against our bodies. I stole a quick glance into the stands. Thousands of people, all jumping and flailing, dressed in red, seemed to meld into each other like a massive glob of quivering strawberry Jell-O.

Southern Illinois came back on the court and quickly tied us at 13–13 on a succession of jumpers. This then silenced the crowd to a low murmur for the first time since we'd taken the court.

The score tied five more times that half, the last one being 26–26. Five minutes remained before the break. By this time, organized cheering had vanished. It was as if the Redshirts had lost their will and could only react reflexively to what happened on the court. I had the sense that SIU and the Aces were simply continuing what we had started two weeks before in Carbondale. I knew it would come down to who would deliver, not who would outsmart the other.

When Watkins brought the ball up the court, McCutchan stood and yelled, "Let's win the rest of the half!" We then traded baskets before I hit two free throws and Williams leaped high to tip in a missed Watkins jumper to give us a 39–35 lead at the buzzer.

In the locker room, we sat on gray metal folding chairs, gathering our thoughts and our energy. Student managers dispensed cups of ice, Coke, and water. We could hear the hum from thirteen thousand people courtside. The weight of the situation hung heavy over the room like freeway smog.

In walked Coach McCutchan, still dapper in his sport coat, vest, and slacks. He wrote "1140/20" on the chalkboard in large digits.

"Boys," he said, "this is how many minutes we've played already this year." He pointed to the number 1140. "And this here," he said, stepping aside and pointing to the 20, "is how many minutes are still left in the season."

He paused, the only sound being the buzz from the crowd far away.

Then he spoke. "Twenty more minutes. Twenty! If you play them with just a little more intensity, just a little bit better, you'll be national champions. I guarantee it. Now go get it."

Williams controlled the opening tip, which went to Sloan, who then batted the ball to Humes, streaking down the right side toward the basket. But gnat-like David Lee anticipated this maneuver and zipped in front of Humes to intercept the ball. The Redshirts' burst of glee abruptly turned to a collective groan of disappointment.

Lee dribbled over the centerline and bounced a pass to Walt Frazier, who promptly swished a jumper from deep in the right corner. After Humes missed his shot, Joe Ramsey canned his own twenty-footer from the left side, which tied the game 39–39. Eighteen minutes showed on the game clock. We started from scratch.

For the next ten minutes, the Aces and the Salukis slugged it out toe to toe. SIU kept in motion on offense, taking their time, settling only for the shot they wanted. I stayed alert on defense, shuttling close to Lee when he had the ball, switching off onto O'Neil, Frazier, or Ramsey when a teammate ran into a block.

Despite our best efforts, Southern Illinois hit the basket with deadly accuracy, easing ahead first by two, then four, up to six, and finally to eight, 67–59. The clock blinked to 8:27.

Except for the cheers from the Salukis fans, the stadium grew quiet. Running down the court, a dazed emptiness filled my chest, the kind I would next feel on the night my father died years later. I knew it signaled dread but was unwilling to consider the possibility that our undefeated season and national championship might be slipping away.

No one said a word as Sloan dribbled the perimeter, probing for an opening. Humes struggled to get position underneath. Sloan passed the ball to Watkins above the free-throw circle, who then threw it to me in the right corner. I held the ball over my head, watching Humes. Once he had his man on his hip, I bulleted an overhead two-hander to him close to the basket. He elongated his lean body as high as he could and missed his shot but was fouled. His two free throws narrowed the gap to 67–61.

"Bear down!" I yelled as we ran back on defense. I knew no one on our team would dispute that command.

We crouched low on defense and forced the Saluki to take an off-balance shot. Sloan snatched the ball off the rim and took it up court. We again passed the ball around the perimeter until I launched a running jumper from the left baseline. It bounced off the metal toward Humes, who leaped and tipped it back in: 67–63.

With that basket, the Redshirts lit up like dynamite, sending an explosion to the rafters.

"Once more!" I yelled to the guys.

We played tenacious defense, double-stepping our feet and keeping our arms in motion. Saluki Joe Ramsey missed his jumper from the left corner, and Herb Williams bounded high to capture it.

Humes ran to his familiar position under the basket, then yelled, "Get me the ball!"

Sloan hustled the ball over the centerline and bounced it to Williams at the top of the key, who, in turn, shot it to me on the right sideline. Humes flung his right arm back to hold his defender in place behind him. I took a dribble to my right to get a good angle to him, pivoted left, and flipped the ball over my defender's shoulder into Humes. He leaped up and laid the ball up and in over his head while being fouled. He didn't even look at the basket.

The Redshirts sprang to their feet and screamed at the top of their lungs, continuing to do so while Humes toed the line and sank his free throw. This drew us within one point, 67–66. They kept up their rampage as Humes made two more free throws on our next possession to put us ahead, 68–67 with only 5:15 left.

The bedlam in the stadium matched anything I'd ever seen or heard. No one stood still, including the Aces on the sidelines and the reporters on press row. Behind our bench, the purple-clad cheerleaders shook their pom-poms, stomped their feet, and yelled words that no one could hear.

I ran back to play defense and looked from Sloan and Humes to Watkins and Williams. Our backs had been to the wall; we could have easily given up. But we hadn't. Each of us had summoned an inner resolve and fought all the way back. I felt a bond with them I knew I would never lose.

From there we traded points. Humes dropped two more free throws, but SIU's Boyd O'Neal tipped in an SIU miss to tie the score 70–70. Williams dropped a jumper from the free-throw line, and Saluki George McNeil countered with a twenty-footer from the left wing: 72–72. Sloan cashed in on two free throws, and O'Neil swished another twenty-footer from the top of the key, making it 74–74. The clock blinked down to 1:39.

Watkins brought the ball up the court, the Aces determined to get either a layup or the last shot. But the referee whistled a three-second violation. The crowd hooted and groaned in equal measure.

Salukis coach Jack Hartman was quoted in the morning paper as musing before the game, "We'll have to get the last basket." That's what the Salukis intended to do. They held the basketball on the outside, taking time off the clock. We played them tight but cautiously, neither giving them an opening nor fouling them. I felt helpless, only able to hope we'd get another chance.

The clock ticked below a minute, then to thirty seconds, and then to twenty. Southern Illinois held the ball and our fate in their hands. With Humes in his face, George McNeil's bid for the national championship from twenty feet arched up through the air and then down with the swiftness of a falling guillotine. I watched it, my emotions blunted as if in a fugue state. Nothing else existed beyond the flight of the basketball. It hit the back of the rim and bounced off. Sloan grabbed the rebound as the buzzer blared, the sweetest sound I had ever heard in my life.

There would be overtime.

Drenched in sweat, towels draped around our necks, we sat in a line on the bench—Williams, Watkins, me, Humes, Sloan. Coach McCutchan stood in front of me, bent over at the waist, swiveling his head left and right, shouting instructions over the unflagging din of the thirteen thousand inmates in the world's biggest madhouse. Semicircled behind him stood our satin-robed teammates, leaning forward to hear.

I wiped sweat off my forehead for the umpteenth time as the buzzer summoned us to the court. As we walked to the center circle, Sam Watkins said to no one in particular, "The time comes for something to be done."

"Damn straight," I said, though not exactly knowing what he meant.

Williams toed the centerline one last time and crouched low to gather as much spring in his legs as nature gave him. So did big Boyd O'Neal for Southern Illinois. The Redshirts repeated "Aces, Aces" as we took our positions.

The referee tossed the ball up for grabs. Williams jumped as high as he could and tipped the ball forward. The Aces and Salukis scrambled for possession before Sloan slapped the ball toward our basket. Watkins grabbed it, wheeled around, and laid it in uncontested for a 76–74 lead.

The Aces on the bench sprang to their feet. The cheerleaders danced. The Redshirts delivered a blast of noise that scorched the court.

"Yes!" I said under my breath, giving an abrupt, closed-fist pump of my forearm.

The Salukis weaved and cut to free themselves for an open shot. With Watkins and me out front, and Sloan and Humes on the wings, we refused to yield an inch. After SIU wasted forty precious seconds of game time, I corralled an errant shot near the free-throw line.

The Redshirts cheered so loudly that, if it had had weight, the noise would have crushed us.

Sloan brought the ball over the centerline, slowly and deliberately. He bounced it to Humes on the right side of the free-throw lane. I saw him start to shoot a long, sweeping hook shot that I considered unwise and improbable. Before I could get the word "no" out of my mouth, he slid the ball high off the glass and into the basket. The Aces now led 78–74 with 4:04 left for the national championship.

"Great shot," I yelled as Humes strutted past me, relieved that my lack of faith had stuck in my throat.

A minute later Saluki Boyd O'Neal tipped in a missed shot, his first basket of the night, but Sloan countered with two free throws. Aces 80–76. By this time, there was no letup in the earsplitting clamor that filled Roberts Stadium.

Somehow, despite the hysteria, the game continued. Humes dropped the first of two free throws at 1:37 to extend our lead to 81–76. We sensed victory, but SIU's Walt Frazier immediately stuffed in a missed shot: 81–78. We played keep-away until SIU fouled Watkins on a reach-in. Cool as an icicle, he converted both free throws to put us back ahead by five, 83–78. Only thirty-five seconds remained in the game. We could taste victory. But SIU's Frazier again connected from beyond the free-throw arc to bring the score back to 83–80.

The deafening noise made coaching from the sidelines impossible. All ten of us on the court now played out of instinct, from a lifetime of hardwood experience drummed into our DNA.

After Sloan brought the ball up the court, David Lee got caught grabbing Jerry's arm while trying to wrestle it out of his hands. He fouled out and took a seat on his bench, throwing his towel to the floor. SIU grabbed Sloan's free throw when it bounced off the front rim and hustled the ball toward their basket. Joe Ramsey tipped the ball back in after a missed Saluki shot to narrow our lead to 83–82. The game clock showed seven seconds left.

I rushed to grab the ball before anyone else could. I held onto it out of bounds, counting out loud, "One thousand one, one thousand two, one thousand three," taking precious seconds off the clock. At three, I ran to my left and tossed the ball inbound to Sloan in the corner. Two Salukis immediately mauled him with only one second of overtime remaining.

The fans exploded. I took a deep breath and let it out as slowly as I could, sensing victory.

Sloan stood at the free-throw line, Humes in the left lane, Williams in the right. The stadium hushed. Jerry bounced the ball three times, took aim, and hit nothing but net. Humes and Williams lifted their arms. Another full-throated explosion blanketed the court, only to quiet when the referee once more handed the ball to Jerry. He took a deep breath, again bounced the ball three times, and swished his second free throw. He leaped into the air, his hands raised, his head thrown back.

The buzzer sounded at exactly 11:27 p.m.

The Aces won the game, 85–82.

The Aces completed their season, undefeated, at 29–0.

The Aces were national champions.

• • •

THE ACES BENCH RAN ONTO the court, jumping together and hugging each other. I grabbed Sloan's face and yelled, "We did it!" I gave Coach McCutchan a bear hug and he hugged me back. I found Watkins and Humes and Williams and embraced each of them as well.

All around us, Redshirts stood and chanted "Aces, Aces! Aces, Aces!" The thought never crossed my mind that this would be the last time—ever—that I would stand on this court and be at the center of such adulation.

We sat together on our bench as hundreds of kids ran from the stands and crowded behind us, too awestruck to touch us. Someone put a white cowboy hat on both Sloan's and Humes's heads.

The Redshirts refused to quiet down, only doing so when McCutchan stood and gestured for them to settle. The announcer called out the Salukis one by one, shook their hands, and gave each their consolation medal. I clapped politely but thought, *Thank God that's not us.*

Once they settled back on their bench, the announcer said, in a voice fit for introducing the president, "And now, welcome the NCAA champions, the Evansville College Purple Aces."

The fury that cascaded down was greater than anything I'd heard all season. I tried to absorb it all, the look, the sound, the feel, hoping to be able to retrieve the thrill anytime I wanted for the rest of my life.

The announcer called us to center court one by one, shook our hands, and gave us a gold watch inscribed with the words "NCAA Champions, 1964–1965." The Redshirts stood and cheered for a solid two minutes for Sloan when it was his turn, as we on the bench joined them.

The announcer then summoned Coach McCutchan to center court and presented him with the NCAA trophy. He motioned for us to join him, and we all assembled together. Sloan held the trophy over his head in triumph, the rest of us reached out to put our hands on it along with his.

That ended the ceremonies. As a group we walked off the court to our dressing room, packed with Redshirts unwilling to end their celebrating. Slowly, unperceptively, it eventually emptied of fans, leaving us mostly there by ourselves. Sweaty uniforms and damp towels littered the floor. Exhausted, we finished dressing in silence. No sound came from the long-abandoned playing area. Players drifted out one by one, leaving me with only Sloan, Watkins, and Humes. I slipped on my letter jacket and approached each of the guys, shook their hands, and thanked them.

Silence and darkness surrounded me when I sat behind the wheel of my car outside the stadium. A yellow hue from an overhead light dropped through the windshield and onto my lap. An occasional horn sounded from traffic on Division Street, faraway and forlorn. I took a deep breath and let it out. I rested both hands on the steering wheel, feeling an emptiness expand in my chest, the emptiness one might feel returning to a childhood home and finding it vacant.

I had no idea what to make of this feeling, where to go, what to do. My parents' house? Art and Helen's? Any number of bars? I knew there would be heavy-duty celebrating everywhere in town, and I'd be welcomed with open arms anywhere I went.

None of these appealed to me. I eased out of the parking lot and drove to Evansville College. I eased my way onto its semicircle drive shadowed by oak trees and gray limestone buildings. No one was there. I felt alone.

I parked in front of the student union building, where we had lunched earlier that day. It seemed months ago. I leaned back in my seat, confused. *What gives? This should be the best night of my life.*

Then it hit me. It was over. For the first time since I'd put on my Christ the King grade-school uniform, I was an ex-basketball player. I could no longer look forward to a practice or a game. No longer could I feel the thrill of shooting a basketball in competition, of running up and down the court in perfect rhythm with treasured teammates, of hearing a crowd of strangers chant my name. If no longer a basketball player, who was I? I felt an overwhelming sense of loss, not only of the game, but of myself as well.

I got out of the car and walked the campus. Cold wind slapped my face, and moonlight fell between tree branches. I passed the building where I'd attended my psychology classes, the library where I'd studied for tests, the engineering building where I'd never set foot.

I found myself outside the one-story, white clapboard building that housed both the English literature and the drama departments. Was this my destination all along? I sat on a bench outside its entrance, then pictured Dr. Grabill in his office, me sitting knee to knee in front of him. I saw his ravaged body nestled into his leather chair, his gnarled hand making a point with a crooked finger, his ruddy complexion, his curly red hair, and, above all, his eyes filled with a mixture of passion and mirth.

I remembered when he told me about his University of Illinois roommate, an All-Big Ten football player who'd returned to school his junior year to completely give up football. "Just a game," he'd explained. Dr. Grabill had told me not to think of myself as a basketball player but, rather, as a person for whom basketball player was only one of my many roles. He had looked me squarely in the eye and said, "You're more than just a basketball player, Russ."

I sat on that bench, my hands deep in my pockets, my jacket snapped tight at my neck. Wind gusted my hair. Tree branches rustled and a faraway dog let out a lonely bark.

In that moment, I made Dr. Grabill's words my own. I understood, as fully and deeply as I'd ever understood anything, that, while basketball may be over, I wasn't. This ending was a beginning. My next adventure would be graduate school, where I'd prepare for my career as a psychologist, and then on to another adventure, then others, whatever they may be.

As I thought this, I felt a mixture of excitement and peace flow through me. New life. I smiled, looked at the building, and nodded a salute.

I retraced my steps back to the car and pulled onto Lincoln Avenue. Few cars traveled the road as I realized it was close to two in the morning. I noticed that the street was bathed in moonlight so bright I could have navigated without headlights. I found my way east to Chandler Avenue and home. There I saw Dad slumped, snoozing in his La-Z-Boy. The TV filled the room with static.

"Dad," I said softly, so as not to startle him.

He woke and smiled. "Just getting in?"

"Yeah," I said, smiling back.

Rubbing his eyes and shaking his head, he said, "What a game!"

"Yeah, what a game."

"You did it, boy—you won the championship."

"I sure did."

"And undefeated, to boot."

"Yep."

"What a season."

"Yeah, a perfect season," I said. And then I walked over to him and gave him the biggest hug I ever had.

A native of Evansville, Indiana, Russell Grieger was a starting guard on the undefeated 1964–1965 Evansville College NCAA Championship Purple Aces basketball team. After graduation, he obtained his MA and PhD from The Ohio State University. Since 1974, he has practiced as a licensed clinical psychologist in private practice, consults with businesses and organizations of all sizes, and teaches as an adjunct professor at the University of Virginia. He lives in Charlottesville, Virginia, with his wife and two sons.

★ ★ ★

Printed and bound by CPI Group (UK) Ltd, Croydon, CR0 4YY

13/04/2025

14656547-0005